The Templars

and the

Shroud of Christ

THE TEMPLARS
AND THE
SHROUD OF CHRIST

*A Priceless Relic in the Dawn of the Christian Era and
the Men Who Swore to Protect It*

Barbara Frale

Skyhorse Publishing

Skyhorse Publishing books may be purchased in bulk at special discounts for sales promotion, corporate gifts, fund-raising, or educational purposes. Special editions can also be created to specifications. For details, contact the Special Sales Department, Skyhorse Publishing, 307 West 36th Street, 11th Floor, New York, NY 10018 or info@skyhorsepublishing.com.

Skyhorse® and Skyhorse Publishing® are registered trademarks of Skyhorse Publishing, Inc.®, a Delaware corporation.

www.skyhorsepublishing.com

10 9 8 7 6 5 4 3 2 1

Library of Congress Cataloging-in-Publication Data available on file.

Print ISBN: 978-1-63450-270-2
Ebook ISBN: 978-1-5107-0209-7

Printed in the United States of America.

"... the track of its course through the generations is not that of earthly glory and earthly power, but the track of the Cross."
—Joseph Ratzinger (Benedict XVI), *Jesus of Nazareth*, p. 346

"The Cross alone is our theology."
—Martin Luther, *Operationes in Psalmos,* WA 5, 176, 32-33

CONTENTS

Introduction

As I worked on this book, I noticed a curious fact. Several experts who had glanced at the title while being shown the work got the immediate impression that it dealt with the Turin Shroud as the true funeral shroud of Jesus Christ.

I therefore feel the need to warn the reader from the very first page that the title says *The Templars and the Shroud of Christ* because these medieval warrior monks did almost certainly keep the Shroud for some time, and believed in the evidence that the Christ (not simply Jesus of Nazareth) had indeed passed through death.

The reader may think this a futile distinction, but it is not, and this book will give ample reasons for it.

The question of whether the Shroud of Turin is genuine or not is still unanswered and at any rate, beyond the purpose of this book. What my research sought to study is the cult of the Shroud among the Templars. There is no doubt that as far as the Templars were concerned, the cloth came from the Holy Sepulchre and had been used to wrap the body of Christ before he rose from the dead. This reality forces the readers to put themselves, as it were, in the shoes of the Templar Knights, even if they have to pretend to believe something they don't. If we wish to study a certain world and understand the way it thought, we must make ourselves at one with it and try to see reality as that world saw it. Many passages in this book will, for this reason, refer to the Shroud as the chief relic of the Passion, for that is how the Templars saw it.

In 1988, the cloth was subjected to a radiocarbon dating test called C-14, which gives reliable results, albeit with some margin of uncertainty, assuming the object has been kept in particular conditions and has not suffered contaminations from organic materials. A good example of its accuracy was an untouched Etruscan tome, sealed in the 6th century BC and only reopened by the archaeologist who discovered it. The analyses of the Shroud were entrusted to three laboratories that specialize in these kinds of investigations, and the result they reached dated the Shroud to the later middle ages, with an approximation of 130 years (1260–1390 AD).

The issue, however, was not settled at all: While on one side the radiocarbon analyses roused a storm of polemics, since some people claimed that the methods used did not respect the rules of scientific procedure, on the other, many asserted that radiocarbon simply could not give any reliable results in the matter of the Shroud, an archaeological relic that has suffered a huge number of contaminations and whose history is still largely to be discovered. Indeed, even the Nobel Laureate Willard Frank Libby, who invented and perfected the C-14 archaeological dating test, had earlier declared himself against the experiment.

Under the late Pope John Paul II, who was devoted to the Shroud because it had given him a vivid and realistic sense of Jesus Christ's sufferings, the then papal guardian of the Shroud, Cardinal Anastasio Ballestrero, stated that the cloth was "a venerable icon of the Christ." Many of the faithful took these words with a tangible sense of disappointment; they had hoped for something different, hoped, in short, that the pope would officially declare the Shroud to be the most important relic of Jesus in our possession. In those hot-headed days, it even happened that Ballestrero, until then every liberal's reactionary Catholic bogeyman, was labeled "an Enlightenment intellectual in purple" (*La Repubblica*, October 14, 1988, issue), a title that no priest enjoys being stuck with.

In fact, that definition of the Shroud is best understood if we try to understand the theological concept of Icon, which is not simply the same as any holy image. The cardinal's words were not at all intended to place the Shroud on the same level as Michelangelo's *Pietà*, or of any work of art that tries to represent the Passion credibly and poetically. Christian theology—Eastern theology, in particular—sees icons as something more than images. Icons, in a sense, live and can give life; they can bestow real benefits on the spirituality of the faithful. None of the many who have written about the Shroud noticed this fact, and yet it is not without importance. Calling it "a venerable icon" was a choice born of long, careful study by experts who certainly did not suffer from a shortage of vocabulary. That expression directly calls up the thought of the theologians of the Second Ecumenical Council of Nicaea (787 AD), to whom the prodigious image of Christ is how we achieve contact with the divine; it expresses the will to look at that object in the same manner full of astonishment and wonder in which the ancient Church looked at it. It all turns on a very simple concept: to seriously study the Shroud means, in any case, to meditate on the wounds of Jesus Christ. Cardinal Ballestrero's was a most delicate definition, respectful of the depths of mystery that this object involves, but possibly a bit too erudite to be universally understood. For their part, several popes have stated their views unhesitatingly: Already Pius XI had spoken of it as an image "surely not of human making," and John Paul II clearly described it as "the most splendid relic of both Passion and Resurrection" (*L'Osservatore Romano*, in September 7, 1936, and April 21–22, 1980).

I myself suspect that there may be something else at issue. If and when the Church ever officially declares the Shroud to be the one true winding sheet of Jesus, it could become very difficult, maybe even impossible, to continue to make scientific studies of it. It would then be absolutely the holiest relic owned by Christendom, thick with Christ's own blood, and any manipulation would be seen as disrespectful. Yet Christendom still wants to examine this enigmatic object because it still has plenty of questions to ask: There is a widespread feeling that it may have plenty to tell about Roman-age Judaism—the very context of the life, preaching, and death of Jesus of Nazareth. This, apart from any religious evaluation, is a most interesting field of study. We know very little of that period of Jewish history because of the devastations carried out by the Roman emperors Vespasian (70 AD) and Hadrian (132 AD), which involved the destruction of Jerusalem and all its archives and the deportation of the Jewish population away from Syria-Palestine. Some important clues to be found on the Turin sheet promise to have a lot to say about Judaic usages in the age of the Second Temple. One of ancient Hebraism's greatest historians, Paolo Sacchi, writes: "Whether we believe or not in the divinity of Jesus of Nazareth, he spoke the language of his time to the men of his time, dealing directly with issues of his time" (*Storia del Secondo Tempio,* p. 17). If we question it delicately and respectfully, the Shroud will answer.

This book will not tackle any of the complex issues to do with the cloth's authenticity and religious significance. Anyone wishing to enlarge their understanding of these areas will find sufficient answers in the books of Monsignor Giuseppe Ghiberti: *Sindone, vangeli e vita cristiana* and *Dalle cose che patì: Evangelizzare con la sindone.* This book is only intended as a discussion along historical lines; there can be no doubt that, to historians, the Shroud of Turin (whatever it may be) is a piece of material evidence of immense interest.

This book is the first part of a study that is completed by a second volume, *The Shroud of Jesus of Nazareth,* dedicated entirely to the new historical questions that arise from recent discoveries made about the cloth. Some of the main arguments treated there are only hinted at here, and this was inevitable, for the argument enters into issues concerning Jewish and Greco-Roman archaeology from the 1st century AD—themes far too distant from the story of the Templars to place them all in a single volume.

My research began more than ten years ago, in 1996. Then, in the spring of 1998, a news program from Italy's state broadcaster, RAI, carried a story about how traces of ancient writing had been identified on the linen Shroud.

I was then reading for a Ph.D. in history at the University Ca' Foscari of Venice, working on a thesis on the Templars. I had long since noticed that in the original documents of the trial against them, some witnesses described an object exactly similar to the Shroud of Turin. When I heard that an Oxford graduate scholar, Ian Wilson, had found interesting suggestions that the Shroud had been among the Templars at some point, I thought of running a check on the issue, and I started looking into the enigmatic Shroud writings, thinking that they had been put there by the Temple's warrior monks. The results impressed me; they were so complex and involved that I decided this was going to be a long-term research project, and that I would not tackle the question until I had satisfactory evidence.

Today I think I can conscientiously say that the evidence is there, and maybe much more than I had originally hoped, and this is largely thanks to some scholars whose wonderful kindness has provided precious contributions.

I wish to underline that the ideas set out in this book reflect my own opinions and are not the property or responsibility of anyone else. Whatever the value of my results, I don't think that even ten years of obstinate and passionate investigation could have led anywhere had I not had the advantage of many authoritative suggestions, advice, and sometimes illuminating criticism.

My biggest debt of gratitude is to Professor Franco Cardini, who trusted my research as it was taking its first stumbling steps, and to His Eminence Raffaele Cardinal Farina, archivist and librarian of the Catholic Church, who supported it when the delicate time of conclusion had come. From these two great scholars, so different from each other, yet both enamored with the human figure of Jesus, I have learned very, very much, even on a human level.

Father Marcel Chappin SJ (vice-prefect of the Secret Vatican Archive and the Pontifical Gregorian University) revised the book's proofs from top to bottom, enriching it with abundant clarifications and advice.

A special thanks goes to my colleagues Simone Venturini (Secret Vatican Archive) and Marco Buonocore (Apostolic Vatican Library) for the patience with which they have helped me to study Hebrew, ancient Middle Eastern civilizations, Greco-Roman archaeology, and epigraphy, which I had studied in university but had then neglected in order to dedicate myself to the Middle Ages. Emanuela Marinelli (*Collegamento pro Sindone*) has generously made available her study experience and an enormous library of specialist studies on the Shroud.

I also wish to thank Marcel Alonso (*Centre International d'Études sur le Linceul de Turin*), Gianfranco Armando (Secret Vatican Archive), Pier Luigi Baima Bollone (University of Turin), Luca Becchetti (Secret Vatican Archive), Luigi Boneschi, Fr. Claudio Bottini OFM, (*Studium Biblicum Franciscanum of Jerusalem*), Thierry Castex (*Centre International d'Études sur le Linceul de Turin*), Simonetta Cerrini (University of Paris-IV), Paolo Cherubini (University of Palermo), Willy Clarysse (Catholic University of Louvain), Tiziana Cuccagna (Liceo Ginnasio "G. C. Tacito" di Terni), Alain Demurger, (University of Paris-IV), Ivan Di Stefano Manzella (University of Tuscia-Viterbo), Enrico Flaiani (Secret Vatican Archive), Stefano Gasparri (University Ca'

Foscari of Venice), Giuseppe Lo Bianco (Secret Vatican Archive), Don Franco Manzi (Archiepiscopal Seminary of Milan), Monsignor Aldo Martini (Vatican Secret Archive), Remo Martini (University of Siena), Tommaso Miglietta (University of Trento), Giovanna Nicolaj (University La Sapienza of Rome), Franco Nugnes (*Velocità*) Gherardo Ortalli (University Ca' Foscari of Venice), Monsignor Romano Penna (Pontifical Lateran University), Don Luca Pieralli (Pontifical Oriental Institute), Monsignor Sergio Pagano (Vatican Secret Archive), Alessandro Pratesi (Vatican School of Palaeography, Diplomatics and Archival Studies), Delio Proverbio (*Biblioteca Apostolica Vaticana*), Émile Puech OFP (*École Biblique de Jerusalem*), Monsignor Gianfranco Ravasi (Pontifical Commission for Culture), Fr. Vincenzo Ruggieri SJ (Pontifical Oriental Institute), His Eminence Christoph Cardinal (Cardinal Archbishop of Vienna), Renata Segre Berengo (University Ca' Foscari of Venice), Francesco Tommasi (University of Perugia), Paolo Vian (Vatican Apostolic Library), and Gian Maria Vian (*Osservatore Romano*).

To the late and much missed Marino Berengo, Marco Tangheroni, and André Marion, who passed away before this text was completed, I send my lasting affection, and I miss you. I wished to consult many other authorities and was unable to do so for various practical reasons; I hope I shall be able to in the future.

My husband, Marco Palmerini, who is remarkably well-read in the sciences and knows the Shroud well, has given an impressive contribution to the quality of my research, passing it through the sieve of his meticulous criticism. My colleague Nadia Fracassi has also practically lived through the development of this book and taken an active part in its creation. Exchanging views with them on many and various matters has allowed me to clarify my thoughts, and at least on the moral level I regard them as joint authors. Ugo Berti Arnoaldi, my trusted reference for the publishing industry, has contributed decisively by improving the quality of my writing from the narrative point of view: I could never give a precise account of the number of times he has read my work over and over again to help me turn my always overly erudite first drafts into a pleasantly readable essay.

I dedicate this book to my friend Claudio Cetorelli, a brilliant young Roman antiquarian. In the summer of 2000, during a seaside holiday, he threw himself into the water and managed to save a drowning man, but his heart could not stand the strain. Those who tried to help him say that his last expression was a smile.

I

The Mysterious Idol of the Templars

Fascination with a Myth

It was Christmas in 1806. The French emperor Napoleon Bonaparte was camped with his army near the Polish castle of Pultusk, on the shores of the river Narew, some 43 miles north of Warsaw.

He was at the height of his power: One year earlier, his great victory at Austerlitz and the following Treaty of Pressburg had allowed him to extend his control to cover almost the whole of Europe.

That August, the Confederation of the Rhine had decreed at a gathering in Regensburg the entrance of the various German states into the French political orbit, putting an end to the 1,000-year history of the Holy Roman Empire.

Again, on October 14, he had inflicted a morally and materially shattering defeat on the Prussian army in the neighborhood of a town called Jena; now he was preparing to meet the Russian troops, who had enlisted to stop his worrisome advance into Polish land. They, too, were to suffer a mighty defeat at Pultusk, on St. Stephen's Day (Boxing Day). But at this moment the situation was still serious: The French troops were frightened by the cold and lack of supplies, and yet the emperor was taking a bit of time to deal with a matter that clearly concerned him.

The emperor kept thinking of a tragedy titled *Les Templiers*, written by a fellow Frenchman named François Raynouard, a lawyer of Provençal origin with a passion for history. The play covered the grim events of the trial ordered by the king of France, Philip IV the Fair, against the most powerful monastic and military order of the Middle Ages, the "poor fellow-soldiers of Christ," better known as the Templars. The tragedy described the unjust destruction of this order of knight-monks, who were also clever diplomats and expert bankers, and in Raynouard's view, the innocent victims of the French king who had treacherously assaulted them to make himself master of their wealth. The emperor had not liked the play: First because Napoleon, having crowned himself emperor in Notre Dame Cathedral on December 2, 1804, in the presence of Pope Pius VII, saw himself as the moral heir of the charisma of the French sovereigns of the Dark and Middle Ages, along with the consecrated oil that, according to legend, had been miraculously brought down from Heaven by a white dove during the baptism of King Clovis. Napoleon found the cynical and cruel depiction of Philip the Fair really out of place. Above all, though, Raynouard had mercilessly disappointed the solid beliefs felt by a whole culture—of which Napoleon himself was an illustrious representative—about that celebrated order of monks who carried swords, so suddenly fallen from the height of power, wealth, and prestige into ruin and the disgraceful charge of heresy. It was an adventurous story, full of mysteries and hints of dark things, and it was magnetically attractive to the rising romantic taste, glad to color everything with touches of the irrational. The emperor was a pragmatic soul, and his interest in the affair was wholly different. The doom of the Templars had been, in its time, the herald of a clear political plan. And paradoxically it went on being so, although the issue was five centuries old.[1]

That fanciful, nostalgic way of looking at the ancient military order had appeared in Europe in the early years of the 18th century, born of the encounter between a genuine desire to renew society and a not wholly objective reading of history. By the end of the 1600s, all Western countries had a bourgeoisie that had grown rich on trade and the beginnings of industrial production, amassed genuine fortunes, and given their children the best educations along with the children of the most ancient nobility. Wealthy and highly prepared, the members of this emerging social group felt ready to take part in the governance of the country but rarely achieved it because society was still structured in the ancient fashion, in a stiff and closed system that concentrated political power in the hands of the aristocracy. The heirs of fortunes built on degrading, plebeian "trade" could only hope to enter the elite by marrying the daughter of some illustrious and recently ruined house, ready to let its blue blood be diluted with fluids of humbler origin. After the wedding, the bridegroom would start living as his new friends and relatives did, and was absorbed into the system. The renewal of thought caused by the Enlightenment led this new, emerging class to look for an independent way to gain power, a way that allowed them to work effectively

---

1   Partner, *I Templari*, pp. 155-159.

to increase their societies and make them fairer. People looked back admiringly to the pasts of certain European regions such as Flanders, Germany, England, or the French area, where powerful corporations of merchants and artisans had been able to form and, through group solidarity, defend themselves against the arrogance of aristocrats. The corporations of builders who had raised great Gothic cathedrals such as Chartres, in particular, were suspected of owning scientific knowledge in advance of their age, and to have handed them down through the centuries under the most jealous secrecy. Legitimate historical curiosity mixed with the need to find illustrious origins, and in the early 18th century, this brought about the formation of actual clubs, motivated by Enlightenment ideals yet certain that they were carrying on a hidden tradition of secret societies going all the way back to Biblical antiquity. Their name was taken from that of ancient guilds of master builders, in French, *maçonnerie*—freemasonry. Eighteenth-century society still had a passion for the concept of nobility, especially of ancient origins, as when in the midst of the Dark Ages the ancestors of the great dynasties had performed the deeds that would build a future of renown and privilege for their descendants. An immense fascination was attached to ancient orders of chivalry; even though their reputation was imprecise, they were seen as a kind of privileged channel, a fast track to the heights of society for persons of natural talent unlucky enough to be born outside the aristocratic caste. And the Templar order, the most famous and debated of them all, seemed to lie exactly where all these interests converged.

From Legend to Politics

Maybe the scientific knowledge that had allowed the great cathedrals to be built was the same with which the legendary Phoenician architect Hiram had constructed in Jerusalem the most celebrated building in all of history, the Temple of Solomon. The temple was not only a colossal piece of architecture: It was the holy sanctuary built to contain the Arcane Presence, the Living God, and as such was not supposed to be touched except by the hands of those initiated into the highest mysteries. It was imagined that Hiram's ancient teachings had reached the European Middle Ages at a particular time, when the Westerners had arrived in Jerusalem for the First Crusade (1095–1099), establishing a Christian kingdom in the Holy Land. The history of the Middle Ages and of the Crusades in the Holy Land featured a particular presence that had even drawn its name from that of Solomon's Temple: the *Militia Salomonica Templi*, better known as the Order of Templars. Founded in Jerusalem immediately after the First Crusade to defend pilgrims to the Holy Land, the Templars had experienced a practically unstoppable growth that had made it, barely fifty years after its founding, the most powerful military religious order in the Middle Ages until it was overwhelmed, about two centuries later, by a mysterious and grim affair of heresy and dark magic that ended with the death by burning of its last grand master.[2]

Celebrated intellectuals of the time, such as Dante Alighieri, had accused the Templar trial, without mincing words, of being essentially a monumental

---

2   Partner, *I Templari*, pp. 115-132.

frame-up ordered by the French King Philip IV the Fair, who wished to take over the Order's patrimony, most of which lay in French territory. But in the 16th century, some lovers of magic such as the philosopher Cornelius Agrippa raised the possibility that the Order might have practiced strange and hidden rites, ones celebrated by the dim light of candles where mysterious idols and even black cats would appear.[3]

There was no clear idea what role the pope, then Gascon Clemens V (1305–1314), had played in the affair. This man seemed ever hesitant, ever supine before royal will, and yet he had dragged on the trial of the Templars over no less than seven years, practically until his death, which took place only a month after that of the last Templar grand master. Many sources now readily accessible were then unknown, but even those that were known were studied using methods wholly different from today's.

History was treated as a literary endeavor, or a pastime meant to entertain and enlighten the spirit. Therefore, facts were selected from the past according to whether any moral teaching could be gotten from them, or whether they could stimulate the imagination like an adventure novel could.

What was known of this pontiff, whose lay name was Bertrand de Got, was that he had been born in France, that he had started the papal exile in Avignon, and that he had released Guillaume de Nogaret—the true "evil spirit" of Philip's reign, whom the king used for his most shameless actions—from excommunication. The king of France had

---

3   Ibid. pp. 106-109.

been victorious in every confrontation with papal authority, and even in the matter of the Templars' trial, many facts seemed to indicate that the Church had easily bent to sovereign demands. But there was another fact that made minds lean toward this idea, a fact that had nothing to do with historical studies proper, but could have a major effect on them. The Church's attitude in the early 1700s was hugely cautious toward the aggressively rising new Enlightenment ideas—ideas that intended to promote a renewal of thought and of many social dynamics. At the root of this rejection lay several factors. Many of the high prelates who had leading roles in the hierarchy came from the same noble houses that managed secular power, and had a similar mentality and the same way of looking at the world. The Church had always been exempt from the social conditions that dominated the centuries, in the sense that it was possible to reach the height of spiritual and temporal power with one's own natural qualities, however humble one's origins. Many of the most famous popes were from decidedly poor families; we just have to think of the legendary Gregory VII, who, as a child, had to work as a porter, or the recent John XXIII, who came from a large peasant family that was not always certain where the next meal would come from. This, at least, was the theory, but in fact things were often very different: The immense patrimonies connected with so many Church positions made them very desirable prey for the nobility, who, by placing their younger sons within the hierarchy, could ensure a privileged life for them without making a dent in the family capital. The highest point of corruption in this sense had taken place in the Renaissance, when it became the practice to actually sell the most important posts—such as bishoprics, the richest abbotships, and the title of cardinal.[4]

The scandals, and the impossibility of swiftly reforming such customs, had raised political as well as religious protests, and had resulted in the Protestant schism. At the beginning of the 1700s, no less than two centuries after Luther's protest, the violent polemics raised by Protestant thought in the 1500s and 1600s had hardly died down. The papacy was accused of having trapped mankind in a network of inventions set up for its own advantage, built upon the only real weave of Christian doctrine—the primitive Church. A school of historical studies had been set up in Magdeburg in Germany for the purpose of showing the whole endless queue of falsehoods that were believed to have been piled up by the Catholic Church over 1,000 years for the sole purpose of bending the faithful to its own material interests. Its members, called the Centuriators of Magdeburg from the name of their published works (*The Centuries*), had indubitable intellectual qualities, and as they had stuffed their writings with considerable imagination, they gave plenty of trouble to generations of Catholic scholars.[5]

In short, the wounds opened by Luther's mighty schism were far from closed, and any innovation that seemed to place the well-established and reassuring Catholic tradition of thought in any doubt seemed the flag of yet another onslaught. Galileo Galilei had been among the most illustrious victims of this reaction. The tendency

---

4   *Capitani, Gregorio VII*, pp. 189, 203; *Traniello, Giovanni XXIII*, p. 646; *Rapp, Il consolidamento del papato*, pp. 119-123.

5   Stöve, *Magdeburger Centuriatoren*, col. 1185.

quickly established itself to see the Church as an ally of that oppressive secular power that needed to be overthrown, and several Freemason groups took a strongly anticlerical tinge that they had not had at their start. From the idea that reason was the favored, if not the only way to improve human life, there progressively developed a near-divine concept of intellect itself—reason as the spark of divinity entrusted to man by God. God himself was pure reason, praised as the Grand Architect who had built the universe. The mysteries whereby the highest builder had raised the cosmos called back to mind those by which another architect of legend, Hiram of Phoenicia, had built the Temple in the Holy City Jerusalem. Solomon, to whom divine wisdom had granted measureless wealth, had raised the temple, and the temple brought back to mind the Templars, also destroyed because they owned fabulous wealth, and possibly—everything seemed to prove it—were possessors of Hiram's secrets. That same Catholic Church that seemed then to be in the way of any progress, however small, was nothing less than the heir of the medieval papacy—an institution that had covered up the fragile bases of its historical claims for centuries by unleashing its most terrible weapon, the Inquisition, against those who held the proofs that could have unmasked it.

All these diverse ideas, born independently of each other but within the same context, ended up merging, and their outlines adapted till they fit each other like the pieces of a complicated puzzle. As simple victims of raison d'état and because of Clemens V's political weakness, the Templars became, bit by bit, the unlucky heroes of a wisdom many thousands of years old, older than

Christianity, that could have spread progress and social welfare, but had instead been sacrificed to destroy the unjust privileges of an institution everlastingly allied with absolute power and its manifold abuses. Templarism—a highly colored, romantic view of the old order projected in the social reality of the 1700s—became so compulsively fascinating a phenomenon as to take a protagonist's role in the history of European popular culture, but there were serious differences in the shape taken by the phenomenon in various countries. If in France, the Templars appeared as champions of free thought against the oppression of the twin dinosaurs of the ancient regime—Crown and Church—in Germany, to the contrary, studies on the Templars were promoted exactly to strike at those very radical and subversive groups whom they inspired.

Prince von Metternich, the leader of the reaction against the upsets caused by Napoleon all over Europe, had started a cultural policy intended to destroy the credibility of the contemporary Freemason and neo-Templar groups. The intention was to prove that those heroic brethren of a secret order from which the French and the Revolution were proud to be derived, were in fact nothing but a bunch of heretics and perverts, the enemies of God, of the Church, of the State.

From champions of free thought and guardians of sublime knowledge as they had been in France and England, the Templars became in Austria the stronghold of the most unyielding heresy. Napoleon was probably aware of this political exploitation of the legend, and if he was, that must have increased his interest.[6]

---

6 Partner, *I Templari*, pp. 133-154.

About Baphomet and Other Demons

In the same year the French emperor was to write his review of François Raynouard's none too brilliant tragedy on the Templars, the London publishers Bulmer & Cleveland published a book by Joseph Hammer (later Joseph von Hammer-Purgstall), called *Ancient Alphabets and Hieroglyphic Characters Explained*, with an account of the Egyptian priests. The author was a young Austrian scholar from the town of Graz in Steyermark who had joined the diplomatic service in 1796 and, three years later, became a member of an embassy to Constantinople. He was later to take part in several British expeditions against Napoleon in the Middle East, meanwhile studying the ancient civilizations and traveling widely. This intense research, and the remarkable openness of his mind, would lead him to become, over the next fifty years, one of the greatest Oriental scholars of his time, author of (among other things) a textbook on the history of the Ottoman Empire, which is recognized as the first significant treatment of a previously unexplored field. In 1847–1849, he was to crown his career by becoming chairman of the immensely prestigious Austrian Academy of Sciences, which was to count among its members such figures as Christian Doppler and Konrad Lorenz.[7] What he had printed in 1806 were his first experiences of research and, possibly to support the wishes of his mighty patron Metternich and surely under the influence of the "black legend" of the Templars in his time, he placed in this review of ancient scripts a hypothesis born from a

---

7   Koch, *Hammer-Purgstall, Joseph Frh. von*, p. 401.

mere similarity in sound, which would however rouse great shock and interest. Hammer-Purgstall had in fact identified a word written in hieroglyphics, which in his reading sounded like *bahúmíd*, and which, if translated into Arabic, meant "calf."

Today we can reconstruct his work's development, and this scholar's oddities acquire a logical explanation. We do in fact find that some witnesses, not members of the Order, who testified in the trial of the Templars in England, had mentioned strange rumors including that the Templars kept an idol in the shape of a calf. Furthermore, some testimonies in the trial carried out in southern France featured that strange name, Baphomet, which made such an impression on Hammer-Purgstall because it seemed to approximate his mysterious word. These few witnesses of obscure notions are at most ten or so, and are really a droplet in the more than 1,000 testimonies (affidavits) still preserved today from the Templar trials, in most of which neither fiends nor calves appear. But the 19th-century scholar, drawn by the romantic taste of his time and by a really quite unscientific research method, fell victim in good faith to a magnetic fascination with an idea: He paid no attention to proportion, seeing only the tiny number of descriptions with disquieting details, and forgot a whole world of much more reliable and rational confessions. And, to the pleasure of Prince von Metternich, he designed for the Templars an exoteric and decidedly grim aspect.[8]

The pieces of the mosaic struck him as fitting each other perfectly, and the pull of the idea drove him further into

---

8   Schottmüller, II, p. 90; Finke, II, p. 323.

his investigations. But it was only in 1818, after Waterloo and Napoleon's exile to St. Helena, after the Congress of Vienna and the dawn of the Restoration, that Hammer-Purgstall's theories started taking a mature shape; they did so by heftily drawing from other sources. In that year, he published the work fated to achieve the highest fame in this area, whose eloquent title was *Mysterium Baphometis Revelatum—The Mystery of Baphomet Revealed.* The author gave up his former belief that the Templar idol's strange name came from an ancient hieroglyphic term, and embraced a more complex theory: The word was no longer from the Egyptian language, but was a compound of two Greek terms joined to mean a "baptism of the spirit." He claimed that it proved that the Templars had inherited from antiquity, through the Cathar heretics of southern France, the doctrines of the ancient Ophite sect. The latter took their name from the special cult they offered to the snake (Greek Ophis) from the Biblical book of Genesis. To them, the God of the Bible was not the principle of good, but of evil, who out of petty jealousy had kept man in a condition of ignorance; it had been the snake, who was not the enemy but the friend of humankind, who had revealed the path of truth—*gnosis* (Greek for "knowledge"), divine knowledge.[9]

This was the primeval religion, the most ancient one known; it always survived in the shadows with its secrets, escaping throughout the millenia from the persecutions by the Church and by the various powers that relied on the Church. One of the worst charges the king of France had made against the Templars was that they forced their

---

9   Peterson, *Ofiti*, coll. 80-81; Camelot, *Ophites*, coll. 100-101.

novices to deny Jesus and spit on the Cross; this could be matched with information from Origen (who had lived in the early 3rd century AD) that the Ophites forced their new members to blaspheme Jesus.

Shortly after the publication of Hammer-Purgstall's theories, it happened that the duke of Blacas, a famous collector of exoteric-type objects, found, as if by magic, two extremely strange little caskets supposedly dated to the Middle Ages and representing some sort of devil cult. The Baphomet received public consecration at that point, which none of the Templar sources, rare and mutually contradictory as they were, could ever grant the henceforth famous shape. It was depicted as a kind of devil with the horns and legs of a ram, the breasts of a woman, and the genitals of a man.[10] The brilliant and dishonest occultist Eliphas Levi rediscovered these fascinating fakes in the late 1800s, finding material in them that was most useful for his speculations; he dressed the ill-defined Baphomet in that threatening devilish majesty in which it towers to this day in so many fantasy pictures. Fans of the occult are free to believe what they wish, but historical evidence leaves no reasonable doubt that Baphomet was nothing but an ugly doll invented—more or less—by romantic fantasy, and still in use to this day to profitably catch the simple-minded.[11]

The truth about the "mysterious idol of the Templars" must be sought in a wholly different direction.

---

10   Hammer-Purgstall, *Mémoire sur deux coffrets*, pp. 84-134; *Mignard, Monographie du coffret*, pp. 136-221.

11   Partner, *I Templari*, pp. 160-162; Introvigne, *Il Codice da Vinci*, pp. 116-129.

Paper Secrets

Although his writings sounded like genuine revelations at the time, Hammer-Purgstall had invented very little, and the bulk of his content was anything but of his own making. The idea that the Templars were the secret guardians of a most ancient religious wisdom had already been proposed some twenty years earlier, in a less extensive form, by the German book dealer Christian Friedrich Nicolai. Nicolai owned a tavern in Berlin that was a favorite meeting place for intellectuals. Among them was a personal friend of Nicolai's named Gotthold Ephraim Lessing, possibly the most outstanding personality of the German Enlightenment.[12]

In 1778, Lessing wrote a genuinely explosive book. It was part of a much larger text written years earlier by Samuel Reimarus, professor of Eastern languages, and bore the provocative title: *An Apology for the Rational Worshippers of God*. Its original author had kept it secret; Lessing published it posthumously with the more reassuring title: *The Goals of Jesus and His Disciples—Another Fragment from the Anonymous Wolfenbüttel*. Reimarus argued that Jesus had nothing divine about him: His activity had been simply that of a political Messiah, a kind of patriotic leader who wanted to free the Jews from Roman rule. When he died, his disciples refused to accept the facts and decided to steal his body, and went on to invent the news that he had risen, eventually founding a new religion. Samuel Reimarus was the first

---

12 Jung, *Nicolai (Christoph) Friedrich*, p. 446; Schilson, *Lessing, Gotthold Ephraim*, coll. 851-852.

member of Western Christian culture to separate Jesus from the Christ, terms that had for so many centuries meant one and the same thing. That moment marks the start of the "quest for the historical Jesus," a new direction in research intended to reconstruct the historical visage of Jesus beyond what was held to have been invented by the Catholic Church with its dogmas; before then, there had only been a Christology—the study of the life of Jesus in light of theology and the Gospels.[13] Both Lessing and Nicolai subscribed to what used to be called "rational Christianity," something very close to Deist philosophy, which substantially denied the divinity of the Christ to assert the existence of a single and sole creator God, the rational principle of absolute goodness and the origin of all things. Some radical circles reached the conviction that the Church and papacy had stubbornly and dishonestly hidden a frightening truth for no better reason than to ennoble their historically dubious origins, based on God himself. The strongly reactionary attitude of some Catholics, clinging to total denial strengthened their opponents' belief that they had something to hide.

By 1810, Napoleon had become the master of most of Europe, and he decreed that all the documents of conquered kingdoms, including the states of the Church, were to be taken to Paris to become part of the vast Central Archive of the Empire. So it was that the colossal bulk of papers accumulated by the popes were packaged up and sent to France. Thanks to the exoteric tradition that had been growing, the

---

13   Penna, *I ritratti*, I, pp. 11-13.

arrival of the documents concerned with the trial of the Templars was surrounded by great expectations and even a morbid kind of curiosity: Those papers, kept safe for so long within the mighty walls of the Vatican, would certainly have revealed disconcerting facts. It was widely and largely correctly believed that the papal archive had always been *secretum*, or reserved for the Roman curia, and that no outsider would ever be allowed a view of them. A kind of frenzy arose among the French officials charged with the expedition; it seemed clear that the truth about that obscure and complicated affair would appear, whole and inviolate, to the first man who could lay his hands on the minutes of the trial. Monsignor Marino Marini, personal manservant of the prefect of the Vatican Archives, had plenty of trouble with certain generals who insisted on opening particular crates of documents even before the convoy left Rome; while the pragmatic Miollis was looking for the bull of excommunication against Napoleon, intending to quietly get rid of a most uncomfortable fact, Baron Étienne Radet was poking around elsewhere, eager to lay his hands on the trial of the Templars.

Even after the fall of Napoleon and the restoration of the monarchy, when the papal archive was allowed to return home, Monsignor Marini was still fighting to prevent the new government from "carelessly" keeping a number of documents of the highest historical interest, including the Inquisition's trial of Galileo Galilei and the trial of the Templar order. He only got them back by a crafty suggestion: He saw fit to point out to the new government that the actions of Philip the Fair threw a decidedly nasty light on that very image of French monarchy that they intended to rehabilitate. It was therefore rather better, ultimately, that they should go back to the Vatican Archives, which were then closed to the public.[14]

The duc de Richelieu felt it wiser to yield to the Holy See's complaints, as well as to Monsignor Marini's witty arguments, but he surely looked on with great regret as the documents of the Templar trial, which Raynouard had meanwhile studied without finding hidden truths, left Paris to return at last to the safe recesses of the Vatican where the mysteries of Baphomet and many other demons would have been hidden away for many more centuries. And yet what really happened was that on December 10, 1879, the brand-new register of requests to consult the Vatican Secret Archive recorded its first request. Over the course of centuries, many people had been given special permission to visit the great palace where the documents of the popes' thousands of years of history were kept, but only then were scholars first allowed regular and continuous access to the precious papers.[15] From the middle of the 19th century, historical studies had made a quantum leap because the general trend of thought, thanks in part to the rising tide of positivism, had lost the taste for irrationalism that had fascinated early Romanticism, in favor of a much more realistic approach. Paleography and diplomatics—the disciplines that teach how to decipher the complex writings of

---

14   Marini, *Memorie storiche*, pp. CCXXIII-CCXLIX; about the Galileo
     trial, see Pagano, *I documenti del processo*.
15   See veda Pagano, *Leone XIII e l'apertura dell'Archivio Segreto*,
     pp. 44-63.

the past and to reliably distinguish genuine from false documents—had been taking giant strides. This was the start of a brilliant cultural period that witnessed the systematic publication of many medieval sources, no longer by private and sometimes amateurish learned gentlemen, but by professional historians who produced systematic collections valid to this day, such as the German-area *Monumenta Germaniae Historica*, which, among other things, contains many edicts of Charlemagne and an enormous number of immensely important texts from the Holy Roman Empire.

Between 1841 and 1851, the French historian Jules Michelet published, in an equally authoritative and prestigious series—*Collection des Documents Inédits sur l'Histoire de France*—the contents of an ancient register from the reign of Philip the Fair, which was then preserved in the Royal Library of Paris, and some other similar documents; it was an excellent edition for its time, which finally gave a scholarly picture of some of the most important documents of the trial against the Templars. The Michelet edition is still in use, although it is not widely known that its main item, the minutes of the long trial that took place in Paris between 1309 and 1312, came from a copy that the king had made for his own chancellery, while the original, which had been sent to the pope, is in the Vatican Archives and still unpublished. The documents show no trace of Baphomet, of the magic Gnostic caskets, or of the other dark mysteries that people connected with the Templars; nor would a character like Michelet's, or the earnest spirit of the historical collection, have allowed such fantasies. Even popular contemporary culture had noticeably matured such that themes that had been so fashionable twenty years earlier no longer interested people. It was exactly thanks to that improvement in historical method that Pope Leo had made the anything-but-easy decision to open the gates of the Secret Archives.

The sudden death on June 10, 1879, of Monsignor Rosi Bernardini, the prefect of the Archive, led to the choice of a successor who was not only a scholar but a major figure in contemporary German culture: Cardinal Josef Hergenröther; years later, Ludwig von Pastor, a famous historian specializing in the papacy, was to call this nomination the dawn of a new age for studies in Catholicism and in Western civilization.[16] As soon as the Archives were opened, the Austrian historian Konrad Schottmüller, a fellow countryman of Joseph von Hammer-Purgstall, started a work of several years' duration, using modern historical methods to find and publish what he thought were the main records of the trial against the Templars. His work was carried on in the early 1900s by Heinrich Finke, and their overall result was the most complete and reliable edition of Vatican sources on the trial available to this day. Large-scale study of the documents relating to the Templars' trial surely turned out to be a severe disappointment to many: When the first scholarly editions started placing in the public domain the contents of those ancient parchments once kept in the fortress of Castel Sant'Angelo, no trace could be found of the sensational revelations expected by some; however, many truths thus far unknown came

16   Gualdo, *Sussidi per la consultazione,* pp. 34-40; Gadille, *Le grandi correnti dottrinali,* pp. 111-132, also p. 113.

to light, making it at last possible to write the history of the trial with accurate and modern criteria.

In 1978, Cambridge University Press published *The Trial of the Templars* by Malcolm Barber, which was to be the start of a new and very fertile season in this field of medieval studies. For the first time, it was possible to follow the process of the trial as a whole, thanks to the authentic documents. A few years later, in 1985, the Sorbonne historian Alain Demurger published another fundamental text, titled *Vie et Mort de l'Ordre du Temple*, which picked up the thread from Barber and developed further aspects with the same scholarly rigor.

When the historian Peter Partner published *The Murdered Magicians: The Templars and Their Myth* with Oxford University Press, the world's scholars were also given a clear account of how many exoteric legends about the Templars had enchanted and animated intellectual and political groups for two centuries—sometimes by culture-driven suggestions, sometimes by downright conscious invention. The original documents, properly read and inspected, left no more room for those magic-tinged, chivalric fancies that past writers had indulged while trying to interpret the history of the Templars using caskets, hieroglyphic writings, or dubious texts written at least 300 years after the end of the Order.

These three monuments of historical method and research would not allow the collective view of this ancient, notorious order of knights to stay the same. There was now certain evidence that the trial had been nothing but a colossal, tragic conspiracy with political reasons and strong economic interests, though several points were still obscure, and that was pretty much the opinion clearly stated by a number of illustrious contemporaries, such as Dante Alighieri, who saw, one way or another, the unfolding of the trial and bore witness to their views. The great Tuscan poet makes the founder of the French Royal House, Hugh Capet, say in so many words that (among the many crimes of his descendants) Philip the Fair had destroyed the Templars for no other reason than greed. [17]

The Brothers of the Glorious Baussant

The Order of the Temple was founded at the beginning of the 12th century. In the years that followed the First Crusade, a French knight named Hugues de Payns, lord of a fief near the city of Troyes and vassal of the Count of Champagne, had brought together a few comrades in the city of Jerusalem, just taken back by Christians, to found a brotherhood of lay soldiers who lived as lay people with the Canons of the Holy Sepulchre.

In 1119, a gang of Saracen robbers slaughtered a caravan of Christian pilgrims traveling to the Holy Places. The event had an enormous resonance; even in the distant lands of the West, Christian society wept over those unarmed, butchered travelers. The government of the Kingdom of Jerusalem was growing increasingly concerned about a problem that was to become chronic in the history of the Holy Land: The troops available were wholly inadequate to efficiently defend the country, so its population was under the constant threat

---

17   Dante Alighieri, *Purgatorio* XX 91-96.

of attack. It was maybe as a result of this tragedy that the following year, 1120, Hugues de Payns and his comrades committed themselves before the patriarch of Jerusalem to fight in defense of Christian pilgrims. Having voluntarily given up the prosperity of their noble estate and having embraced poverty as a mark of conversion to atone for their sins, Hugues de Payns's *lay* knights had taken the name of "poor fellow soldiers of Christ"; they lived on alms from the population and wore clothes thrown away by others that had also been given to them as alms.[18]

A few years later, the group grew till they amounted to some thirty people. They were too many to remain with the Canons in the basilica of the Holy Sepulchre, or it might have been that the king of Jerusalem had felt the potential in the brotherhood and decided to take it under his wing; at any rate, the "poor fellow soldiers of Christ" moved to a wing of the royal palace, which the sovereign had earlier used as royal quarters.

The building stood near some ruins that were identified as the remains of the ancient Temple of Solomon, so people started calling them *Militia Salomonica Templi*, or even *Milites Templi*, and later, more commonly, Templars.[19]

Hugues de Payns and his companions had taken the three monastic vows of poverty, obedience, and chastity before the patriarch of Jerusalem; without being

---

18　On their origins, see, for instance, Barber, *The New Knighthood,* pp. 1-37; Demurger, *Vita e morte,* pp. 20-23, and Ibid. *Chevaliers du Christ,* pp. 36-40.

19　Demurger, *Vita e morte,* pp. 54-57. The original name is reconstructed by Tommasi, *Pauperes commilitones Christi,* pp. 443-475.

ordained priests, which would have been incompatible with the profession of arms that was at the heart of their mission, they were members of a kind of brotherhood in the service of the Holy Sepulchre and had achieved a Church dignity comparable with that of the many lay-brother monks who, without becoming priests, lived out their lives of penance and prayer in the convents of various religious orders. It may have been this special vocation of theirs that suggested to Baldwin II, king of Jerusalem, the next step: If the brotherhood became a genuine order of the Church of Rome, with all the exemptions and privileges that went with it, the new body would be free of possible external interests. They would be a mighty resource for the defense of the Holy Land.

The project faced many difficulties. In the 1,000-year history of Christianity, the profession of arms had never had favorable press, and some of the ancient Fathers of the Church even regarded soldiering as an offense against God. To deal with the issue, the greatest mystic of the time, Bernard the Abbot of Clairvaux, was called upon. Some scholars hold that he was related to the family of Hugues de Payns. The king of Jerusalem seems to have written a letter to him, asking him to patronize the new order's birth and work out a special religious rule in which service to God "should not be in contrast with the noise of war."[20]

In 1126 or 1127, Hugues de Payns left the East and traveled to Europe to canvass his project with the various feudal lords and find new followers. He also met the

---

20 Demurger, *Vita e morte*, p. 22.

celebrated abbot, who had thus far proved deaf to his prayers; it may have been then, speaking in person with the head of the religious brotherhood and hearing from his own lips the difficulties faced by the Christians in Jerusalem, that Bernard reconsidered the king's proposal. He realized that the military activity of these monks, if restricted purely to the defense of pilgrims and of other defenseless Christians, could be seen as a good thing, and very useful for the kingdom in the Holy Land. From then on, the abbot threw the whole weight of his authority behind the establishment of the new order. Bernard explained his great enthusiasm for the new project in a treatise titled *De Laude Novae Militiae*, in which the Templar Knight was celebrated as a warrior *saing*. He also brought in other religious celebrities of the time, such as the aged and venerated Stephen Harding who had written rules for important monastic foundations; he gained the papacy's support through the help of Aymeric of Burgundy, head of the papal chancery and right-hand man of Pope Honorius II. Thanks to his precious patronage, in January 1129, during an ecumenical council held in Troyes, the papal legate, Cardinal Matthew of Albano, granted pontifical approval to the new Order of the Templar militia, and approved its rule in the pope's name. A fine recent book by Simonetta Cerrini gives a clear account of the genuine spirit of the Templar rule, and the context of its approval.[21]

The brothers of the Temple lived in communities separate from the world and divided their time between

---

21 Hiestand, *Kardinalbischof Matthäus von Albano*, pp. 17-37; Cardini, I *poveri commilitoni*, pp. 81-114; Cerrini, *La rivoluzione dei Templari.*

prayer and armed service in defense of the Christian population. They were divided into two main groups: the milites—those who had received the investiture as knights and who wore white clothes as a mark of purity and perfection—and the sergeants, who had to be satisfied with darker clothes and who carried out essentially working tasks. Their popularity and protection from rulers made the Order a mighty institution, and their power grew in time, thanks to the special immunities they received: In 1139, Pope Innocent II, a disciple of St. Bernard, granted the Templars a privilege titled *Omne Datum Optimum*, which laid the groundwork for the Order's independence from any lay or ecclesiastical authority. This was later strengthened by several successive concessions that made the Templars a wholly autonomous body, subject only to the authority of the pope.[22] In 1147, Pope Eugenius III decreed that the Templar habit was to carry a red cross as a distinctive sign, in memory of the blood that the warrior monks shed in defense of the faith.[23] To be brief, the new order adopted the principle of *ora et labora* that regulated the life of all Benedictine monasteries, but in this case the manual labor carried out by the Temple monks took the form of military activity. Barely thirty years after its foundation, the Order had grown so swiftly that it was necessary to divide its establishments into a number of provinces, and its development continued throughout the 12th century. By about 1200, the Temple was present throughout the

---

22 D'Albon, *Cartulaire général de l'Ordre du Temple*, nn. 5, 8, 10.

23 Curzon, *Règle*, § 16; Cerrini, *Une expérience neuve*, § 6; Barbero, *L'aristocrazia nella società francese*, pp. 243-324; Demurger, *Vita e morte*, pp. 66-67.

whole Mediterranean basin, from northern Europe to Sicily and from England to Armenia, with hundreds of properties including fortresses, commands, and landed estates of various kinds. The provinces were under the control of a general overseer called the Visitor, who was charged—exactly—with visiting the various regions of the Templar world and referring back to the grand master and to the general chapter of the Order, which met once a year. By the end of the 1200s, there actually were two Visitors, one for the East and the other for the West.[24] The Templars were admired for their reputation as heroes of the faith and envied for their riches and the many privileges bestowed on the Order, and they also had a considerable religious charisma in contemporary society: Their leaders were regarded as highly authoritative experts in recognizing genuine relics, of which the Order had a vast store. It is legitimate to wonder on what basis their contemporaries developed this view or how the Templars went about distinguishing the authenticity of such objects. They certainly were greatly helped by their profound knowledge of the Eastern world, in which the Order had been born, but according to some sources, it seems that the Order's priests used relics of Jesus because their sacred power strengthened the force of prayer during exorcisms.[25]

The warriors of the Temple were subject to a strict military discipline that made them, when the time to fight came, a tight force with great capacity for coordination. Their military skills came with a great deal of *esprit de*

---

24 Curzon, *Règle*, §§ 87-88; Michelet, *Le procès*, II, pp. 361-363.
25 See, for instance, Michelet, *Le procès*, I, pp. 646-647; Schottmüller, II, pp. 392-393.

corps, which the rules tried to encourage in every way, and obedience to a most rigid code of honor from which no deviation was allowed. Their flag was the glorious banner called the *Baussant* because it was half-white, half-black, the symbol of Templar pride and excellence. Together with the fighters of the other great military religious order, the Hospitallers, they were the backbone of the Christian armed forces in the Holy Land, but there was an important difference between the two orders. While the Temple was, from the beginning, an institution designed for the military defense of the Holy Land, the Hospital of St. John had been born as a brotherhood to care for sick pilgrims and had only later also become a military order for the defense of the realm.[26]

Losing the Sepulchre, Losing Honor

In 1187, the sultan of Egypt, Saladin, who had managed to unite Muslims into a single front against the crusader states, annihilated the Christian army at a place called the Horns of Hattin. All captured Templars and Hospitallers were slaughtered, several fortresses fell to the Muslims, Jerusalem was lost, and the Holy Sepulchre taken from the Christians for good, save for a brief spell in the time of Emperor Frederick II, who made a special agreement with Sultan al-Kamil that seemed like treachery of a kind to many.[27] The loss of Jerusalem was a colossal injury to the Templar order, born exactly to defend the Holy

---

26 Gaier, *Armes et combats*, pp. 47-56; Demurger, *Chevaliers du Christ*, pp. 41-43, 131-147.

27 See *The Horns of Hattin*, ed. B. Z. Kedar, Jerusalem 1988, passim, and Lyons & Jackson, *Saladin*, pp. 255-277.

Land. Historians have abundantly documented its grave material losses, but there may yet be more to say about what we would call the troops' morale. The Templars had an extremely close bond with the tomb of Christ; in that ultimately sacred place, the ideal and material center of Hugues de Payns's first brotherhood had been born. Losing the Sepulchre meant losing their own honor. At the beginning of the 13th century, there was a great collective movement to restart the Crusades and recover the Holy City, and Pope Innocent III, who felt very strongly about this matter, tried to help the military orders, which were on their knees after Saladin's victory. Between 1199 and 1203, a new expedition to the East was set up under the leadership of the city of Venice and of some great French barons, but once it had reached Constantinople, the crusader host took advantage of the grave political decline of the Byzantine Empire, whose immense wealth excited the crusaders' greed. Though excommunicated by Innocent III, what was to be the Fourth Crusade for the recovery of the Holy Sepulchre turned into an ugly bloodbath at the expense of fellow Christians, even though their Church was supposed to have broken away from Rome with the Schism of 1054. The Venetians, who had driven the shift of object from Jerusalem to the wealth of Byzantium, shared the immense loot of the city—incalculable amounts of precious metals, artworks, unique relics—with the French, and they also partitioned the territories of the former empire, creating a new Latin Empire of the East. The event left a dark shadow over the image of crusading in general; it had become clear that some ideas no longer had the same hold over people's hearts, that political and economic interests stood now above everything else. From then on, Christian society started doubting whether it would ever be able to really retake the Holy Sepulchre.[28]

The Islamic re-conquest of the Holy Land went on apace throughout the 1200s, and the military orders were forced to become used to defeat after defeat. The Order of the Temple had to adapt itself to changing conditions by changing, for its part, its functions; if it was no longer possible to focus on military service, since the Islamic front was too strong, it was still possible to advance the financial activities that one day, when the time was right, could serve to reconquer Jerusalem. The Temple thus became a kind of bank in the service of the Crusades; popes used it to keep and invest the alms collected for the Holy Land, and the Order was also used as a treasury by Christian sovereigns.[29]

Between 1260 and 1270, Sultan Baibars cut the Christian kingdom down to a thin strip of coast land headed by the town of Acre in Syria. Western society started having serious doubts about the utility of military orders; many wondered whether it was right to keep these gigantic enterprises, loaded with privileges, going, when all they seemed to do was take one defeat after another and be wholly unable to recover the Holy Places. In 1291, Acre was also taken in spite of a desperate resistance in which the Templars proved heroic and Grand Master Guillaume de Beaujeu died fighting to cover the retreat of others. The last bulwark in the Holy Land was now gone, and the

---

28 See the items collected in *Quarta crociata*.
29 Demurger, *Trésor des templiers*, pp. 73-85; Di Fazio, *Lombardi e Templari*; Metcalf, *The Templars as Bankers*; Piquet, *Des banquiers au moyen âge*.

crusading age closed with defeat.[30] The event immediately had serious consequences for the military orders, who were forced to find other Eastern seats. The Templars and Hospitallers moved to Cyprus, while the Teutonic Knights, an order founded in the middle of the 13th century, shifted their activities to the frontier of northeastern Europe.[31]

The fall of Acre convinced Pope Nicholas IV that it was necessary to join the Templars and the Hospitallers into a new single order, larger and stronger and finally able to recover the Holy Land. This project had already been mooted in the Council of Lyons, in 1274, when it had also been suggested that the leadership of the new order be offered to one of the Christian sovereigns, possibly a widower or someone unmarried in order to respect the monastic nature of the institutions. Nothing had come of this initiative because the grand masters of both Temple and Hospital had opposed it fiercely. In 1305, the new Pope Clemens V started the discussion of fusion again and requested that the heads of Temple and Hospital offer a view on the matter and also produce a plan for a new crusade. Templar Grand Master Jacques de Molay declared himself firmly against it: If the two orders had been united and placed under a European sovereign, the latter would have made the new order a tool for his own political goals and forgotten all about Jerusalem and the Holy Land.

As for the new crusader expedition, the Templar leader suggested to the pope that its military leadership

---

30   Demurger, *Vita e morte*, pp. 235-236; Barber, *The New Knighthood*, pp. 119-220.

31   Ibid., see, for instance, pp. 213, 217, 236-237; Favreau-Lilie, *The Military*, pp. 201-227; Edbury, *The Templars in Cyprus*, pp. 189-195.

not be entrusted to Philip the Fair, but rather to James II of Aragon. The Catalan sovereign would have been very useful thanks to his powerful fleet, and besides—and this was very important—he was known to be very respectful of apostolic authority and to have a mind in line with that of the Templars, who regarded the pope as the Order's lord and master. Philip the Fair, on the other hand, declared himself openly autonomous of papal authority. Only a few years earlier, from 1294 to 1303, the king of France had been in open conflict with Pope Boniface VIII and had been excommunicated; the assault of Anagni, intended to arrest the pope and take him prisoner beyond the Alps, had prevented the bull of excommunication from being published, but the king's position was still very dubious. There also was a fact that should not be neglected: Philip the Fair wanted to pass the crusader troops through Armenia, with the intention of conquering that kingdom, which was Christian though not Catholic, and make it a French dependency. The Temple had a province of its own in Armenia, and the local leaders had informed the Templars that they would never admit French cavalry within their fortresses, for fear of being treacherously attacked. The memorial written by Jacques de Molay unmasked the French monarchy's true intentions in the crusade to come and no doubt put a major spike in Philip the Fair's plans; the king and his advisers surely saw the Order as a serious obstacle in their international policy. Still, in 1306, Philip the Fair found himself beset by popular revolt because of some financial maneuvers of his that had unleashed horrendous inflation on the kingdom. The king badly needed good money to stop the hole, and in the Paris Temple Tower—a fortress of awe-inspiring size—vast liquid capital was kept. That was when plotting against the Order began.[32]

Early in 1307, Jacques de Molay sailed from Cyprus to the European mainland to meet with Clemens V, while the leader of the Hospitallers had put off the trip because he had been forced to take command of certain military operations involving his order. The grand master of the Temple would never come back to the East again; a few months later, the long trial was to start, whose notorious events may be summed up in a few essential phases.

Under a Cloak of Infamy

At dawn on October 13, 1307, the king of France's soldiers appeared in full battle dress at all Templar commands in the kingdom to arrest all the monks in residence; they immediately started questioning them, tortured confessions out of them, and had them written up in official form so as to send them to the pope as evidence. They were following, word by word, the warrant of arrest signed by Philip the Fair and secretly sent out on the previous September 14. The king claimed to have acted after consultation with the pope and on a direct request by the French Inquisition because a strong suspicion of heresy had arisen in the Order. He said:

> They who are received within the Order ask thrice
> for bread and water; then the preceptor or master
> who receives them leads them secretly behind the

---

32   Frale, *L'ultima battaglia dei Templari*, pp. 43-48; Lizérand, *Le dossier*, pp. 2-15.

altar or in the sacristy; then, still in secret, he shows them the cross and image of Our Lord Jesus Christ and orders them to thrice deny the Prophet, that is, Our Lord whose image is present, and to thrice spit on the cross; then they are made to strip their clothes off, and he who receives them kisses them at the end of the spine, under the pants, then on the umbilicus, and finally on the mouth, and says that if any brother of the Order wants to be joined with them carnally, they must not deny themselves, for under the statutes of the Order they are required to bear it. For this reason, many of them practice sodomy. And each of them wears over his shirt a thin strand of rope which he is always to bear, his whole life long; these strands have been touched and placed around an idol of the head of a man with a long beard, a head they kiss and worship in their provincial chapters: but this is not known to all the brothers, but only to the grand master and the elders. Furthermore, the priests of their order do not consecrate the Body of Our Lord; this will have to be investigated most especially when Templar priests will be questioned.[33]

With incredible speed for that time, the fruit of a detailed strategy worked out in advance over years, Philip the Fair's officials gathered hundreds of confessions across the kingdom, which were presented to Clemens V as evidence of heresy before the Curia had time to react. The lawmen of the Crown had meant this to tie the pope's hands, leaving him little or no room for autonomous

---

33 Lizérand, *Le dossier*, pp. 16-19.

action: Immediately after the arrests, Guillaume de Nogaret, the royal lawyer who had been sent to Anagni to arrest Boniface VIII, organized some popular assemblies in which the Templars' guilt was advertised as certain. Franciscan and Dominican friars were ordered to preach to the people of the Templars' heresy, so as to create a true prejudice among the commoners.

Inquiries went on throughout France at a frantic pace till the start of the next year; in a short time, the dossier of accusations set up by the king's men of law swelled to monstrous proportions, and the charges already set out in the indictment of October 1307 were joined by new ones, formed from materials gathered here and there as pressure and torture produced their crop of confessions. It was an obscene crescendo, greedily fed by popular imagination that was to continue throughout the length of the trial like a river bursting its banks, dragging all kinds of detritus on its rabid way to the sea. It wasn't enough to have denied Christ and outraged the Cross: The charges against the Templars were to eventually grow from seven to more than seventy.[34]

Clemens V went from a state of utter confusion in the weeks that followed the arrests to a suspicion that the king was acting entirely in bad faith—a suspicion that turned into certainty when, toward the end of November 1307, two cardinals, sent to Paris to question the local Templar prisoners and so clarify the situation, came back to the Curia with the news that they had not been allowed to even see the prisoners. In December, a second delegation of the same prelates reached Paris,

---

34   Frale, *L'ultima battaglia dei Templari*, pp. 311-323.

this time with the power to excommunicate Philip the Fair if prevented again from meeting the prisoners. This allowed Jacques de Molay to denounce all the violence and grave irregularities he had suffered. The following February, the pope suspended the whole French Inquisition for grave irregularities and abuses of power, which stopped the trial in its tracks. The whole spring that followed was spent in a heated diplomatic war between the king, who had taken over the Temple's goods and wanted the Order condemned, and the pontiff, who refused to make any decision before he had personally examined the prisoners. Faced with Clemens V's obstinacy, the king understood that he had no choice so he allowed a minority of Templars, including the grand master and other high officials of the Order, to leave Paris under escort to reach the Roman Curia, then resident in Poitiers, and be questioned by the pope. Between June 28 and July 2, 1308, Clemens V was at last able to conduct his own investigation of the Templars; although the pope was the only person who had the legal authority to investigate the Order, paradoxically it was only then that he was able even to see the accused in person after months during which the confessions that had been tortured out of them had been spreading openly all over Europe. The evidence was by now as polluted as it could possibly be; the Order's honor had been crushed under a colossal cloak of infamy.

After finding that the officers of the king of France had made extensive use of torture, Clemens V found that, beyond the falsehoods constructed by the royal lawmen, the Templars admitted that a tradition existed, handed down in strict secrecy, that obliged new members to deny Christ and to carry out some kind of outrage against the Cross (generally spitting). The brothers explained it by saying, *modus est ordinis nostri*, or "It's a habit of our order." The existence of this secret ceremony, a kind of test of obedience placed at the end of the actual ceremony of admission, shifted the responsibility onto the Order itself; it was clear that the fault could not be ascribed to the individual brothers if they had been forced into those unworthy acts by their own seniors just to obey some Order custom. The Saracens used to torture Christian prisoners to compel them to reject Christianity, and as a tangible sign of apostasy, they required them to spit on the Crucifix: The Templars' odd ritual repeated this custom in a highly realistic, theatrical manner, including threats, beatings, and even isolation in a jail cell. Its purpose was to steel the new member's character through a traumatic experience by putting him immediately in the presence of what he would suffer if he ever fell into enemy hands; it probably also served to inculcate that total obedience that the Order demanded, surrendering his own freedom to hand himself over to the judgment of his superiors in practically total subjection. The denial of Christ and the spitting on the Cross had later been joined by elements of other origins, of the kind of senior-to-junior bullying and "initiations" well-known in armed formations, gross and humiliating practical jokes performed by veterans on recruits: These included the three kisses (on the mouth, on the umbilicus, and on the buttocks) and the warning not to deny oneself to brothers in search of homosexual sex. The invitation to sodomy was a simple verbal humiliation, never followed by concrete acts; only six Templars out of more than 1,000 who confessed in the trial ever actually spoke of homosexual relations with fellow knights.[35]

A Trial without a Verdict

In the pope's presence, the Templars had the opportunity to explain that the gestures of the admission ritual were nothing more than a stage performance that had nothing to do with intimate belief, a very unpleasant nuisance that had to be accepted because the Order required it. The fact that the denial happened under constricting terms excluded personal responsibility, and there could be no real guilt if the outrage against religion had not been done of one's own will. Clemens V became convinced that the Templars were not heretics, even though the Order could not be absolved because it had allowed a vulgar and violent military tradition, wholly unworthy of men under vows, to exist. His final judgment was severe but not condemning, not heretical but hardly without stain: The Templars had to offer solemn repentance, begging the Church's pardon for their faults; then they would be absolved and taken back into the Catholic communion. Between July 2 and 10, 1308, the pope heard out in person these requests for forgiveness and absolved the Templars as penitents, but an important part of the Order had not been reached by his operation. The grand master and the Order's highest officers, who had left Paris with the rest of the convoy, had been kept by royal soldiers in the fortress of Chinon

---

35   Ibid., pp. 169-205.

on the shores of the Loire, under the excuse that they were too ill to ride all the way to Poitiers. Clemens V immediately understood that the king intended to cut off the significance of the papal investigation at the neck, for if the pope had not been able to hear the leaders of the Temple, those who knew the whole truth, it was always possible to claim that his verdict was not complete or significant, since it had come from minor witnesses. After completing his investigation of the Templars who had reached him, Clemens V secretly sent to the Chinon castle three cardinals who heard out the Templar leaders from August 17 to 20, 1308, received their demand for forgiveness, and absolved them in the pope's name. It was not what we would call a quashing of the sentence, but rather a sacramental act that, however, had juridical features as well: The charge moved against the Templars had been for crimes against religion.[36]

Assaulted in his rights by the illegal arrest of the Templars, then once again deceived by the king's fraudulent effort to prevent him from meeting the heads of the Order, the pope could consider the Chinon inquiry as a forceful moral victory—the only kind of victory, alas, open to him, given his extreme political weakness. No later than the following October, shortly after the events of Chinon became widely known, Philip the Fair's strategists set out on a long-prepared action that directly attacked the Church of Rome: Bishop Guichard di Troyes, who had earlier fallen into disgrace at the court of France and had then been involved in a financial scandal, was charged with sorcery and burned

---

36   Frale, *Il papato e il processo ai Templari*, pp. 139-192.

alive by royal decree, even though Clemens V himself had previously cleared him of the charges. This repeated the plot of a trial from a few years earlier, of the bishop of Pamiers Bernard Saisset, whom Philip the Fair had hounded on charges of lèse-majesté and condemned to death against the will of the pope.

This fact was connected with the trial against Boniface VIII and that against the Templars, amounting as a whole to a plan to destabilize a bishop, a pope, and a whole religious order that had fallen under accusation of terrible crimes such as heresy and sorcery, and thus showed that the Church of Rome was riddled with corruption in every part of its body. Philip the Fair's lawmen were planning to dig up the body of Boniface VIII to subject it to a public trial, at whose end it was to be burned under the charge of heresy, sorcery, and blasphemy. The dead pope's burning would have placed the whole Church in an illegal position: The whole reign of Boniface VIII would have been considered invalid, and everything that had happened after the abdication of Celestine V, including the election of Clemens V, would have been proved null and void. With the College of Cardinals split and most French bishops loyal to Philip, the king threatened a schism that would separate the Church of France from that of Rome. Clemens V was faced with a dreadful dilemma: He had to choose whether to condemn the Order of the Temple as the sovereign demanded, or save it and risk the burning of Boniface VIII's body and the French schism with all its consequences.[37]

---

37   Frale, *L'ultima battaglia dei Templari*, pp. 265-299.

The pontiff chose to protect the unity of the institution for which he was responsible, sacrificing a part to preserve the whole. The Order of the Temple was by now effectively destroyed, blasted by the waves of scandal and defamation. Many brothers had died in the king's jails; many more had lost their motivation for good. In the spring of 1312, an Ecumenical Council was gathered in Vienne to decide, among other things, the fate of the Templar order; the pope did not conceal that the judgment was most controversial and a large part of the Council opposed its condemnation. After long thought, he felt there was only one way to solve the issue, avert irreparable scandal, and serve the interest of the Crusades: avoid a verdict and act instead by way of administrative decision—an official act required for practical reasons. Being a great expert in canon law, he sought an expedient not to condemn the Order of the Temple, of whose innocence, at least where the most serious charges were concerned, he was certain: In the bull *Vox in excelso*, the pope declared that the Order could not be condemned for heresy and was therefore "closed" by administrative fiat and without a verdict, to avoid grave danger to the Church. The goods of the Templars were handed over to the other great religious-military order, the Hospitallers; that at least made them safe from the greed of the French crown, and so they might possibly still serve the cause of retaking the Sepulchre and Jerusalem, the reason why so many people had donated gifts to the Temple in the past. Philip the Fair did not exactly accept that decision happily; in the end, however, the Hospitallers were able to have a consistent part of what had been the Temple's patrimony.[38]

---

38   The bull's text is in Villanueva, *Viaje literario, V*, pp. 207-221; Barber, *The Trial*, pp. 227-234.

Though unjust, the end of the Templar order proved historically convenient: The scandal roused by the trial had to be placated, and the doubts created by the Templars' confessions needed to be silenced. The scandal had made the Order odious to sovereigns and to all Catholics; it would no longer be possible to find an honest man willing to become a Templar. The Order had therefore lost its usefulness to the crusader cause for which it had been established, and furthermore, if a swift decision on the issue had not been reached, the king would have completely squandered its goods. Clemens V therefore decided to get the Templar order "out of the way" by refusing to issue a final sentence, but he forbade any further use of the name, habit, and distinctive signs of the Temple under the penalty of automatic excommunication for anyone who ever dared proclaim himself a Templar in the future. The pope thus eliminated the Order from contemporary reality, but by not issuing a formal sentence, he left judgment of the Order in abeyance.

In the end, then, there was no conviction or convict, but a defendant severely punished for crimes different from those he had been indicted for. Something of the same kind also happened with the trial against the late Boniface VIII, which is hardly surprising since the two issues were intimately bound up with each other, and their resolution was the result of a long diplomatic struggle made up not just of negotiations, but also of actual blackmail from both sides.

The fate of the leading Templars was still undecided, and they were awaiting the pope's judgment, when, on March 18, 1314, after the Order had been proclaimed innocent, Grand Master Jacques de Molay and Preceptor of Normandy Geoffroy de Charny were abducted by royal soldiers and condemned to be burned on a little island in the Seine without any reference to the pontiff. Old, sick for years, and severely tested by that long clash with the French monarchy, Clemens V was no longer in any condition to exert influence; he died about a month later, and his death marked the start of the Church of Rome's exile in Avignon. Later popes, pressed by other emergencies, preferred not to deal with the odd situation of the Templar order—never condemned but practically shut down by virtue of a wholly exceptional decision.[39]

The Mysterious Presence

The most recent research into the documents of the Templar trial has allowed many points to be clarified. The documents proved, among other things, that the construct of Philip the Fair's indictment had an explosive impact because it was built on some foundation of fact; certain charges such as the denial of Christ, the obscene kisses, and the spitting on the Cross came from a few actual facts, suitably distorted and reworked into evidence of heresy. A few years before he moved openly against the Temple, the king of France had secretly intruded into the Order some spies to collect any kind of information that might help damage it; then a group of royal men of law led by Guillaume de Nogaret had worked the information into a detailed and imposing

---

39 Frale, *L'ultima battaglia dei Templari*, pp. 300-304; Demurger, *Jacques de Molay*, pp. 263-277.

castle of accusations. These clever technicians of the law started with a few basic points and derived facts from them just as is done in mathematical sciences when building a theorem. It's no exaggeration to say that Nogaret and Co. built the "theorem of Templar heresy." Their technique was that of the half-truth: Every charge they wanted to prove must have a hook in genuine fact, unpleasant or censurable, but committed without intention of sin, and the Templars would admit to the fact itself under questioning—such as that they had been forced to deny Christ—but they would then deny the charge that hung from it, that they did not believe in Christ. But at that point, their position hardly looked solid.[40] The very same scheme was employed to argue that the Templars had turned their back on Christ en masse to indulge in the worship of a mysterious idol.

The charge started with a material and evident fact. The Templars wore a little strand of linen string over their tunics. That was something nobody could deny because everyone had seen it. Indeed it was clearly mentioned in the part of Templar statutes dealing with the brothers' dress. The Templars knew that it had some kind of symbolic rather than practical value since they were under obligation never to take it off—even when they slept at night—but they did not have any clear idea what it was. Leaning on this unarguable fact of this little linen string, Nogaret and the king's other strategists would argue that that object had in fact a perverted meaning, and stated that it had been in contact with a devilish object, a dark and mysterious idol in the shape

---

40   Frale, *L'ultima battaglia dei Templari*, pp. 207-263.

of the head of a man with a long beard. According to the charge, the Templars offered this idol special liturgies reserved only for the highest dignitaries. These were solemn ceremonies during which it was worshipped, kissed, and rubbed with the linen strands that would later be distributed to all brothers in the Order.

The linen belt was a most banal little object which could never in itself have been used to defame the Templars, but it was something that concerned the whole Order, all its members, one after another. The idol, on the other hand, was a wholly exclusive matter that could only be used against the higher officials. Making the Templar linen strands somehow "fouled" by contact with the dark idol, however, Nogaret threw the charge of idolatry at every single monk of the Temple "contaminated" by the idol, possibly without knowing it thanks precisely to that little belt he had worn every day.

Of all the charges thrown at the Templars, idolatry was no doubt the darkest, and it is not at all strange that such a suggestion inspired so many novelists. Curiously, however, this charge was not Nogaret's *pièce de résistance* in the trial, not his chief weapon, but a little side corollary stuck on as a kind of tail to so many other charges: In his indictment, Philip the Fair made it quite clear that only a very few Templars knew of the idol. Why such a disagreement between potential effect and actual work? The answer is simple: The prosecution, who had built a theorem on solid bases from a decade's worth of reports from its moles, knew quite well that the three disgusting acts of the ritual of admission were common matters practiced in every command of the Temple. Practically every Templar could be led by threats or other methods to admit facts that were part of the daily life of the Temple, facts that could be manipulated and distorted, but the existence of the idol, whatever it was, was an issue purely for the elite, and the hope of wringing out any confession seemed very distant indeed. Rumors about that mysterious object were, to Nogaret, very attractive; they would have allowed him to create a theatrically effective comparison to shock the pope: Just as Moses came back to find, to his rage and grief, that the Jews had, in his absence, abandoned the cult of the sole God and had built themselves a golden calf, so too Pope Clemens V was to have the evidence that the Templars, themselves monks in a religious order, secretly worshipped a strange idol that had fallen into their hands. There was, however, a severe problem: If only the leaders of the Temple knew of the idol, it could be expected that only a very few confessions would be gathered.

What Philip the Fair wanted was the entire demolition of the Order, so he had to convince the pope that the whole Templar body was poisoned by corruption and heresy; the condemnation of the leaders alone was no good to the king. They would have been removed and replaced, while only a mass indictment of the whole Order would have allowed him to demand from the pope its total extinction. A few confessions, however red-hot, were worth little to the prosecution: Even if ten or twenty Templars could be found admitting that they practiced sorcery and raised devils, that would have amounted to nothing because it would have seemed a sin—although a dire and inexcusable one—that affected only the culprits. At that point, the Inquisition would have convicted the individuals. Nogaret and Philip the Fair, however, needed large numbers and had to find charges that, even if less serious, were so widespread in the Order as to let them say that one could hardly find even one Templar innocent of them. The military ritual of admission suited this need exactly; the secret ceremony, with its apparent outrages against Christian religion, was ideal. The ritual was known to be commonly practiced, though in widely divergent forms, so nearly every member of the Order could admit that they had carried out at least some of those guilty acts, such as denying Christ or spitting on the Cross, and since judicial procedures at the time weren't too refined, the general confusion raised by the scandal could well be used to suggest that the whole order was affected by anti-Christianity. Emphasis on the idol in the prosecution's scheme would have been ill-advised, since it risked suggesting that the whole castle of charges was built on mere calumny. Like the smart lawyer he was, Nogaret preferred to bet on charges that the monks themselves were more likely to confirm, and so he reduced the matter of the idol to an obscure, if chilling, detail: He made it clear in the indictment that the existence of this simulacrum was unknown to the vast majority of monks. As had been expected, the harvest of reports of idolatry was exceedingly small, scarce, and mutually highly contradictory, though Philip the Fair's strategists did what they could to manipulate and paint them in the grimmest possible colors.

A Mosaic of Fragments

Examination of the documents leaves no doubts whatsoever. Only a small, tiny minority of the Templars who appeared in the trial were able to say anything at all about this phantom object. And even within this tiny minority, many mentioned it only because they had heard talk about it from others, that is, from no personal knowledge at all. That is a pretty sad haul when compared to the near totality of testimonies that have nothing whatsoever to say about it. Out of 1,114 Templar testimonies recorded during the trial, only 130 included even a hint of the idol, and most of those did nothing but repeat what the prosecution said; clearly, these were the miserable products of torture and other forms of violence. Only fifty-two statements gave any information at all about the idol—4.6 percent of the total. About this, at least, Philip the Fair did not lie: Very few Order members were aware of the matter, as compared to the immense majority that had no idea whatsoever. We may take this as reliable since the inquisitors and the royal lawmen were hardly short of means of persuasion. These very few witnesses, utter exceptions to the rule, didn't even describe the same object, giving in fact the most wildly different details. This must have discouraged historians from looking with due scholarly care into this field: In effect, the great variety of images makes it all seem like a big hodgepodge of things said at random. So the whole trial was condemned without distinction as a set of tragic lies caused by torture.

Matters are further complicated by the fact that some monks gave more than one statement over the course of the trial, changing their stories from one inquiry to another for reasons that we can sometimes only guess at (torture, promised rewards, the desire to avenge some personal wrong, etc.). A classic case is that of Brother

Raoul de Gisy, preceptor of the command of Latigny and charged with exacting the king's taxes in the county of Champagne: This man went from a red-hot first account of events, in which he claimed to have seen the idol no less than seven times and that it was the image of a devil, to a wholly different one in which he said he had seen it only once, by chance, and had no idea what it really was. The explanation lies in the fact that Raoul de Gisy made his first confession on November 9, 1307, under pressure from Guillaume de Nogaret and the Inquisitor of France—an interrogation carried out immediately after the wave of illegal arrests, when the king needed the most serious evidence against the Order, and fast, to justify before the pope his violation of the rights of the Church; the second was released on January 15, 1312, in an inquiry carried out by a commission of bishops when the pope had already taken control of the trial and interrogations were taking place with greater guarantees.[41]

Historians may find themselves as disconcerted as archaeologists would when, on opening the site of an ancient garbage pit, they meet with thousands of tiny pieces of pottery, different in make, material, and color, each of which will have to be carefully identified and re-made. In spite of the difference between the disciplines, there is only one way to make order out of chaos and reach a sufficiently valid understanding: One has to work with minute patience, bringing all fragments of the same type together and at the same time discarding extraneous material that does not help and that has found its way into the heap by chance.

---

41   Michelet, *Le procès,* II, 363-365; I, 394-402.

Some certainties may be reached as soon as we start reading with care the circumstances in which individual question sessions with the Templars took place, and they greatly help us understand many things about the trial. We know, for instance, that in some cases Templars were questioned once, but the inquisitors were not satisfied with their statements. Instead of taking the testimonies as they were, they had the brothers tortured, then gave them time to think it over, and finally staged a second question session: This time, their confessions, full of detail that their tormentors found satisfactory, were accepted and taken down as evidence. We also know that the trial went through several phases, and that these phases were widely different both in the methods used by the questioners and in their good faith. Therefore, the statements sought by the questioners also changed widely according to date and place; he who asked the question was very able to influence the answer.[42]

The issue of the idol is one of the most complex, since it was a charge that lent itself more than any other to becoming colored by fantasy, in part because of the violence used to question the Templars, and in part because of the power of psychological suggestion—a mighty power and never to be underestimated—that rose everywhere in the dark climate of the scandal. Once we get over the first, disconcerting impact, it becomes clear that behind all the descriptions of the idol there are only five kinds of objects that appeared over and over again, if maybe with varying details. Three of these were cult objects, items basically not too different from many others that the medieval faithful saw every day in

---

42   See, for instance, Frale, *L'interrogatorio ai Templari*, pp. 243, 253-254, 258, 259, etc.

their churches: a reliquary-sculpture showing a head, neck, upper chest, and shoulders; a painting on wood; and, finally, the portrait of a man with a rather strange and ill-defined frame. No doubt, if such portraits were worshipped in secret, it made it all the more urgent for investigators to know who the man was that they represented, but the presence alone of such objects in Templar churches was not enough to support a charge of heresy. On the other hand, the reliquary and painting lent themselves to it wonderfully, for they were things that could make an enormous impression on the minds of medieval men: Had the prosecution only been able to find any such things in a Templar command and take them to the pope, it might have been enough to get a swift condemnation of the entire Order. The first of these supposed "idols" that the questioners tried to make the captive monks describe as a bust of Mohammed, was presented as evidence that the Templars had betrayed the Christian faith and gone over secretly to Islam. The second was supposedly some kind of monstrous or even devilish image, useful in proving that the Templars had been practicing sorcery.

Idols of Islam

The identification of the idol with a bust sacred to Islam is found in six testimonies, but it is not certain or identical in all cases. Brother Sergeant Guillaume Collier from Buis-les-Baronnies said explicitly that the brothers called the strange head *Magometum*, while two monks questioned in Florence and Clermont said they had each seen an idol called, respectively, *Maguineth* and *Mandaguorra*; in the inquiry that took place in Carcassonne, the monks Gaucerand de Montpézat and Raymond Rubei stated that it was made *in figura baffometi*, and the latter specified that it was addressed as *Yalla*, an Arabic word.[43] In the inquest carried out in Tuscia, near Rome, the sergeant Gualtiero di Giovanni from Naples said that during his ceremony of admission to the Temple, there had been a real theological discussion to deny the dogmas of Christianity, and the idol, a figure of Allah, had been at the center of the debate: He said that brother Alberto made him deny Christ and told him that he should not believe in him. Brother Gualtiero then asked: "And in whom should I believe, then?" The same brother Alberto answered: "In that great and single God that the Saracens worship."

He then added that it was wrong to believe in the Father, the Son, and the Holy Ghost, because they amounted to no less than three different gods, and he ended by stating that the grand master of the Temple and the preceptors in charge of a province had an image that represented that same God, worshipped him as creator, and exhibited his bust in general chapters and in the most important assemblies. This testimony may perhaps be connected with that of Pierre Segron, who was told by the preceptor that he should not believe in Jesus Christ but only in the Almighty Father: This confession, however, contains no reference to Islam.[44]

About the name of this supposed reliquary, there is one clear testimony that calls it *Magometum*, a form very

43   Ibid., pp. 243-245; Bini, *Dei Tempieri*, p. 474; Sève, *Le procès*, p. 114; Finke, II, p. 323.
44   Gilmour-Bryson, *The Trial*, p. 255; Frale, *L'interrogatorio ai Templari*, pp. 252-253.

close to the genuine pronunciation; according to two brothers in Carcassonne, it was called *Baffometum*, a word that comes from the former but is distorted on account of the translation from Arabic to French. It is this form that has given rise to the fanciful etymologies once proposed by Hammer-Purgstall and accepted today only by readers of fantasy fiction. The other two variants, *Maguineth* and *Mandaguorra*, are also deformations of the original word, while the strange invocation of the idol supplied by another Templar, *Yalla*, seeks to replicate the Arabic form *Allah* with a strong initial aspiration that the notary who had to write the minutes in Latin rendered with the letter Y. But is it conceivable that the Templars, maybe even a small part of them, had become Muslims? Their strange, secret admission ritual practiced after the licit ceremony did indeed have a direct relationship with the Muslim world: In the East, it was known that Saracens forced Christian prisoners to deny Jesus Christ and to spit on the Cross, on pain of death if they refused. This is described in the chronicle of the Franciscan Fidenzio da Padova, and the ritual of obedience invented by the Templars to test their recruits repeated these gestures in a kind of theatrical performance. The king of France's lawyers had found out about it after years of secret investigations: Managing to confirm that the Templars had gone over to Islam en masse would have been vitally important to get the condemnation they were seeking, even better if they could prove that the mysterious idols on which the king had gathered a few scraps of information were in fact of Mohammed.

Two facts prove that this charge was utterly false— incoherent elements incompatible with each other yet liable to be brought together somehow by a 14th-century European mind. To begin with, it is well known that the Islamic religion utterly forbids images of the Prophet, and all images of Mohammed are actually figures of his body with his face hidden by holy fire. The "idol" ascribed to the Templars, however, was clearly the bust of a normal human being with a bearded face; it cannot in any way be considered an image of Mohammed. The same is true of the testimony of that Templar who claimed the idol was an image of Allah: The Qur'an utterly forbids any representation of God whatsoever, for this would be idolatry, and Islamic civilization has always been most careful to respect this rule. The second feature is even more definite: According to one witness, the idol of this supposed *Machomet* had horns[45]! That proves beyond a reasonable doubt that the tale has no relationship whatsoever with real Islam; it was the fruit of tortures carried out by inquisitors and went exactly where the torturers wanted their witness to go, for their own reasons. No Christian who had anything actually to do with any Muslim group could ever have imagined them worshipping the Devil; in spite of all their strong religious differences, Muslims were highly devout and had a few essential points of faith in common with Christians—in particular, a single creator God who is a benevolent and just Father. Unarguable historical evidence tells us that a certain amount of inter-religious debate went on in Jerusalem, and it is at any rate well

---

45   Ibid., pp. 245-246.

known that St. Francis of Assisi was received by the sultan of Egypt and took part in a theological debate with him. In the Holy Land, Muslims were essentially political opponents, people who governed Jerusalem and Syria-Palestine alongside Christians; the whole history of the Kingdom of Jerusalem is full of alliances between Christian rulers and various local emirs, alliances based on common interests and setting religious differences aside.[46] In a country such as France, where no Muslim communities existed among the population, the common people had the most vague and bizarre ideas of Islamic religious traditions: The largely illiterate commoners, used to the simplistic idea that one went to the Holy Land to kill enemies of the faith, could easily be led to believe that those enemies of the faith had something dark and devilish about them. It is probably not a chance occurrence that this kind of rumor found no fertile ground either in Spain or in Cyprus where contact with Muslims was frequent and Christians had a much clearer view of them. Not that it made any difference to Nogaret whether or not the brothers worshipped Mohammed or even the Devil, as long as they could be charged with an unforgivable crime that struck deep into the imagination of the popular masses.

The Shadow of Ridefort

In the current state of research, I think that the Templars who said that the idol was a bust of *Mahomet* may have seen a vaguely human image, but strange or at least

---

46 Tommaso da Celano, *San Francesco*, p. 73; Cardini, *Francesco d'Assisi*, pp. 178-208.

unlike those of the saints seen everywhere in churches. Pressed by torture, and having no understanding whatsoever of the identity of the man represented, they were forced to make statements of that kind. Without a doubt, it was the portrait of a man, but since nobody understood who it was, it must inevitably have been something illicit. The fact is that there was no way to freely interpret a work of art in the medieval world because all images were rigidly controlled, and therefore every personage could be recognized on sight. Medieval sacred art had fixed iconographic forms because its purpose was not just to guide but to educate souls; already, Pope Gregory I the Great (590–604) had strongly recommended respecting this precept: The faithful were largely illiterate and did not have the ability to understand too elaborate a set of concepts, so the figures that illustrated sacred history on the walls of churches were a great treasure store for the people, forming the doctrine of the common person.[47]

There was an ancient, consolidated tradition, known to everyone and used as a guide: St. Peter must always carry a large key in his hand, as the symbol of his power, and St. Anthony the Abbot had to wear his monk's hood and have a meek little pig sitting by his feet, so that the faithful could recognize them immediately. Artists had to follow fixed schemes; their interpretative liberty was limited to secondary details, and at any rate their work was evaluated by relevant Church authorities. A representation of holy subjects that did not conform to Church tradition appeared suspicious and would be condemned, for it could create confusion among those

---

47 Gregory the Great, *Letters*, IX, epist. LII, in PL 77, 971.

who did not have enough culture to defend themselves against error. Had the Templar idol been a traditional image of any saint, the monks would have recognized him; instead, everyone who saw this portrait agreed that they could not tell who it was, that there were no elements to help identify him. Showings often took place at night: In the dark church, lit only by the irregular light of candles, the atmosphere became that of a mysterious and grim cult. Required to worship the portrait of someone they did not recognize, and conscious that it was a secret cult, the monks were awestruck and experienced these liturgies as terrible things.

The king of France's agents took advantage of this fact and tied it to the charge that the Templars had gone over to Islam, thanks to an easy (and unhistorical) syllogism: The Order of the Temple is friendly with Muslims; in its ceremonies a man of unknown identity is worshipped; therefore, that mysterious man must be the prophet of Islam, Mohammed. The accusation obviously had no roots in reality, since Islamic religion forbids the portraiture of Mohammed, and therefore even if many Templars had indeed gone over to Islam, this cult described in the trial would have been utterly impossible. But Nogaret was not concerned about the charge being true, so long as it could be believed by the Western world that was being asked to condemn the Order. The king's grand strategist had dusted off the shelf a rumor already more than 100 years old, which had been popular for a while and had momentarily stained the Order's good name. When, in 1187, Saladin had won his memorable triumph at the Horns of Hattin and taken back Jerusalem for Islam, he had always behaved most generously to the local Christians, granting freedom not only to the rich who could pay their ransoms, but also to the poor, for the mere love of God; it was only to the Templars and Hospitallers, the true thorns in his military side, that he had shown no mercy whatsoever, and had them beheaded. In that context, Templar Grand Master Gérard de Ridefort, captured by the enemy, had been returning to his people unhurt when everyone already believed him dead. As everyone knew how the sultan saw the Templars, this had immediately struck everyone as most suspicious. Besides, Ridefort was well known as an adventurer, an opportunist, and a traitor of friends who had risen in Templar ranks without gaining anything like a good reputation on his way up. His reputation grew even worse when it became known that he had bartered his freedom for the surrender of Templar fortresses. In a word, he had betrayed the Order in the vilest of manners.[48] The conditions agreed upon at the time between Ridefort and the sultan had shocked Christian society so much that the echo of the scandal was recorded in the Chronicle of St. Denis; besides, Christian society was appalled by the disaster just suffered, the military orders were being singled out by everyone as the main culprits in the failure, and a scapegoat hunt seemed inevitable. The cowardly, arrogant, unworthy Ridefort seemed born for the role.

This was the source that Guillaume de Nogaret pulled from shelves to charge the Templars of having gone over to Islam. A few similar rumors had spread again toward the end of the 13th century, when certain diplomatic

---

48   Runciman, *Storia delle crociate,* II, pp. 628, 660-675; Lyons & Jackson, *Saladin,* pp. 250, 303-304.

agreements made by Christian leaders in the Holy Land with the Muslim enemy had not been understood in the West and had caused intense polemics. During the trial, Guillaume de Nogaret suddenly turned up and resurrected the whole affair, to which Jacques de Molay had to give an answer:

> In the chronicles kept at the abbey of Saint-Denis, it was written that in the time of Saladin, sultan of Babylon, the Templar grand master of the time and the other heads of the Order had paid homage to Saladin. Saladin in turn, having heard of the grave adversities being suffered by the Templars, said in public that they were meeting all that trouble because they had fallen into the vice of Sodom and prevaricated their faith and their laws. The grand master [Jacques de Molay] was astonished at those words, and he answered that he had never heard anything of the kind.

> On the other hand, he knew that once upon a time, Guillaume de Beaujeu, the master of the Temple, used to murmur against the grand master, that he had served the sultan and kept him sweet.

> In the end, though, both he and the others were happy with that policy, because they understood that the grand master had had no choice. In those days, the Templar order held several towns and fortresses, which he named, at the border of the

---

49   Michelet, *Le procès*, I, pp. 44-45.

sultan's land, which could not have been defended by the Christians had the king of England not sent supplies.[49]

In the Holy Land, diplomacy was as much a weapon of war as weapons themselves, perhaps even more so: The first decades of the crusader kingdom had enjoyed comparative quiet just because the Muslim powers abutting it had often preferred to make alliances with the Christians and remain autonomous rather than fall under the sway of a much bigger Islamic power. The work of Grand Master Beaujeu, who later died heroically at Saracen hands while protecting the flight of civilians by the sea, had been dictated by political reasons, and at the news of his odd Islam alliance, his full good faith became suspect among the ill-disposed who began to think the Templars were not inept, but rather had no intention of attacking Islam because it had covertly gained their sympathies. The context and dynamics of the trial were to turn this scrap of gossip into a black accusation.[50]

Many Faces

The Templars who described the idol as if it were a bust of the Devil were full of surreal detail: The monster had many faces; he was associated with a black cat who always appeared mysteriously; he was worshipped during the witches' Sabbath; and he was even said to answer the monk who prayed to him and to promise him hefty material advantages. Any historian would be immediately tempted

---

50   See, for instance, Michelet, *Le procès*, I, p. 187; II, pp. 209, 215.

to reject such descriptions, taking them for nothing but the sorry fruit of torture; however, it is better to avoid quick judgments, because experience shows that even the most absurd statements may sometimes conceal grains of truth in their depths, real facts that have to be brought to light by cleansing them of the many dark details added by torture, psychological violence, and the awful suggestions raised in the atmosphere of the trial.

We know, for instance, that medieval Christian tradition used to represent the dogma of the Trinity by means of three separate but identical figures, or even of one body with three faces. It was the *vultus trifrons*, an arrangement thought up in the 1200s to somehow give a visual account of the complex concept of a single God in three Persons. During the Council of Trent (1545–1563), many features of popular religion that had previously been accepted by everyone were weighed and discussed, and among them was the three-faced head: It was seen that this image was too much like certain ancient representations of pagan gods, such as the Roman Diana, whom Virgil calls in the *Aeneid* (IV, 511) "Virgin with three faces," or the Greek Hekate, goddess of the Lower World, associated with the moon and represented with three faces to allude to its three phases—crescent, full, waning. Hekate was the queen of the Otherworld, and in some pagan magical texts, she was called upon by magicians and sorcerers; in the Roman imagination and in that of early Christianity, she was seen as an image of the Devil, even though the deity did not originally have anything evil about her, and in the tradition of medieval art, three-headed demonic monsters can sometimes be found (as, for instance, in the front of the Church of St. Peter in Tuscania). In 1628,

Pope Urbanus VIII forbade any further representation of the Trinity under that pagan-originated and, all things considered, monstrous scheme, and in 1745, Benedict XIV ordered that the three Persons should be only represented according to images found in Holy Scripture: the Father as a venerable elder, the "Ancient of Days" of the book of the prophet Daniel; the Son as a young man; and the Spirit in the shape of a dove. We know that the Order of the Temple was originally dedicated to the Holy Trinity, and in the text approved at Troyes, the founder and his followers are called, exactly, Knights of the Holy Trinity; we cannot in the least exclude that the churches of the Order included some sculptures of this very peculiar kind, little used in Gothic art but absolutely licit, seen as late as the Renaissance in Donatello's decorations of the tabernacle of St. Thomas the Apostle in Orsanmichele, Florence.[51]

A magnificent manuscript from the Vatican Library, painted in Naples by Matteo Planisio in 1362, features a cycle of miniatures representing the creation of the world: God is represented as the Three Persons of the Trinity, a venerable elder with a two-faced head, one as an old man (the Father) and the other as a beardless teenaged boy (the Son), while the dove that represents the Holy Spirit rests on his shoulder.[52] If we exclude the dove, which is not equally visible in all the miniatures, one must admit that the Creator appears as a strange being with one head and two faces: The smooth-featured boy's face, with no facial hair, does in effect seem like a woman's. Medieval art does from time to time come up with this kind of

---

51 Wehr, *Trinità, arte*, coll. 544-545; Naz, *Images*, coll. 1257-1258; Curzon, *La Règle*, §9.
52 Biblioteca Apostolica Vaticana, Vat. Lat. 3550, f. 5r.

invention. It does not find it so important to represent things realistically as much as bring out symbolic and spiritual meanings. Certainly such images must have seemed monstrous to anyone who saw them without adequate preparation.

It's hard to tell what these simulacra, described by some Templars as having two, three, or even four faces, ever stood for. Some testimonies certainly spoke of real things, sacred goods used for liturgy and cult, while others were no more than the deformed result of terror and violence. For this purpose, it can be very useful to consider the geographical areas where the various questionings took place. The trial took place practically all over Christendom, with inquiries in France, England, Scotland, Italy, Germany, the Spanish peninsula, and Cyprus. And yet all the scary and filthy testimonies were concentrated in France, especially in the historical region of Midi, which was the headquarters of the dreaded Inquisition. From this region comes an unfortunately incomplete document, which can only be called the "Languedoc Inquiry" since it lacks any reference to the place and date of questioning. However, many clues suggest that the well-known inquisitor Bernard Gui was involved at least in the information-gathering stage. This document is an absolute mine of information about the factors that affected the trial, and does much to explain why scholars such as Nicolai, Hammer-Purgstall, and many more had such a grim picture of the ceremonies that took place in the Temple.[53]

---

53   See, for instance, Frale, *L'interrogatorio ai Templari*, pp. 254, 255, etc.
Ménard, *Histoire civile, Preuves*, p. 210; Michelet, *Le procès*, II, p. 363.

Right from the first affidavit to survive without damage from the Languedoc Inquiry, the interrogated monk, a sergeant named Guillaume Collier from Buis-le-Baronnies (Drôme), said that he was admitted with a normal ceremony, but that immediately after, the preceptor refuted some fundamental dogmas of Christianity, such as the divinity of Jesus and the Virgin Birth; then he opened a secret window in a part of the church, where a silver idol with no less than three faces was kept. He was told that that idol represented a mighty patron of the Order who could get them any kind of grace from Heaven. Then, suddenly, he saw a mysterious red cat appear near the idol; immediately, the preceptor and all those present doffed their caps and paid homage to the idol, whose name was Mahomet (*Magometum*).[54]

This is a genuine cliché that formed a pattern for the path of confession and was repeated from affidavit to affidavit; however, as each successive Templar spoke, the pattern grew more elaborate and more gross, as in a kind of ghastly crescendo. According to the next monk to be questioned, another sergeant, named Ponce de Alundo from Montélimar (again in the Drôme), the idol even had horns; indeed, it was no longer a simple image, but a real demon that even lived and spoke: The candidate spoke to it as one would to a real person, asked it for material favors, and was promised its support. This time, the mysterious cat that appeared by the idol was black, more similar to the animal that contemporaneous imagination placed with witches; by the preceptor's order, the devil-cat was to be adored and kissed on its anus. As we go on reading other testimonies, we

---

54   Frale, *L'interrogatorio ai Templari*, pp. 243-245.
55   Ibid., pp. 245-246.

find that the obscene detail of the kiss of the cat is a constant, and that the animal also seemed to be nearly always black. However, two theatrical details appeared: The magical feline vanished miraculously as soon as he had received the new monk's homage, and someone concluded that it must in effect be the Devil in the shape of a cat.[55]

The records then brought in a further sensational development: A knight by the name of Geoffroy de Pierrevert, preceptor of the mansion of Rué in the department of Var, said that he had been present at an admission ceremony during which, apart from an idol with no less than four faces and a devil-cat, the demonic presence was also manifest in the apparition of some women in black mantles, who materialized in the room even though all the doors had been closed and barred. According to him, the strange women had no carnal relations with the monks present at the ceremony. This surely disappointed the inquisitors greatly but they were soon satisfied when, during another session, Garnier de Luglet, from the diocese of Langres, said the witches who had appeared had indeed been allowed to corrupt the monks, vanishing immediately after they had dragged them into deadly sin.[56]

In short, the questions were built according to a scheme that tended to dig through successive layers: First, the accused was questioned about the idol's presence, then the questioner asked whether a cat was also present, and if the answer was positive, they proceeded to investigate the animal's role in the ceremony and its real nature. With those who proved ready to give a positive answer in this crescendo, the questioning moved further, asking first about the apparition of witches, then hammering on the question about celebrating a

---

56   Ibid., pp. 256-257, 267-269.

demonic orgy. The procedures employed in Languedoc had unique features in the context of the broader trial. It seems to be the area where the evidence was most polluted by the conscious intervention of the inquisitors: Here, the charges against the monks were much more serious than those conceived by Philip the Fair in his order of arrest, which was intended to get the Templars condemned as fast as possible. The very minutes of the investigation said it in so many words: Witnesses would be first properly prepared with suitable tortures, then they were left for several days to reflect (or recover at least enough to be able to speak), and finally were questioned again.

The way such trials were managed speaks volumes: During the inquest held in Poitiers from June 28 to July 2, 1308, Clemens V interrogated, with the help of his assistant cardinals, seventy-two Templars within five days; Philip the Fair himself and Inquisitor of France Guillaume de Paris, immediately after the arrests, had questioned no less than 138 brothers captured in the Temple of Paris in barely a month, from October 19 to November 24, 1307. The investigators who managed the Languedoc Inquiry, however, took an amazing two months to question barely twenty-five persons; the "preparation" of witnesses must have been horrendous.[57]

A letter written by the inquisitor of France, Guillaume de Paris to Bernard Gui, the most famous inquisitor of the 1300s, entrusted him with some

---

57   Archivio Segreto Vaticano, *Archivum Arcis*, Armarium D 208, 209, 210 (number 217 is the Chinon parchment), and Reg. Av. 48, ff. 437r-451v): about the edition, see Schottmüller, II, pp. 9-71; Finke, II, pp. 324-342; Michelet, *Le procès*, II, pp. 275-420; Frale, *L'interrogatorio ai Templari*, pp. 199-272, also p. 226.

operations in the trial against the Templars, and rouses a legitimate suspicion: The Languedoc Inquiry, Languedoc being Bernard Gui's headquarters, did not follow the scheme of Guillaume de Nogaret, but rather another drawn up by the dreadful inquisitor who pursued charges of sorcery and devil-raising.[58] In the indictment written in Paris by the royal lawyers, the idol is in fact quite a marginal issue and there is no trace whatsoever of devils; whereas, in the confession extracted from the Templars in Languedoc, the strange idol was described with reports of the Devil in the shape of a cat and of witches, and the description of these sinister rituals takes up a great deal of the text. To the contrary, in the north of France, the charge of sodomy was placed very much in the forefront, as if it alone were enough to blast the Order's reputation beyond remedy, and a boy was even found who was ready to confess that Jacques de Molay (who was well over 60) had abused him no less than three times in a single night.[59]

In the south, on the other hand, sodomy went altogether unmentioned: Maybe the ordinary mentality was more tolerant, or else it was simply decided to go for something much more "explosive." In a way, the idol had indeed many faces—faces different from each other, indeed sometimes incompatible—which the prosecutors hid or showed depending on what the tastes and fears of the public were.

---

58 Frale, *Du catharisme à la sorcellerie*, pp. 168-186; Frale, *L'interrogatorio ai Templari*, pp. 199-242. On the myth of the idol, see also Reinach, *La tête magique*, pp. 25-39.

59 Michelet, *Le procès*, II, pp. 289-290.

II

Behold the Man!

A Peculiar Sacredness

Once we have cleared the field of all confusion and ascertained the origin of the charges of Islamism and black magic, the other descriptions of the Templars' idol seem suddenly very concrete; it's simply a bust of a human, made of diverse materials and representing an unknown man. It's in this group of realistic observations, descriptions of simple objects of sacred art, that we find the most interesting data. The idol is a simple object, although for some reason the Templars seemed to think it incomparably valuable. That it was a portrait came out immediately, during the very first interrogations that followed the arrests of October 1307, but the sensationalism with which the Templars' arrest had been advertised confused everyone. People had started yelling about heresy and sorcery, and now they saw them everywhere.

Sergeant Rayner de Larchent saw the bust twelve times during twelve separate general chapters, and the last was the one held in Paris the Tuesday after the feast of the apostles Peter and Paul, the July before the arrest. As he described it, it was a bearded head that the monks kissed, calling it their "savior"; he did not know where it was placed or who kept it, but he guessed that it was the grand master or the officer who oversaw the general chapter. It was also seen in Paris by brothers Gautier de Liencourt, Jean de La Tour, Jean le Duc, Guillaume d'Erreblay, Raoul de Gisy, and Jean de Le Puy. The ceremonial display was presided over by the grand master, or more often by the Visitor of the West, Hugues de Pérraud, who was second in the Templar hierarchy and became the most powerful Templar in Europe when the grand master happened to be in the East.[1] When questioned, Hugues de Pérraud admitted the existence of this idol and its cult, but said precious little to help us in our modern historical research.

> Of the head we just mentioned, he said under oath that he saw, held, and touched it near Montpellier during a chapter. Both he and the other brothers worshipped it: he, however, only pretended adoration, acting with the mouth but not with the heart, and could not say who else offered adoration from the heart. Asked where the idol was, he said that he left it with Brother Pierre Allemandin, who was preceptor of the mansion of Montpellier, but he could not say whether the king's agents would find it. He said that this head had four feet, two in front on the side of the face, and two behind.[2]

The testimony does not specify what kind of simulacrum this was. However, it states that it had four feet, which points at a three-dimensional object held up by supports.

---

1   Michelet, *Le procès*, II, pp. 279, 299, 300, 313, 315-316, 364, 367.
2   Ibid., 363.

At the end of his and the Roman Curia's inquest in the summer of 1308, the pope took over the investigation from the inquisitors and decreed that it was to be handed over in each territory to special commissions formed by the local bishops. These were not dependent on the king of France and did not have to follow the plans of his legal strategists; the pope only tasked them with shedding light on the thorny affair. Some of these bishops may not have loved the Templars for personal reasons; it is well known that there was widespread envy of this rich and powerful religious order with its many privileges, but they had no direct interest in persecuting it—as was the case with the king and with Guillaume de Nogaret's group. It's hardly surprising that it is during the investigations carried out by diocesan bishops that many of the accusations thrown previously started to totter, while others suddenly took a more rational and credible aspect. The diocesan bishops swiftly came to understand that the Templars' notorious idol-head was in fact a reliquary, an upper bust sculpture containing the remains of some saint, a very widespread class of object in medieval sacred art: This came out clearly as soon as the management of interrogations was handed over to the pope, and in the very inquiry held in Poitiers in June 1308, Clemens V was able to come to the conclusion himself. In his presence, the sergeant brother Étienne de Troyes spoke of the idol:

> Concerning the head, he said that it was the Order's custom to celebrate each year a general chapter on the day of the apostles Peter and Paul, and one of those was held in Paris the year he was admitted into the Order. He took part in the chapter all three

days it lasted: They would begin in the first watch of the night and went on until the first hour of day. During the first night of the chapter they carried a head: It was borne by a priest, who was preceded as he moved forth by two brothers who held large torches and burning candles in silver candelabra. The priest laid the head over the altar, on two pillows and a silken carpet. The witness thought it was a head of human flesh, from the top of the skull to the knot of the epiglottis; it had white hair, and nothing covered it. The face also was of human flesh, and seemed to him very livid and discolored, with a beard of mixed white and dark hair, similar to the beard that Templars wear. Then the Order's Visitor said, "Let us worship him and pay him homage, for it is he who made us and it is he who can dismiss us." They all approached it with the highest reverence and paid it homage and worshipped that head. He heard someone say that that skull had belonged to the first master of the Order, Brother Hugues de Payns: From the Adam's apple to its shoulder blades, it was covered in gold and silver and studded with precious stones.[3]

The same object, in all likelihood a reliquary of the founder, Hugues de Payns, was also seen in the Temple of Paris by Brother Bartholomé Bocher of the Chartres diocese, who joined the Order in 1270; according to him, the reliquary did not stay in that place, but was only carried there during special occasions and was then taken away and put elsewhere:

---

3   Archivio Segreto Vaticano, Reg. Aven. 48, ff. 449-450r.

The Templar who welcomed him into the Order showed him a certain head that someone had placed on the altar of that little chapel by the sanctuary and the vases with the relics; he was told that when he was in difficulty, he should call on the help of that head. Asked how that head was made, he answered that it looked like the head of a Templar, with the head cover and a hoary and long beard; but he could not tell whether it was made of metal, wood, bone, or human flesh, and his preceptor did not explain whose head it was. He had never seen it before nor did he see it afterwards, although he must have been in that chapel at least a hundred times.[4]

There was a certain suggestive power to this tale, told in the pope's presence, as he had the opportunity for the first time to personally listen to the Templars after nearly a year of hearing accusations and dreadful rumors. The scene of that mysterious cult, emerging from the dark into the shaky light of candles, indubitably could not have made a positive impression on him. But in and of itself, the evidence was not very damning. The Templars paid special homage to their founder Hugues de Payns, revering him as a great saint during certain nocturnal liturgies, when they would expose his head, whether mummified or naturally preserved, within a large and precious reliquary. Hugues de Payns had never been officially canonized, and to the Church of Rome, he remained simply a *conversus* who had chosen to serve God in the same way countless other unknown priests and monks had. Hugues de Payns had never been raised to the honor of altars, and Clemens V,

---

4   Michelet, *Le procès*, II, pp. 192-193.

as a specialist in canon law, could not look kindly on such solemn veneration. But in the Middle Ages, people used to regard some people as saints purely for their simple lifestyle, even during their lifetimes. As soon as they died, their bodies and the objects they had owned immediately became precious relics; people would start coming to pray on their graves, asking for miracles and intercessions with God, without waiting for the Church to complete its long, prudent bureaucratic process. Saints were made by popular acclamation. When the rumor spread through Assisi that Francis was dying in the Porziuncola, people began praying, waiting impatiently to finally be allowed to see and worship the stigmata on his body: This is a famous and peculiar case, but many more of its kind exist.[5]

The idea that contact with the bodies of saints had beneficent effects was certainly no medieval innovation. It belonged to the most ancient Christian tradition: The Book of Acts tells that people approached Paul as he was preaching, and the faithful would touch his clothes with silken handkerchiefs, because they were certain that they were making relics for themselves. The apostle's divine charisma passed from his body to clothes and kerchiefs.[6] It might be that the worship of their founder, Hugues de Payns, whom they held to be a holy man, may have led Clemens V to admonish the Templars to reduce the homage to more sober proportions, but it was very, very far from evidence of heresy. As a matter of fact, in the Cyprus interrogations, carried out by a commission of local prelates 1,000 miles from Philip the Fair and his

---

5 Tommaso da Celano, *San Francesco*, pp. 130-138; see also Cardini, *Francesco d'Assisi*, pp. 231-273.

6 19, 11-12 (Nestle-Aland, p. 1167).

influence, the Templars absolutely denied any charges of deviant behaviors or ideas where religion was concerned. Furthermore, many secular nobles, priests, and religious leaders from other orders offered to testify, declaring that the Templars observed religious rituals with exemplary devotion. It seems that they practiced very peculiar and beautiful liturgies of the adoration of the Cross during Good Friday, in which others who were not Order members would also take part. A priest said that he would celebrate Mass in Temple churches, and had from time to time celebrated jointly with Order chaplains: The formulas of the consecration of the Host were spoken exactly as required. A Dominican who often carried out religious service with the Templars said that he had heard many of them in confession, both in Cyprus and in France, and none of them had heretical attitudes on their conscience.[7]

The charge of idolatry and disbelief in the Eucharist soon proved utterly hollow. And yet Guillaume de Nogaret and his assistants had gone about building it just as they had done with the other charges, with the method of half-truths. They had started with a core of actual facts, a bread crumb of truth, suitably amplified and distorted.

Intuitions

In 1978, Ian Wilson published an essay titled *The Shroud of Turin: The Burial Cloth of Jesus Christ?* It was a well-written and a rather well-researched book following the

---

7   Schottmüller, II, pp. 375-400, 379-380, 392-398.

story of the Shroud over almost 2,000 years, from Gospel descriptions to the latest scientific investigations of 1973. Out of this broad panorama, the author dedicated a chapter of some fifteen pages to the investigation of a rather bold theory of his: There was, in the history of the Shroud, a "hole," an empty space of about a century and a half (from 1204 to 1353) during which this object seems to disappear from historical sources. On the basis of evidence drawn both from documents and from objects the Templars had owned, the author maintained that the mysterious "idol" worshipped by the Templars was in fact the shroud kept at present in Turin, folded on itself and kept in a container designed to show only the face. The theory made a great impression because in its light, several obscure points in the story of the Templars also became easily understandable; Wilson, however, did not specialize in this subject and knew only the most famous sources of the trial, so a lot of precious data escaped him. In any case, those fifteen pages contained an intuition of immense historical interest and left the scholarly community with a burning curiosity that the few bits of evidence used could not possibly satisfy. In recent years, the sources of the trial against the Templars have been investigated, both in much greater depth and more systematically than had been the case in the past, and this has led us to bring to light historical truths that once seemed dubious or out of focus—indeed, shadowy. Can they also tell us something about the relationship between the Templars and the Shroud? Luckily, yes, quite a bit—thanks mainly to some testimonies left "hidden," as it were, in an authentic document little known to experts. A document that seemed to have little to offer to the study of the political and judicial aspects of the trial but that could not matter more in the study of Templar spirituality. Templar experts barely mention these facts in their studies. The same happens in another area that has been investigated by scientific methods for over a century— sindonology, the complex study of the Shroud of Turin. I think it better to show the reader this new evidence of Templar matters by discussing it on its own, without reference to Wilson's theory: This is to avoid two strands of argument superimposing themselves on each other and conditioning each other. We shall therefore look at the bare sources, just as they appear to a researcher who first reads them, without influences gained from reading other studies. Later, the material will be compared to Wilson's intuitions, and we can verify what historical scenario arises from it.

Throughout the second phase of the trial against the Templars, the one that took place after the summer of 1308 when the investigations were being carried out by diocesan bishops, the investigators began to ascertain that the Templars' "head" was in fact the reliquary of some saint, and started asking clear-headed questions to this purpose. A significant case is that of Sergeant Guillaume d'Erreblay, a sometime alms-giver for the king of France, who was questioned by the commission of bishops who managed the Paris investigation in 1309–1311. This man had often seen a handsome reliquary of silver used in the normal Temple liturgies, exhibited for the veneration of the faithful who came to pray in the Order's churches. Some said that it was the reliquary of the 11,000 virgin companions of St. Ursula, who were martyred in Cologne, and that was what he too had believed. However, after the arrest, and under the psychological power of the prosecution, it occurred to him that there were many odd things about it: He seemed to recall that that reliquary had a monstrous aspect, with two faces, even of which one had a beard.[8] A modern historian will suspect that the witness had been badly affected by the context of the trial, to the point of talking nonsense: How could anyone exhibit for the veneration of the faithful the portrait of a girl saint with two faces and a beard? In fact, this Templar must have described two different objects. It was only from other brothers that he heard of the reliquary of the Eleven Thousand Virgins, while what he saw himself with his own eyes may indeed have had two faces. His description is identical to the miniatures painted by the painter Matteo Planisio on the manuscript *Vaticano Latino 3550,* in which the Creator is shown with two faces, one bearded and masculine (the Person of the Father) and one of an adolescent youth (the Son) who may well look like a woman. The superb Neapolitan miniature is one example, but who knows how many similar objects existed in medieval churches?

The commissioner bishops took the statement and immediately ordered a check; it was thus found that the Temple of Paris really did hold a reliquary with the bones of one of the Eleven Thousand Virgins, but that far from being monstrous, it was handsome and represented a perfectly normal young woman's face.

> At that point, the designated guardian of the Order's goods after the arrest, a certain Guillaume Pidoye, who held the crates containing the relics found in the Templar mansion of Paris, was called to the hearing.

---

8   Michelet, *Le procès*, I, p. 502; II, p. 218.

The guardian was ordered to take to the trial every
object shaped as a head, whether of wood or metal,
that was found in that building; he then handed over
to the commissioners a large, handsome, gold-plated
silver reliquary that represented a girl. Inside they
found bones that seemed to be part of a skull, sewn
in a white linen cloth and then placed in another
red cloth. Along with the cloth there was a small
ticket that said "testa LVIII M." The head seemed
to belong to a girl child, and some said it was a relic
of one of the Eleven Thousand Virgins. Since the
guardian stated that there was no other head-shaped
object, the commissioners summoned Guillaume
d'Erreblay and showed him the reliquary, but the
Templar said it was not the same and that he doubted
he had ever seen that one in the Temple's mansion.[9]

Discovering that the Templars' mysterious head was
in fact a silver reliquary weakened the prosecution's
structure of accusations, since it roused suspicions that
the other charges against the Templars could have been
the result of similar distortions. It is, however, true that
the commissioners noticed that the Order had peculiar
liturgies and cults that the brothers did not clearly
understand. Sergeant Pierre Maurin had been inducted
into the Order by Grand Master Thibaut Gaudin in
about 1286, in a room of the great Templar mansion of
Château-Pélerin in the Holy Land; on that occasion, he
was shown no simulacra of any kind, but he became very
curious when he was handed the little linen strand, which
he had the duty never to take off despite nobody being

---

9   Ibid.; Gugumus, *Orsola e compagne*, coll. 1252-1267.

clear on just what it was for. When two or three years had passed one day, while he was in Château-Pélerin, he found out from fellow brother Pierre de Vienne that a mysterious cult object was preserved in the central treasury of the Temple in Acre, and that this object was in the shape of a head; all the Templars' linen strands were consecrated by touching this head. The reliquary was said to contain remains from the head of St. Blaise or of St. Peter, but from that day on, he started feeling a strong unease and no longer wanted to wear the strand on his body.[10]

On the other hand, the treasurer of the Paris Temple, Jean de La Tour, saw a portrait painted on a board that was hung in the Order's chapel near the central crucifix. He could not find out whom the representation was of, but he thought that it must be the image of some saint: He was, however, certain that the man could not be a Templar, for he did not wear the typical Templar dress. Nevertheless, it was certainly not monstrous, and though he refused to worship it, the sight of it caused no kind of fear.[11]

The trail of the male portrait, with the figure of a man whose identity was unknown to the Templars themselves, is surely most interesting; it seems to point straight to the notion of a most sacred figure, worshipped by the Templars with the highest devotion, even though only a very few among them knew who he was, and in fact he was not easy to recognize: Those who saw him had trouble describing him. Who was he?

---

10   Michelet, *Le procès*, II, p. 240.
11   Ibid., I, p. 597.

A Man's Image on a Cloth

The records of the interrogations carried out of the Templars jailed in Carcassonne in the winter of 1307, a few months after the arrests, have survived in a single document kept in the Paris National Archives—a copy on paper made to be sent to Philip the Fair. The material is much darkened and is not in a good state of preservation, but it is perfectly readable to anyone who is familiar with the sources of the trial against the Order of the Temple. Early in the 20th century, Heinrich Finke tried to publish it but found it exhausting and finally made a somewhat questionable decision to transcribe only a few passages he had identified in his edition of the Templar trial. These were bitten-off chunks of sentences, stitched together with dotted lines to indicate the many things he had not managed to read. These brief gobbets of Latin in the middle of a flow of academic German form a bizarre linguistic patchwork: The whole thing is far from the norm of today's historians and really quite disjointed enough to confuse anyone. That may be why this has been, thus far, practically ignored by historians as a source. I have presented and discussed this source, along with many others, in my doctoral thesis at the University of Venice (1996–1999), when I was collecting all surviving evidence from the trial to make a systematic analysis of the data and compare them to each other. Its content struck me immediately as of immense interest, because I think that, together with so much other data, it proves that the mysterious idol of the Templars was a very famous object with a well-defined identity. It was effectively a portrait, but the least that can be said is that it was not just any portrait.

The Templar brother Guillaume Bos, who around 1297 received the Templar command of Perouse near Narbonne, was shown an "idol" of peculiar shape, a very different image from the others, which were mostly reliquaries worked in bas-relief. It was a kind of monochromatic drawing, a dark image on a light background of a cloth that seemed to his eyes to be made of cotton (*signum fustanium*):

> And immediately a kind of drawing on a cloth was taken to the same place and spread out in front of him. Asked whose figure it represented, he answered that he was so astonished at what he had been told to do that he could hardly see it, nor could he distinguish very well what person was represented in the drawing; it seemed to him, however, to be made of white and black, and he paid it worship.[12]

Jean Taylafer, heard in Paris during the long inquiry of 1309–1311, saw the same kind of object: It was a kind of drawing with an ill-defined shape, made of a tint that seemed reddish to him, and he could only distinguish the image of a face that had the natural dimensions of a human head. Like Guillaume Bos, he could not be sure whether it was a painting or not, but in that case, too, he said it was an image in a single color. Another Templar named Arnaut Sabbatier, on the other hand, said explicitly that he had been shown the whole figure of a man's body on a linen cloth, and then was ordered to worship it three

---

12 Du Fresne, *Glossarium*, p. 447.

times, kissing its feet (*quoddam lineum habentem ymaginem hominis, quod adoravit ter pedes obsculand*).[13]

The document is authentic, and, in spite of its less than perfect condition, the passage can be read clearly. Unless we reject the reality of the historical source, it shows that some Templars in southern France were shown an "idol" identical to the Shroud of Turin, which is precisely a linen cloth showing a man's image. Nor can there be any doubt that the figure contained the entire body, not just the head; the witness says in so many words that the Templars worshipped it by kissing its feet. Nobody can deny that the Shroud, if seen for the first time by someone who has no idea what it is, will seem just like a kind of imprint or large, ill-defined stain on a long piece of linen, a clear imprint with no outline or contour, showing the features of a man's body. It is a characteristic of the image that it becomes visible or invisible according to the distance at which it is seen, which immediately reminds us of the Templar witnesses who remembered that the image of the idol "appeared and disappeared" suddenly. There are many clues to suggest that the various descriptions of this Templar idol are nothing but an account of the Shroud of Turin, rendered in an imprecise and fragmentary manner by persons who could only look at it for a short time, most often in a container that only showed its head; we should not forget that the Templar ceremonies took place in the earliest hours of the morning, before the sun had yet risen; this object was seen, practically speaking, in dark

---

13   Michelet, *Le procès*, I, pp. 190-191; Paris, Archives Nationales, J 413 n. 25, unnumbered folios (f. 9); Finke, II, pp. 323-324.

rooms, and above all, without the faintest clue about what it was. Arnaut Sabbatier's evidence, on the other hand, describes explicitly an obstension (a religious exhibition or display) of the actual Shroud, when the cloth was fully unfolded to show the image of the whole body. It also describes a precise liturgy of worship that involved a threefold kiss on the mark of the feet; curiously enough, the same gesture was offered with the highest devotion by St. Charles Borromeo and his company of priests during their famous pilgrimage on foot from Milan to Turin to see the Shroud in October 1578. The Jesuit Francesco Adorno, who went with St. Charles and wrote an account of the events, knew perfectly well what he was going to see, and yet stated that he was completely astonished, dumbstruck before the cloth—the same kind of emotion described by so many Templars in the trial. Indeed, the Jesuit had already seen a fine copy of the Shroud, made at the order of its owner, Duke Emmanuel Philibert of Savoy. Yet the original was something else: The picture on the cloth of Turin left the impression of a living, suffering man giving up his last breath.[14] The Templars worshipped the Shroud in the same way that St. Charles Borromeo did three centuries or so later, at least those among them who had the privilege to contemplate the original relic and not one of the many copies scattered about the commands of the Order. According to Adorno, St. Charles and a few others also kissed the wound in the side, along with those of the feet, and by the regretful tone easily felt in his words,

---

14 Savio, *Pellegrinaggio di san Carlo*, pp. 447–448.

one can guess that he did not have that great privilege. As of now, we don't know whether the Templars used to kiss the side as well; the monk who left his account of this ritual was fairly low in Templar hierarchy, and everything leads me to think that the privilege of kissing the wound in the side would be, if anything, saved for the highest dignitaries.

The wounded side of Jesus, from which, according to the Gospel of John, had come blood and water, has moved Christian emotions deeply since the most ancient of times. They were certain that it had an immense value and that it was in some way a mark of the divinity of Jesus: Some scholars argue that John the Baptist himself who told the story also ascribed to it a strong theological significance, since in his denomination water is the symbol of the Holy Spirit. Christian tradition claims that the Church itself had been born from that wound, just as a child is born from the pain and the love of a mother. Most monks were uneducated, but among the dignitaries there were some scholarly persons; we can mention, for instance, the poet Ricaut Bonomel, who wrote a poem on the fall of the Holy Land that became and remains famous, or the chaplain Peter of Bologna, an outstanding legal expert who struggled to defend his order during the trial. At any rate, it took no great intellectual to understand that that wound on the side was the source of the Eucharist, which the priest celebrated on the altar by mixing wine and water in memory of that Gospel passage.[15]

15   Demurger, *Vita e morte*, pp. 220-221; *Frale, L'ultima battaglia dei Templari*, pp. 287-293; Brown, *La morte del Messia*, pp. 1330-1338; Id., *Giovanni*, pp. 1181-1195.

For several reasons I will explain comprehensively later on, the Templars were deeply fascinated with that wound through the ribs, and in their eyes it had incomparable value. Perhaps they thought it too holy for anyone to dare touch, at least anyone who was a Templar of the modest rank of the man who had given his testimony in the Carcassonne Inquiry.

The information that the Templars worshipped the image of a man on a linen cloth clearly spread and ended up rousing the curiosity of the commoners, perhaps much more widely than the sources would let us know today. In fact, it was even recorded in the Chronicle of Saint-Denis, the vast book of memories written by the Parisian abbey that was particularly bound to the Crown of France. The monks of St. Denis did not see the Templars' idol either as a likeness of the Devil or as a portrait of Mohammed, but rather described it in essentially two different forms:

> And shortly after they began to worship a false idol. According to some of them this idol was made from a very ancient human skin that seemed embalmed [*une vieille peau ainsi comme toute embalmeé*], or else in the shape of a washed cloth [*toile polie*]: in it do the Templars place all their most vile faith, and in it they believe blindly.[16]

In the end, the matter of the notorious Templar idol was a real fiasco for the prosecution, especially when they tried to color this object with the dark tints of sorcery. Nogaret had felt it from the beginning: During the first

16 Dupuy, *Histoire*, pp. 26-28.

interrogation, carried out in Paris by the Inquisitor of France, the ground had been tested, but Templars who knew anything about it were too few and gave wildly confused descriptions. So the royal lawyers had decided to pass over the matter and aim instead for charges that nearly every brother would be ready to admit to. The inquisitors of the Midi, true professionals of the witch hunt, gave the Templar idol the connotations of incarnate evil according to their own peculiar mentality: Maybe they acted in bad faith, or maybe they had themselves somehow fallen under the spell of their ghastly profession, prisoners of the specters created by their own minds even as they heard out the confessions of their unfortunate victims. At any rate, the idol as an image of the Devil or a portrait of Mohammed did not travel very far beyond the grand inquiry of Languedoc, which was, beyond argument, the most bloodthirsty in the entire trial. Later on, when, after the summer of 1308, Pope Clemens V managed to hand the investigations over to commissions made up of local bishops, the idol's nature grew clearer into an increasingly detailed compound picture of two liturgical objects: The first was a reliquary in bas-relief containing the remains of some saint; the other a very strange linen cloth that bore the mark of the whole figure of a man in monochromatic drawing, a kind of imprint with ill-defined features.

The Power of Contact

Whoever the mysterious man worshipped by the Templars may have been, he was regarded as so sacred and mighty that someone, at some still unknown point in Templar history, had thought it best to make sure that his charisma reach and protect Templars physically throughout their lives. And this even without their knowledge, thanks to a small object that kept and passed on his power. The trial sources include many statements ascribing to the Templars' little linen strand a very special kind of sacredness, derived from contact with an object worthy of the highest reverence: Very few of them knew that it had been consecrated with the power of a most highly venerable object, and within this narrow circle, someone was aware that the strands were themselves potent relics, for they had been made holy thanks to contact with the "idol."[17]

The use of always wearing, even at night, a little strand of linen over one's shirt had been introduced as early as St. Bernard's Rule, approved in Troyes in 1129. Its meaning was chiefly symbolic, for it was a kind of warning to keep the vow of chastity. Sleeping with one's pants on and with the tight belt over one's shirt was seen as a very decent thing, since the brothers slept in dormitories with their beds next to each other; the light of little lanterns would burn all night, to protect honest intimacy and discourage the ill-intentioned of any kind, including persons looking for undesirable encounters.[18]

As time went on, though, the awareness of this ancient meaning was lost, to the point that at the time of the trial only a few remembered it. At some point in the 13th century, a new symbolic tradition having to

---

17 See, for instance, the statements made by the monks questioned at Pont-del'Arche, in Prutz, *Entwicklung*, pp. 334-335, and Dupuy, *Histoire*, p. 22.

18 Curzon, *La Règle*, §§ 21, 37.

do with the linen strand arose and spread, because the original tradition was at this point obsolete; by 1250, the Templars used to consecrate the strands of their habit by placing them into contact with the most important places in the Holy Land connected with Jesus's life, or else with individual relics kept in Outremer and greatly venerated by the Order.

The knight Guy Dauphin, preceptor of the Temple in the French region of Auvergne and member of the general staff, explained it clearly during the trial:

> He said they would wear a thin strand over their shirts with which they slept as a sign of chastity and humility; the strands he himself wore had touched a pillar that stood in Nazareth, exactly in the place where the angel had made his annunciation to the Virgin Mary, while others had touched precious relics kept beyond the sea, such as those of saints Polycarpus and Euphemia.[19]

Guy Dauphin had been received among the Templars in 1281, but the habit of consecrating the strands through contact with relics was older. The knight brother Gérard de Saint-Martial, an old man at the time of the trial, had joined the Temple in 1258 and said that it was usual to turn the strand into a relic by consecrating it with the sacred spirit of the Basilica of Nazareth, where the archangel Gabriel had brought the news of Incarnation to the Virgin.[20]

---

19   Michelet, *Le procès* I, p. 419.
20   Archivio Segreto Vaticano, Reg. Aven. 48, f. 443r; Schottmüller, II, pp. 64-66.

How is this habit to be explained? The answer is very simple and may already be found in the Bible, which expresses the religious mentality of Hebraism, from which comes that of Christianity. When God appeared to Moses on Mount Horeb in the shape of a burning bush that was not consumed, He ordered him to remove his sandals, for that was holy ground (Ex. 3, 1–6). The place would always have kept some of the power of that Supreme Being who had manifested Himself there, and to touch the holy soil would always have been of great benefit to the faithful. After 1250, Jerusalem having been lost for decades and the chance of recovery growing ever more remote, the Templars felt the need to keep physical contact with the place of Christ's life, so they got into the habit of making individual relics to carry constantly on their bodies, as a defense against sins of the soul and the dangers of battle. This, after all, suited the nature of a military and religious order well, and St. Bernard had also emphasized that the Templar was always fighting on two fronts all the days of his life. During the previous decades, when Jerusalem and the Holy Sepulchre had been guarded by Christians, the Templars would go to the great Basilica to celebrate particular nocturnal liturgies of which the sources tell us nothing: They probably consecrated their linen strands, the symbol of the religious vows of the Temple, resting them on that very stone where the corpse of Jesus had been placed after the Crucifixion.[21] If that is the case, they would have made them priceless relics of the Passion of Christ, to be kept forever on themselves, guarding their physical

---

21 Curzon, *La Règle*, § 40.

and spiritual salvation. Later, having lost the Sepulchre to Saladin's re-conquest, they had to resign themselves to consecrating their strands with something different; other Holy Places of the Christian kingdom, which certainly did not have the same value as the Sepulchre, or other relics that the Order had acquired, which formed a treasury kept in the city of Acre during the second half of the 1200s.

Among the Templars, a rumor kept going around that the mysterious "idol" was kept in that treasury of Acre, and everything leads us to believe that its identity was kept secret from most of the monks.[22] Whatever it was, there were several copies owned by the Order and scattered among its commands; these simulacra seem to have been exhibited to be worshipped by the Templars, and also by the secular faithful who used the Order's churches, as if the simulacra belonged to some mysterious, sacred figure who protected the Order especially. The bust was considered more as a relic rather than a simple image; it was kept and exhibited along with other Templar-owned relics, and the liturgy by which it was honored included the ritual kiss traditionally given to relics.[23] According to some Templars, the idol was called "the savior"; it was prayed to not for material benefits such as wealth, success in love, or worldly power, but rather for the highest Christian goal—salvation of the soul.[24]

Can we know with any degree of certainty who the man represented in the portrait was? Fortunately, we

---

22 Sève, *Le procès*, p. 192.
23 Michelet, *Le procès*, I, p. 502, II, pp. 191, 279; Archivio Segreto Vaticano, Reg. Aven. 48 c. 443v; Schotmüller, II, p. 67.
24 Archivio Segreto Vaticano, Reg. Aven 48, f. 444r, lines 15-17.

can. In 1268, Sultan Baibars conquered the fortress of Saphed from the Templars; he was certainly astonished to find, in the fortress' main room—the one where the Order's charter was held—a bas-relief featuring the head of a bearded man. The sultan could not understand who that man was supposed to be, and unfortunately modern historians are no better off, for the monument was destroyed. There are, however, other figurations of the same character, found on objects that certainly belonged to the Templars, objects preserved to this day and which allow us to see—we might even say, touch with our hands—the identity of the mysterious man: some seals of Temple masters kept in German archives, bearing nothing but a portrait of a bearded man on the verso, and a wooden panel found in the church of the Templar mansion of Templecombe in England.

Without any doubt, these are copies of the Face of Christ, represented without aureole or neck, as if the head had been somehow separated from the rest of the body. It is a fairly rare iconographic model for medieval Europe, but extremely widespread in the East, for it reproduces the true aspect of Christ such as it appeared in the *mandylion,* the most precious of all relics owned by the emperors of Byzantium. A very ancient tradition told that it was a portrait of Christ, made not by human hands but created miraculously when Jesus had passed a towel (Greek, *mandylion*) over his face; it was not, properly speaking, a portrait but rather an imprint. Kept in the great sacred treasury of the imperial palace in Constantinople, the *mandylion* was copied in countless frescoes, miniatures, and icons on wooden boards, and the tradition of this miraculous portrait eventually spread to the West. To this day, some of Europe's greatest basilicas have works of art that reproduce it—such as the icon on cloth known as the Holy Face of Manoppello; those kept in Genoa, Jaen, Alicante; and the one preserved in St. Peter's Vatican inside the chapel of Matilda of Canossa—all copies of the *mandylion*, made in the East.[25]

What is particularly interesting about the table of the Templar church of Templecombe is that it reproduces the very shape of the display reliquary in Constantinople, as it is shown in many representations, of which the best is the magnificent miniature on the codex *Rossiano greco 251* of the Vatican Apostolic Library: The Face seems to be inserted in a kind of rectangular container that has the very dimensions of a towel, more long than broad, and this container has an opening in the center that allows only the sight of the Face of Jesus, separated from the neck and from the rest of the body. In the icon of Templecombe, this opening that shows the human features of Jesus and separates them from the rest of the body is an elegant, geometric four-leaf-clover motif widely appreciated in the East and used by the Byzantines since at least the 9th century.[26]

The Templars' mysterious idol, then, was nothing more in and of itself than a portrait of Jesus Christ, of a most unusual type. But in the mess of interrogations, tortured or even only terrified by inquisitors, many monks ended

---

25   These images, which belong to the Byzantine tradition of iconography, have been studied by Wilson, *Holy Faces*.
26   Sterlingova, *The New Testament Relics*, pp. 88-89. I am grateful to Emanuela Marinelli for informing me about this object.

up describing anything that could somehow resemble that strange male head the torturers wanted information on at all costs. It was a portrait that followed an Eastern iconography, imported from Constantinople but little known in Europe, and it was present in many commands of the Order in different forms—as an icon painted on wood, as a bas-relief, and as a linen cloth which bore the representation of the whole body. The last of these was only seen by a few monks in southern France: It did not look like a painting, but rather like an image with ill-defined limits, monochromatic. This was an absolutely peculiar kind of portrait, impossible to understand for anyone who was not aware of certain facts: It represented Christ in a tragically human dimension, enormously distant from that of the Risen Savior that the Templars were used to. And everything suggests that the leaders of the Order had good reasons of their own to keep its existence secret.

A Physical Icon

Ian Wilson argues that the Shroud, folded so as to show only the image of the face, had actually been an object once owned by the Eastern Roman emperors, and considered as one of the most precious and venerable icons of Christianity: an authentic image of Jesus's face, reproducing its physiognomy faithfully. Stolen during the terrible sack of Constantinople in April 1204, the priceless relic ended up in the hands of the Templars, who kept worshipping it in its original container but preferred to keep silent about its existence, since it had reached them through less than clear methods.[27] The next few pages will follow Wilson's reconstruction in its essential lines, but I thought it necessary to discuss several points over again and open a few new parentheses, to make the context clearer.

There is a very long theological tradition connecting this portrait closely to the Gospels and to the life of Christ; in a way, we might say that, to many authoritative theologians of the ancient world, this object was almost a manifesto of Christianity itself.[28] In the ancient town of Edessa, present-day Urfa in Turkey, an image of Jesus on a cloth was worshipped that was said not to have been made by human hands (*acheropita*); the portrait, always called *mandylion* (in Greek, "hand towel" or "handkerchief"), was the holiest of objects to the local Christian community. In 943, Emperor Romanus I Lecapenus sat on the throne of Byzantium, and that year the city was celebrating an especially important anniversary. One hundred years before, in 843, an important imperial decree had finally outlawed and declared heretical the theological current called iconoclasm, literally "image-smashing," which had been favored by several previous emperors over a matter of decades and which had destroyed an incalculable number of works of art with religious fanaticism. The iconoclasts, the image-smashers, based their views on an interpretation of Jesus Christ that was not the one defined by the Council of Nicaea in 325, which had fixed the Christian statement of faith. The

---

27   Wilson, *Le suaire de Turin*, pp. 152-253.

28   The theology of icons is a particularly fascinating chapter of Christian thought. This study has taken as reference the fine volume by Cardinal Schönborn, *L'icona di Cristo*.

Nicene Creed stated that Jesus was both a true man and the true God, that he bore in himself both a human and a divine nature, but the iconoclasts were monophysites, from the Greek *monophysis* or "one nature"; according to their view, the human nature of Jesus, mortal and base, had been absorbed and taken into the divine one, eternal and infinitely superior. The Christ, therefore, had only one nature, the divine one. Like God in all things, Jesus was not to be represented visually, because it was not legitimate to represent God; hence all his images were to be destroyed. On March 25, 717, Leo III Isauricus was crowned Eastern Roman emperor. He had reached the throne from the army, having previously been the commander of the great unit of Anatolia. Leo was of Syrian origin and had brought with him from his native country a certain tendency to look with suspicion on image-worship, for it could contain the seeds of idolatry, which Christians and other Eastern peoples had always been concerned with avoiding. When he became familiar with the usages of Constantinople, Leo III realized that the cult of images had taken a fundamental role even in liturgy, and had practically become one of the main forms of Byzantine religiosity. That hurt the sensibilities of some extreme theologians who saw Christianity as a spiritual religion and who therefore condemned the cult given to images, objects made of matter. Leo III embraced this doctrine, but his choice made the public hostile to him; on January 19, 729, some fanatics even defaced one of the capital's most famous icons of Christ, and the people rose in revolt, which Leo III bloodily suppressed. This also led to a break in relationships with the Church of Rome, led in those years by Pope Gregory II (715–731) and his successor, Gregory III (731–743): Both believed that the human nature of the Christ deserved, without a doubt, to be represented and worshipped by the faithful through the contemplation of sacred art.[29] In actual fact, the worship of images was rooted in an ancient tradition, going back to the very beginnings of the Church. In the 4th century AD, Bishop Athanasius of Antioch extolled the images of Jesus by quoting the Gospel passage in which Christ had said, "He who has seen me, has seen the Father"; therefore, owning faithful portraits of Jesus was a patrimony for the Christian community, and to contemplate his human form could be a valid aid in prayer.[30] Not much later, St. Basil the Great, bishop of Caesarea (330–379 AD), the founder of a monastic movement that spread all over the East, had written a work titled *A Treatise on the Holy Spirit* in which he explained this theological concept with a very effective example. According to St. Basil, when the subjects paid homage to the statue of their emperor, the affection and admiration they bore went from the statue to the person of the emperor himself; so, too, the homage that Christians offer to the portrait of Christ is aimed at the Person of Jesus, and therefore is not idolatrous. In another work, St. Basil maintained that the images of martyrs are able to drive demons off, an idea shared by his brother, St. Gregory, bishop of Nyssa, according to whom representations of saints induce the faithful to imitate them: "The silent

---

29   Jugie, Iconoclastia, coll. 1538-1542; Schönborn, L'icona di Cristo, pp. 131-158.

30   Schönborn, *L'icona di Cristo*, pp. 15-36; *Uspenskij, La teologia dell'icona*, pp. 101-132.

pictures painted on church walls can in fact talk, and are of great advantage."[31]

But probably the most passionate defender of image worship was the monk John of Damascus (about 650–749 AD), one of the most brilliant minds in 2,000 years of Christian history. He had lived in Syria when it was ruled by Muslim Arabs, and paradoxically this had left him free to express his religious views with much greater freedom than his brother monks had while living under the power of Constantinople: The Arabs forced Christians to pay a special tax, after which they were free to follow their own religion without their rulers meddling in dogmatic issues. John's *Treatise on Images* describes these practices of devotion with great theological subtlety and a most agile, even poetic, language: In a word, he was able to reflect the warm love borne by the common people for the most important representations of Christ, of the Virgin, and of the saints. John of Damascus started with a very simple truth that everyone could understand: To the Christian believer, Jesus was also a terrestrial, concrete, and material reality. In his life, he had walked through the roads of Palestine, and his feet had left their prints in that sandy land; after his death and resurrection, through the power of the Spirit, Christ went on living and acting in the lives of his faithful, as he had promised in the Gospel of Matthew: "Behold, I am with you all days, until the ending of the world."[32]

---

31 St. Basil the Great, *A Treatise on the Holy Spirit*, 18, 45; p. 32, col. 149; *Homily for Gordianuss the Martyr*, p. 31, col. 490; St. Gregory, *Solemn Encomium for the Great Martyr Theodore*, p. 46, coll. 737-739.

32 Mt 28:20 (Nestle-Aland, p. 285); Schönborn, *L'icona di Cristo*, pp. 169-175.

The portrait of Jesus preserved by tradition symbolizes and reminds the Christian of this physical, daily, and terrestrial presence, and that contact is the greatest comfort from the difficulties of life. This opportunity of a personal relationship could not be taken from the people in the name of a very abstract piece of reasoning. It was not right; besides, that strange view of faith promoted by certain ultra-refined thinkers was not even close to the original dictates of the Gospels, which had clearly stated that even after his resurrection, Jesus had a concrete and tangible body that could be seen and touched. According to John of Damascus, Jesus was a "physical icon" of the Father (*èikon physikè*), a living image full of Holy Spirit and capable of bringing man closer to God by purifying his soul and thoughts.[33]

"Et habitavit in nobis"

In the early 8th century, the theological line that extolled the spiritual value of icons found a strenuous supporter in the monk Theodore, abbot of the Monastery of Studion in Constantinople, one of the most splendid centers of Byzantine culture. Theodore the Studite was able to fight both intellectually and politically to reassert the need to worship images: If man had been created in the image of God, then surely there was something divine in the art of making sacred images. With amazing insight, he was able to underline a perennially valid, timeless fact: Forbidding

---

33 St. John Damascene, *Treatise on Images* I, 19, on p. 94, col. 1249, but the idea had already been stated by St. Gregory of Nissa, cfr. Schönborn, *L'icona di Cristo*, pp. 27-36; Gordillo, *Giovanni Damasceno*, coll. 547-552; Ozoline, *La théologie de l'icône*, p. 409.

the cult of images can be very dangerous, for it lays the groundwork for the growth of heresies. Rejecting images in the name of a religion made only of ideas and mental concepts prevents contact between believers and the human aspect of Jesus: This leaves believers exposed to the ever-lurking danger of taking Jesus Christ as nothing but a spiritual entity, a symbol of the possible contact between man and God. Jesus, though, was also a concrete flesh-and-blood person; it was his human suffering that had brought about the redemption of others: "As a perfect Man, Christ not only can but must be represented and worshipped in images; deny this, and the whole economy of salvation in Christ is virtually destroyed." [34]

Theodore's ideas triumphed in the great Second Ecumenical Council of Nicaea in 787. At the center of debate was placed the *mandylion*, the most ancient and venerated image of Christ. The term used to describe it is "print" (*charactèr*), the same used for coining money: The word describes the negative image formed thanks to contact with an object. The Council of Nicaea was also highly concerned with the precise regulation of the role of images in the life of the Church so that their religion would not lead toward the sin of idolatry: It specified that it was forbidden to worship idols, for worship belongs exclusively to God, but it recommended a carefully balanced honoring. It insisted that God is certainly not a matter for images: Faith is born from Scripture, which is the Word of God, and nobody should ever feel at ease with his conscience for only being devoted to a sacred image, no matter what it was of. Sacred representations

---

34 Weitzmann, *Le icone*, pp. 5-6; Kazhdan, *Bisanzio e la sua civiltà*, pp. 96-98; Schönborn, *L'icona di Cristo*, pp. 194-210.

essentially had an educational function, useful to make dogmas somehow accessible to the majority of the faithful with insufficient cultural resources; furthermore, they belonged to the Christian tradition, which is itself venerable and a carrier of truth. For all these reasons, there was a detailed settlement of the kind of liturgy to be followed when holy icons were venerated, the same used for relics: It was based on kissing, lighting lamps, and *proskìnesis*, kneeling with one's forehead to the ground, still in use today among Muslims. That was how the Christians of the Holy Land venerated the relic of the true Cross, and the Templars did the same with their "idol," prostrating themselves with their faces to the ground: Certainly in 14th-century Europe, this practice must have left the curious astonished.[35]

The achievement of the Council of Nicaea was the theology of the icon, which is still in place and widely popular to this day: An icon is not merely a portrait of Jesus or of other characters in sacred history, but rather a place of the Spirit, a sanctuary in itself that lets those faithful approaching it step one foot in the dimension of the divine. Contemplation of the icon is communication with God. Only a few people are allowed to paint icons, and they must follow a very ancient ritual governed by cast-iron rules, because the result must be faithful to traditional models. Everything begins with a period

---

35   Johannet, *Un office inédit,* pp. 143-155; Auzépy, *L'iconodulie,* pp. 157-165; Marion, *Le prototype de l'image,* p. 461; Shalina, *The Icon of Christ,* pp. 324-328; Curzon, *La Règle,* § 342; *Cronaca di Imad ad-Din, in Storici arabi delle crociate,* p. 135; statement of Raoul de Gisy, preceptor of Champagne, Paris Inquiry, Autumn 1307, in Michelet, *Le procès,* II, pp. 363-365; Archivio Segreto Vaticano, Reg. Aven. 48, cc. 441r e 443r, edition Schottmüller, II, pp. 30, 68.

of fasting and spiritual purification that the painter is obliged to undergo before he so much as starts the work, and it ends with the addition of writing that can only be done using a liturgical language. The writing seals the truth of the portrait to the original and declares that what can be seen with human eyes is verily and indeed present, and takes part in the heavenly liturgy. Of course these captions that appear on icons are subject to absolute, fixed rules established by Church doctrine. The writings cannot be touched: No painter was allowed to alter them, even with the consent of a bishop or of a patriarch, because they had been studied to synthetically render certain unarguable dogmas of religion. The first and probably the most ancient is the one shortened as IC-XC, which refers to the image of Jesus and is formed by the first and last letters of the Greek words IHCOYC XPICTOC, "Jesus Christ." It appears in icons as early as the 9th century and contains in itself a whole confession of faith—that Jesus was the Son of God, the Messiah (in Greek, *christòs*) awaited for centuries by the people of Israel. It is the first, essential, untouchable truth of Christianity, the basis on which the Church had been built.[36] Possibly the second most ancient and widespread motto was the one that accompanied the image of Mary, MP TY: It stood for MITIIP TEOY, "Mother of God," and it was also obviously the codification, in a simple form, of a dogma. It came from the Council of Ephesus in 431, in whose sessions had raged a furious debate exactly because this title, born among ordinary people and used since time out of mind, had been placed in doubt. Bishop

---

36   Icone, pp. 19-21.

Nestorius, who held the important office of patriarch of Constantinople, wanted to change Mary's title from *theotòkos* ("Mother of God") to *christotòkos*, that is "Mother of Christ," because in his view the Virgin had given birth to the human nature of Jesus, but it was not possible for a young woman, herself a created thing, to give birth to the divine nature of Jesus, to the Logos that was immensely superior to her own nature.

Nestorius's proposal did not go down well at all with theologians such as St. Cyril, bishop of Alexandria, because in practice it amounted to breaking the unity of the Person of Jesus Christ into two parts—one weaker and the other perfect. It pleased the commoners even less: Tradition had it that it was just to Ephesus that the apostle John had taken Mary, entrusted by Jesus on the Cross to his care. The people were long used to honoring her as Mother of God despite all those abstruse reasonings they neither understood nor wanted to understand. The proposal to downgrade the Virgin from "Mother of God" to "Mother of Christ" was rejected under a hail of excommunications, and the city was lit up as if for a festival. The bishops who had defended the traditional title of *theotòkos* were escorted to their homes by a solemn procession with torches and incense smoke, as if they were themselves icons of saints.[37]

On the other hand, the expression *Jesus Christ* (in Greek, *Ièsus Christòs*) was never challenged because it was too ancient, too vital, and too central. The Gospels took it back to the time of Jesus's preaching itself. One day the Nazarene had asked his disciples, "Who do people

---

37   Jugie, *Concilio di Efeso*, coll. 114-119.

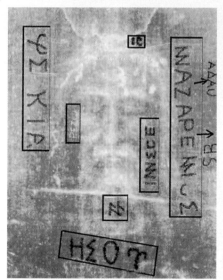

The human face of the Shroud with traces of Scripture in Greek and Latin, identified by André Marion and Anne-Laure Courage.

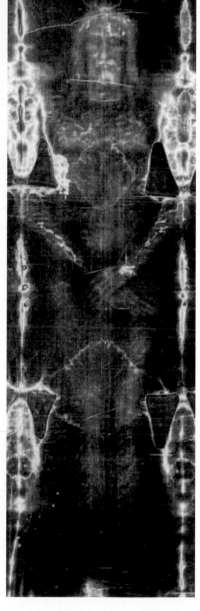

Right: The Shroud of Turin—the pale, indistinct, yellowish image perceived by the naked eye is changed by photography into a clear, hyper-realistic picture, full of striking detail.

A Matteo Planiso miniature depicting the Creator as a man with two faces. Vatican Apostolic Library, ms Vat. lat 3550, f. 5v.

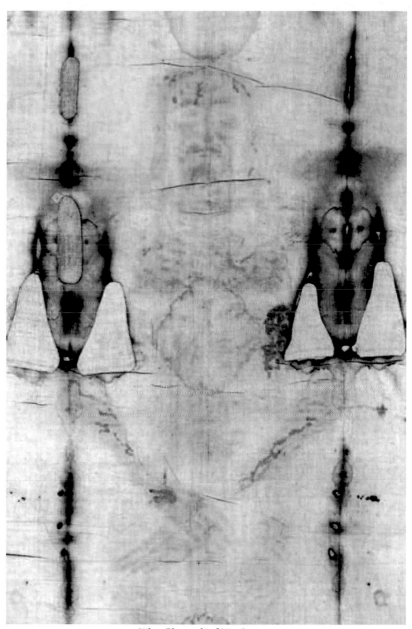

The Shroud of Turin.

Innocent III wrote a hymn to celebrate the Veronica, a famous image of the Face of Jesus kept in Rome.

Knights of the Temple on a war footing. Miniature from a manuscript from the 13th century of the *Cantigas* of King Alfonso the Wise.

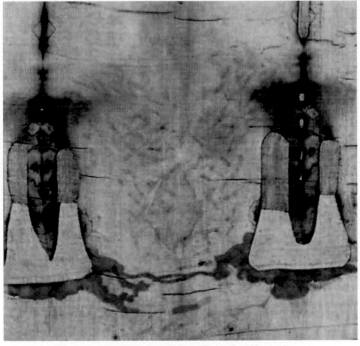

The so-called "belt of blood" on the Shroud.

A shroud with the exact kind of holes the Shroud of Turin has is represented in a miniature of the striking Pray Manuscript.

From the earliest days, Christians used to keep portraits of Jesus. This icon was preserved by the monastery of Saint Catherine on Mount Sinai. Even a layman can tell that they were drawn from realistic portraits.

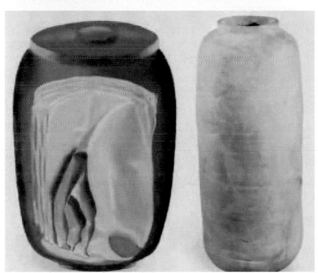

A jar-like object (the same type found at Qumran) was the first container of the shroud, according to a reconstruction made by Aldo Guerreschi and Michele Salcito.

Above: Miniature from a manuscript depicting Byzantine Emperor Constantine VII receiving the holy *mandylion* on his arrival from Edessa.

Right: Byzantine miniature of the 12th-century manuscript *Rossiano Greco 251* of the Vatican Library.

say I am?" Peter had eventually answered, "You are the Christ, the son of the living God." That had been the first Christian profession of faith, synthetic but complete. In the circle of the first Christians, what today's exegetes and theologians call the "post–Paschal Church," already a very short time before the death and the events that followed, the two words *Jesus* (a very widespread man's name) and *Christ* (a sacred adjective) had become indissoluble, one and the same. [38]

In March of 843, the empress Theodora, a widow whose husband had once again persecuted the defenders of images, made a wholly opposite choice and established a solemn ceremony, the Feast of Orthodoxy, meant to remember the final victory of the holy icons.[39] And in the year 943, the first centenary of the Feast, the emperor Romanus I decided to solemnize that anniversary by taking the most famous and venerated of all images of Christ, the one kept in Odessa, into the capital city of the Empire. He therefore entrusted the recovery mission to the best of his generals, John Curcuas. The town was then held by the Arabs, and Curcuas was forced to negotiate the handover of the *mandylion*. In exchange for this single object, the Byzantine emperor set free 200 high-ranking Muslim prisoners, paid 12,000 gold crowns, and furthermore gave the city a guarantee of perpetual immunity. After long examinations—for

---

38 See, for instance, 1 Ts 2, 15; 3, 11; 3, 13; Col 1, 3; 1 Cor, 1, 2; 2, 9; 6, 14, 9, 5. Légasse, *Paolo e l'universalismo cristiano*, pp. 106-158; Trocmé, *Le prime comunità*, pp. 75-105; Jossa, *Introduzione*, pp. 15-29; Ratzinger-Benedetto XVI, *Gesù di Nazareth*, pp. 333-352.

39 Ostrogorsky, *Storia dell'impero bizantino*, pp. 139-202; Jugie, *Iconoclastia*, coll. 1541-1546.

the Arabs had tried to stick the general with a fake—
the famous image was taken into Constantinople in
a memorable procession on August 15, the day of the
Dormition of Mary, and placed in the Church of the
Blachernae, dedicated to the Virgin. The following day,
it was placed on an imperial ship to sail around the city,
finally coming to rest in the imperial chapel of Pharos.
This inaccessible sanctuary was a colossal reliquary
where the emperors had been collecting all the most
precious relics of the lives of Jesus, of the Virgin, and of
the saints for centuries. Several medieval visitors who
had been allowed in, and had been able to contemplate
the collection, stated that the collected objects included
all the relics of the Passion, from the bread consecrated
in the Last Supper to the sponge with which the soldiers
had offered Jesus vinegar, along with a number of other
important mementos, the long result of a centuries-old
campaign of toothcomb searches that had started with
leaders as early as Helena, mother of Constantine.[40] This
patient, continuously and wildly expensive operation
is easily explained. Since, at a certain point in history,
contact with the Holy Land had become difficult, it was
necessary to keep a physical and concrete relationship
with the testimonies of Christ's life. Within barely four
years (636–640 AD), the Arabs, led by Caliph Omar,
tore from the emperors of Byzantium most of Lesser
Asia, including the region of Syria and Palestine; from
that moment on, visits to the Holy Sepulchre and to
the other Holy Places only became possible under
special diplomatic agreements between the court of

---

40   Riant, *Exuviae*, for example pp. 216-217, 218-224, 233-234.

Constantinople and their new masters, and at any rate, it was impossible to stop the utter devastation of the Basilica of Anastasis itself, the location of the Sepulchre. So they studied ways to transfer everything from the life of Jesus that could possibly be moved so as to create a new Jerusalem on the Bosporus, with all the fundamental proofs. In 1201, the imperial guardian of relics, Nicholas Mesarites, had to defend the great Byzantine sanctuary from the danger of looting when a palace revolution tried to seize power; he managed to calm the spirits of rebels because he told them that that chapel was an utterly sacred place, a new Holy Land to honor and respect above any political issue:

> This temple, this place, is a new Sinai; it is Bethlehem, Jordan, Jerusalem, Nazareth, Bethany, Galilee, Tiberias; it is the basin, the Supper, Mount Tabor, the praetorius of Pilate, the Place of the Skull called in Hebrew Golgotha. Here Christ was born, here was he baptized, here did he walk on water and here he has walked on the land. He made wonderful miracles and lowered himself to washing feet [. . .] Here he was crucified, and those who have eyes can see the rest for his feet. Here he was also buried, and the rolled stone by his grave bears witness to it to this day. Here he rose again, and the shroud with the grave-linens proves it to us. [41]

After being transferred to the capital, the *mandylion* remained in Constantinople and soon became the symbol of the city itself, a kind of supreme protector that was

---

41 Ostrogorsky, *Storia dell'impero bizantino,* pp. 97-98; Dubarle, *Storia antica,* pp. 39-41.

featured even on the army's standards; the Byzantine religious mind identified it with the Eucharist, the Body of Christ, and reproduced it in countless copies. From then on, the Byzantine world developed a great passion for the physical features of Jesus: It was a bit like reacting against centuries of a culture that had for so many different reasons ignored if not even refused them. Through the study of relics, they worked out how tall he was: Outside the Hagia Sophia cathedral they erected a life-size reproduction of the Cross, called "Cross of the Measure" (*crux mensuralis*), which allowed everyone to envisage him as he was.[42]

The imperial collection at Pharos filled with testimonies of every kind, including some (like the diapers of Baby Jesus or the milk of the Virgin) that make us smile today. But this must not let us forget the huge historical value of their presence. It had certainly not been ignorant peasants who had wanted them there and had made them precious, but the greatest intellectuals of their times. There was something like a sense of deep emotion in rediscovering this human dimension of Jesus, something that the Eastern Christian world had neglected for centuries. After all, the absolute novelty of Christianity was that God had come to walk among ordinary people: The Greek text of the Gospel of John says literally, "The Word was made flesh, and pitched his tent among us."[43] To contemplate Baby Jesus's diapers was to be reminded that Christ had been a newborn baby like everyone else, and that Mary, whom the Byzantines called the Mother of God, had looked lovingly after him just as other mothers did with their children. Some objects show that God looks after man from nearby, and that He is

---

42   Riant, Exuviae, p. 220.

43   Gv 1, 14: κ⬚ὶ ὁ λόγος σὰρξ εγενετο καὶ εσκηνωσεν εν ημιν (Nestle-Aland, p. 758).

within his reach. And those of the Passion also had another thing to say: There is surely something of the divine in the sick, the dying, the person crushed by suffering—all those whose faces, in the adversities of life, can be superimposed on that unrecognizable face of Christ.

The transfer of the *mandylion* to the capital was a memorable event, during which a considerable amount of writing was produced. The study of all these sources proves of special interest, for the description of the *mandylion* and of its history, as narrated in the days of Constantine VII, do not quite agree with what we know from the oldest sources. Several different things appear in it—details that seem custom-made to "update" the legend in light of a new and disconcerting truth.

Of Flesh and Blood

In 1997, the Roman historian Gino Zaninotto noticed that inside a 10th-century Greek manuscript of the Vatican Apostolic Library there was preserved a solemn speech written by Gregory the Referendarius, the archdeacon of the cathedral of Hagia Sophia in Constantinople, who oversaw the relationship between the emperor and the patriarch Gregory went himself to Edessa in John Curcuas's mission to recover the *mandylion* in 944 and carefully investigated the city archives, looking for the ancient documents telling the story of the image; he then wrote this homily, in which he celebrated the relic's importance and gave a synthetic account of its history. The Referendarius' account was thus far unpublished, one of many unknown treasures in the pontiffs' library. It was published by Byzantine scholar

André-Marie Dubarle in the specialist periodical *Révue des Études Byzantines.* [44]

According to Archdeacon Gregory, the image is in fact an imprint, adorned with the drops of blood that fell from Christ's wounded side: Precedent tradition usually described the *mandylion* as a small piece of linen, as large as a hand towel, as the name itself implies, which bore the only imprint in existence of the Face of Jesus. But the homily of codex *Vaticanus Graecus 511* describes it as an imprint showing the chest with the mark of a spear wound and the flow of blood that had issued from that wound, an image of the body at least from the waist up. According to the most ancient tradition, the *mandylion* had nothing to do with the death of Christ: It was simply a portrait of him when he was alive. The first records of this legend spoke of an exchange of letters between Jesus and Abgar, king of Edessa, identified as Abgar V the Black; the sovereign had heard stories of Jesus's great fame as a healer, and Abgar knew that Jesus was being sought to be killed, so he had a messenger offer Jesus safe refuge in his city.

Eusebius of Caesarea, the very learned bishop who was Constantine the Great's spiritual adviser, inserted the episode in his *Church History*, but with no mention of any image. In fact, this may well be due to Eusebius' own intervention, selecting from tradition only what he appreciated and eliminating (or simply ignoring) what struck him as less worth sharing. We know that the bishop of Caesarea was strongly opposed to image-worship. There is a famous letter of his to Empress Constantia who had heard

---

44   Biblioteca Apostolica Vaticana, Vat. Gr. 511, cc. 143r-150v; Zaninotto, *La traslazione a Costantinopoli*, pp. 344-352; Dubarle, *L'homélie de Grégoire le Référendaire*, pp. 5-51.

that some Christian groups owned the true portrait of Jesus of Nazareth and had asked the bishop to use his influence to let her have a copy. His answer was an undiplomatic, unmitigated reproof:

> And yet if thou now declarest that thou askest me not for the image of the human form turned to God, but the icon of His mortal flesh, just as it was before His Transfiguration, then I answer: knowest thou not the passage where God commands that no image should be done of anything up in the heavens or down on earth?[45]

Such an attitude may strike us as overly cerebral—indeed, unpleasant—but we must try to put ourselves in those people's shoes and take careful note of the realities of their time. Eusebius was certainly no unbeliever, but both a great theologian and most devout person: His basic concern was to ward off the danger of idolatry, a risk that Christians felt to be most serious and ever lurking. In the Roman Empire, it was a widespread custom to make realistic portraits of the dearly departed, and the tablets found in the necropolis of Fayyum in Egypt show that they worked hard to make these portraits as close to the original as possible; many are so accurate that they seem like photographs. The monastery of Saint Catherine on Mount Sinai preserves a couple of superb icons from the age of Emperor Justinian (527–565), representing Jesus and Saint Peter, which clearly come from this very tradition of Roman imperial-age portrait. Even a layman can tell that they are drawn from realistic portraits:

---

45 Schönborn, *L'icona di Cristo*, pp. 74-75.

The icon of Peter bears three round frames on top, which hold the portraits of Saint John (shown as a young man of about fifteen), then Jesus and Mary, whose facial features are strikingly similar.[46] From the earliest days, Christians used to keep portraits of Jesus, and also of Peter and Paul, in their homes, but Eusebius did not approve, for many Christians were freshly converted from paganism on account of Constantine's religious policy, and tended to worship these images no differently from the way they had worshipped pagan idols. Christianity required a total change of mentality, of the way of looking at the world, which could hardly be done in a few months. Meanwhile, as long as the neophytes had not developed a wholly Christian conscience, it was wiser to break altogether from what had been part of their old pagan cult. Following this reasoned judgment, Eusebius preferred not to have realistic figures of Christ at all, only ideal and symbolic figurations. Maybe for the same reason, Christian art from the first to the fourth centuries preferred not to portray Jesus, but rather represent him with symbols (the fish, the anchor), by particular figures that hearkened back to the parables (the Good Shepherd), or again as a young god like Apollo, impersonally and perfectly beautiful with a beauty that has nothing to do with the portraiture of a lowly human. [47]

Around the year 400, the legend of Abgar reappeared in a new version, inside an unknown author's text called *The Doctrine of Addai.* Besides writing a letter to Jesus, according to this tale, King Abgar had sent him a painter who was able to make a very faithful portrait, "picked

---

46   Belting, *Il culto delle immagini,* pp. 105-132.
47   Schönborn, *L'icona di Cristo,* pp. 58-63; Dulaey, *I simboli cristiani,* pp. 52-69; Crippa e Zibawi, *L'arte paleocristiana,* pp. 69-108.

out in marvelous colors"; then, about a hundred years later, Armenian historian Moses of Korene spoke of the *mandylion* as an image painted on a silk curtain. Over the course of the 6th century, and particularly when Edessa suffered a Persian conquest, people began to speak of the *mandylion* no longer as a painter's portrait, but as an *acheropita*, an image made not by human hands but by miracle; according to the Byzantine historian Evagrius who lived in that period, the people of Edessa thought it a relic of immense power and used it in certain rituals, thanks to which they had been saved from the enemies.[48]

It was only with the expedition of General John Curcuas under Romanus I in the year 943, and the transfer of the image to Constantinople, that the *mandylion's* tradition started to be filled with references to the Passion of Christ. These references were very clear, yet there was a clear attempt to gloss over them in embarrassment: Clearly they had found out that the image of Jesus on the cloth was the image of a dead Jesus, a detail of no small importance that tradition had left unmentioned. Gregory the Referendarius and General Curcuas had gone to Edessa with an army to bring back to their homeland a truthful picture of Jesus of immense fame; what they surely expected was an effigy of "Christ Pantocrator," the mighty Lord of the Universe, smiling and blessing the faithful from the shining gold of the mosaics on the wall of great churches—an image on whose pattern the emperor of Constantinople had been represented since the days of Justinian and, in a way, since Constantine had been celebrated as Christ's

---

48   Emmanuel, *The Holy Mandylion*, pp. 292-293.

Vicar on Earth and equal to the apostles.[49] Gregory the Referendarius and John Curcuas expected to see the portrait of a divinely handsome face, a portrait of a living Jesus capable of developing the most profound sense of majesty, such as pertains only to the Lord of the World and his earthly follower, the emperor. Instead they were faced with the frightful imprint of a dead man, the corpse of a man killed on the cross, his whole body tormented with wounds. There was blood on the *mandylion*. Not a few drops here and there, but a vast flood, as visible as what can come out of a human chest torn open. Instead of the King of Kings, they met in Edessa the Man of Sorrows. Nothing could have been further from the glory of the Byzantine emperor than that pitiful view, almost the very symbol of mankind defeated by suffering and by death. And yet the *mandylion* had an ineffable quality the sources don't describe for us, and that something gave the two officials the nerve to appear before the emperor with an object so radically different from anything that had been expected. The documents telling of its arrival contain curious details, hard at first to understand: The children of Emperor Romanus looked at the relic but could not distinguish the details, while his son-in-law Constantine Porphyrogenitus, who was to inherit the throne, immediately saw every detail and felt an immense emotion. What does it mean? When compared with the Shroud of Turin, as Ian Wilson wishes, this account seems very credible, because it is well known that the image of the Shroud has the curious optical property already mentioned: It

---

49   See R. Farina, *L'Impero e l'imperatore cristiano.*

130

is visible only if one stands at least about six feet from it, but swiftly vanishes when one tries to get closer. It is my own personal view that there is something more to be read there—that Constantine VII could see the image because he could accept it as it was. For a special reason, unlike so many of his contemporaries before him, he could appreciate a portrait of Christ with the unmistakable signs of suffering and death. Discovering the *mandylion*'s "true identity" was surely a shock, and also raised the delicate issue of explaining and justifying how tradition seemed to have kept it hidden behind the notion of a simple portrait; nonetheless, Gregory the Referendarius certified it as authentic, for he was sure that the emperor would welcome it with great satisfaction, even after he discovered the incredible news. Romanus I had had a long, hard struggle against Paulicians and other heretical groups that sprang up here and there throughout the empire and exploited religious ideas to challenge imperial authority. Paulicians and other sects of the same kind derived their beliefs from the ancient Gnostic heresy that had spread great confusion in the first centuries of the Christian era, especially among Eastern churches. Though divided into separate groups that followed different Gospels, Gnostics had in common one strong belief: Jesus had not really been a man of flesh and bone, but a pure spirit, a kind of angel who appeared on earth who did not possess a human body but only a human appearance. The Christ was both a symbol and a celestial messenger who had appeared among men to teach them how to reach the knowledge of God (in Greek, *gnòsis*), and once his mission had been accomplished, he had returned to his original dimension. According to the

Gnostics, the Christ had never been incarnated, had never suffered Passion, had never died, and, of course, had never been resurrected.[50] Emperor Romanus I had understood that a religious struggle could not only be fought by armed power, but that a confrontation on the level of ideas was also necessary. Even the famous *mandylion* of tradition could have helped refute the heretics, since it was a realistic portrait of the face of that Christ of whom they said had never had a real human body; this weird, disquieting object from Edessa also showed him in his dreadfully human nature with a stunning and agonized realism. Owning his funeral shroud with all the marks of the Passion, to the point of being soaked with the flow of blood from his ribs, meant proving to the whole world that the heretics preached a falsehood.

Gregory the Referendarius was a regular at Romanus's court because of his diplomatic duties, and he certainly knew the mind and attitudes of the whole imperial family. He was a diplomat and an expert in politics; he judged that the relic could also be a most powerful weapon in the ideological struggle against the proliferating heresies, and at least a few of Romanus I's relatives were sure to appreciate it. It was a smart decision: Within a few months, young Constantine VII Porphyrogenitus rose to the imperial throne of Byzantium and made the *mandylion* the most worshipped and celebrated object in the whole empire.

It is in fact during this man's very long reign that Byzantine religious thinking experienced a remarkable development, which placed at the forefront, in both

---

50   Zaninotto, *La traslazione a Costantinopoli*, pp. 344-352.

liturgy and theology, the figure of the suffering Christ, the dead body tormented by the Passion, whereas before it had practically only extolled the risen one, shining with glory. They also introduced a new piece of liturgical apparel called *epitàphios*, a cloth bearing the embroidered or painted image of Christ in the Sepulchre before the Resurrection, with his hands joined over the pubis just as they are seen in the Shroud of Turin.[51] It is very difficult, perhaps even historically impossible, for this change to have been independent from what they had just discovered from the nature of the *mandylion*. What could be seen on the cloth once unfolded impressed contemporaries so strongly as to stimulate theological research toward hitherto unexplored directions, so powerful as to change the religious sensitivities of a world. Byzantium rediscovered the Crucifix as the image of a man annihilated by the violence of other men, naked, bloodied, his head fallen down on a no longer breathing chest. For centuries, they had represented him with the open eyes of a living man and with a serene face showing no hint of pain, often even richly dressed in purple and wearing a golden diadem instead of a crown of thorns. For nearly a thousand years, the faithful had worshipped the illogical image of an emperor in sumptuous dress, finding himself near the cross almost by chance, majestic and impossible; in the end, even without having to drift into heresy, the idea that the Chosen of God could be executed like a common criminal had trouble being accepted. Now,

---

51   Wilson, *Holy Faces*, pp. 149-151; Dubarle, *Storia antica*, pp. 51-52.

however, theologians looked to a new dimension of the faith, and mystics found themselves weeping at the wounds of Jesus.[52]

Four Times Doubled

Once this new reality with its valuable political aspects was accepted, the problem remained to not make gaping breaks with tradition: The ancient tale of the *mandylion* could hardly be discarded, yet on the other hand, there was no desire to renounce what had just been newly discovered. In 944, an anonymous intellectual at the court of Constantine VII, or possibly even the emperor himself, who was a talented writer, wrote a new version of the legend of Abgar. The ancient tale was preserved, but the miraculous formation of the icon was now set during the Passion: No wonder, then, if the linen cloth of the *mandylion* showed thick drops of blood. The new version had a very sick Abgar resolving to send to Jesus a messenger of his, one Ananias, who also happened to be a painter; Jesus could not go to Edessa because his mission in Jerusalem was coming close to its fulfillment, so he decided to let Ananias paint his portrait for the king to have. Ananias tried desperately to render his features and failed because that face seemed to change mysteriously in shape; then Jesus, touched and wishing to help the ailing king, took a handkerchief and, on his way to Golgotha, rubbed it over his face, so that his features remained miraculously imprinted.

---

52 On this subject, read through Grondijs's magnificent work, *L'iconographie byzantine du crucifié,* and also Shalina, *The Icon of Christ,* pp. 324-336, and Jászai, *Crocifisso,* pp. 577-586.

An interesting and possibly not casual coincidence: A magnificent Byzantine miniature from the 14th century represents the arrival of the *mandylion* in Constantinople, and Emperor Constantine VII receiving from Gregory the Referendarius not a simple towel, but a very long cloth on which the image of the Holy Face can be seen.

The new version of the legend of Abgar sought to reconcile as much as possible the discrepancies between the tangible form of the *mandylion*, bearing the imprint of a man with his chest torn by a spear blow, and the older tradition that made it only a realistic portrait for which Jesus had sat while alive.[53] The result is naïve and hardly believable: Jesus was staggering toward Golgotha, surrounded by mocking soldiers who would not let anyone near him, and those are the conditions in which he would have a towel handed to him to be able to leave his portrait for the king's envoy. At that time, the image was supposed to have formed by a miracle, but the spear thrust that can be seen on the *mandylion* was only inflicted later, after Jesus had died on the Cross. That it was judged acceptable to manipulate the story to this extent surely has an important historical significance. What meaning could this curious contradiction have?

Ian Wilson noticed that as early as the *Doctrine of Addai*, the *mandylion* was described with a strange adjective, *tetràdiplon*, that is to say "folded double four times." It is an adjective that cannot possibly make sense if the *mandylion* had really been a piece of linen the size of a towel or of a handkerchief: Once that had been folded eight times,

---

53   Emmanuel, *The Holy Mandylion*, pp. 291-292.

it would have been smaller than a school notebook and not visible to most. When folded in eight parts, as the ancient sources describe the *mandylion*, the Shroud of Turin takes exactly the appearance of a towel, and all that can be seen is the imprint of the face alone. Linen, if kept folded long enough in the same way, will keep its imprint in the shape of slight deformations that can be seen very well using a grazing, sideways light source: The Shroud retains the marks of these ancient foldings, and among them there is precisely an eightfold mark which, once completed, shows only the face just as it appears in ancient reproductions of the *mandylion*.[54]

Therefore, Ian Wilson felt that in Edessa the cloth was kept in an eightfold form and concealed inside a wooden case covered by a textile that bore on its front an opening through which the head alone could be seen. It was a reliquary, but at the same time also a kind of mask designed to show only the most indispensable features, and above all conceal the most striking bloodstains, which it left inside. We can get a fairly clear idea of the form of this case, which bore decorations similar to those of royal cloths in ancient Turkey: According to Ian Wilson, it was Abgar V himself, or else one of his descendants, who had prepared this purpose-made reliquary to disguise the real nature of the object and make it seem like a towel. [55]

This trick was probably thought up because the Edessa region was rife with Monophysite ideas and tended to see Jesus as a being of wholly and only divine

---

54 Dubarle, *Histoire ancienne*, pp. 105-106; Baima Bollone, *La sindone e la scienza*, pp. 89-94.
55 Wilson, *Le saint suaire*, pp. 152-165.

nature: An image showing him as a corpse riddled with wounds would have seemed disgraceful, and risked even being destroyed. One of the finest representations of the *mandylion* can be found in the manuscript *Rossiano Greco 251* of the Vatican Apostolic Library, and curiously presents it turned over in a peculiar manner, as if it were the negative imprint of a positive real object. This expensive codex was made in Constantinople in the 12th century, and by that time the theology of icons had triumphed long before. Even so, a vandal's hand had ripped into the magnificent Byzantine miniature. This tells us much about the long survival of a certain kind of bitter hostility against the cult of images.

Once it had been triumphantly placed as the central and most precious part of the imperial collection of relics, the *mandylion* was not touched again, even by the emperor himself, and its obstension only took place rarely and under special circumstances. The sanctuary of the Pharos chapel was inviolate, its security awe-inspiring. Experience taught that it had to be defended both from the greed of potential thieves and from the fanaticism of believers. After Helena, the mother of Constantine, had rediscovered the pieces of the True Cross in Jerusalem, these relics used to be freely exhibited to the faithful, who could touch and kiss them without protection, but it was soon discovered that this freedom needed limitation when a pilgrim pretending to kiss the Cross managed to bite off a bit of wood. Sometimes, during ceremonies of particular solemnity, the emperor could grant some illustrious guest, ambassador, or head of State the supreme honor of a visit to the chapel of Pharos—a privilege certainly granted in 1171 to Amaury, king of

Jerusalem, when he visited the court of Emperor Manuel I Komnenos, according to the chronicle of William of Tyre. Additionally, an Arab writer named Abu Nasr Yahya had been able to see the *mandylion* exhibited in Hagia Sophia during a solemn procession in 1058.[56]

The original container made in Edessa was probably preserved, based on the many artistic reproductions, but it is possible that at some point the emperors may have chosen to make an identical copy of the Shroud's face to place in this ancient reliquary, so as to exhibit the Shroud completely open, for the purpose of showing the whole image of the body; in fact, many ancient authors describe a shroud in Constantinople's imperial collection that looked much like that of Turin, and speak of it and of the *mandylion* as two different objects. However, this might have a very simple explanation. According to some Byzantine sources, the usual place for the *mandylion* was the imperial chapel at Pharos, where it was kept together with another famous relic: the *keramion*, the tile that, in the city of Edessa, sealed the hideout where the miraculous icon of Jesus had been kept for a long time. According to tradition, the image of Christ's face had been miraculously impressed on the tile's terracotta, so the *keramion* had also been taken to Constantinople to be exhibited for the veneration of the faithful; placed one next to the other, the two relics formed an impressive whole that focused minds on the Passion. But the Flemish crusader Robert de Clari, the last witness who ever saw

---

56   Egeria, *Diario di viaggio,* p. 83; Frolow, *La relique,* pp. 21-152; Wilson, *Le saint suaire,* pp. 200, 208.

the Shroud before the great looting, describes a peculiar ceremony of obstension:

> Among these is also a monastery called Our Lady of Blachernae, where is found the shroud wherein Our Lord was shrouded: all [Good] Fridays, it is raised wholly upright so that the figure may be seen. Nobody, neither Greek nor French, knows what happened to this shroud when the city was conquered. [57]

In the church of the Blachernae, the Shroud was opened in a frame thanks to a mechanism that slowly lifted it so that the faithful could see the body of Jesus as if he were slowly and gradually rising from the grave. The cloth, therefore, was earlier kept folded, then very slowly spread out. According to Robert de Clari, the Blachernae ceremony took place every Friday, but it is more likely that he intended to mean only Good Friday rather than every week; his description, together with other sources, suggests that on special occasions, the Shroud-*mandylion* was removed from its holder in the chapel of Pharos and taken to Blachernae where the faithful could contemplate it, even spread out, in the impressive liturgy of the "ascent" (in Greek *anàstasis*, "resurrection").[58]

At the present stage of our knowledge, it is clear that the Shroud of Turin had once belonged to the

---

57 Wilson, *Holy Faces*, p. 156, provides a reproduction of the original manuscript that contains the description (Royal Copenhagen Library, ms. 487, fol. 123).

58 I thank Marco Palmerini for pointing me toward this reconstruction; see also Lidov, *The Mandylion*, p. 268, and Shalina, *The Icon of Christ*, pp. 333-334, featuring a scheme of how the elevation was performed.

Byzantine emperors, since the descriptions of ancient authors are fairly precise; on the other hand, it is certain that until the time of Constantine VII Porphyrogenitos, traditions about the *mandylion* speak of a head-and-shoulder portrait of Jesus alive, while later—as I will point out shortly—this object is always described as a cloth on which was the outline of an image of a full body. At present we have no clear idea how this change came about; a credible idea suggested by historians is that in Edessa there was an attempt to mask the funereal nature of the *mandylion* in any possible way, because the marks of suffering and death on the figure of Christ might have created a scandal that would not have been endurable in that particular historical context. But this explanation might be incorrect, or it might be accompanied by other issues unknown to us at present. It is evident that we know some moments of the Shroud's millennia of history in detail, while we know nothing of others. To strain to tell its vicissitudes date after date seems unhelpful because it means, over so many stretches, dressing up incomplete or highly dubious notices as ornately as possible; rather, it is wiser to arrange in their place the pieces of the puzzle on which we can rely, waiting for further discoveries to give us other convincing information.

In effect, the religious tradition that went into the making of some icons of the *mandylion* associates this image with Christ dead in the Sepulchre, as shown for instance by a superb item in the St. Petersburg Russian State Museum, painted by Prokop Tehirin in the early 1600s: The dead body of Jesus, with its hands joined over the pubis as in the Shroud, arises from the Sepulchre, while two angels above him display the *mandylion*, not as a towel but as a fairly long sheet.[59]

Thanks to public showings and the narratives of foreign ambassadors who had been present at private ones, the fame of the *mandylion* spread as far as the West as early as the 11th century, but in Europe it was never described as a towel: It was mentioned from the beginning as a sheet that bore the image of the whole body of Jesus Christ. To the text of a sermon ascribed to Pope Stephen III (768–772 AD), someone in the 11th century added a bit of a speech refurbishing the "updated" version of the legend of Abgar with the extra bits added on in Constantine Porphyrogenitus' time:

> So, to please the sovereign fully, the mediator between God and men lay the full length of his body over a sheet of snow-white linen, and upon this linen, wonderful to relate or to hear, the most noble form of his face and of his whole body was divinely transfigured, so that to see the transfiguration impressed upon that linen would be enough even for those who had not been able to see the Lord in the flesh.[60]

More or less at the same time, between 1130 and 1141, the monk Orderic Vitalis clearly stated, in his *Historia Ecclesiastica*, that the *mandylion* of Edessa bore the image of Jesus's whole body:

---

59   Lidov, *The Mandylion*, pp. 268-280; Bacci, *Relics of the Pharos Chapel*, pp. 234-246; Zocca, *Icone*, coll. 1538-1542.

60   Dobschütz, *Christusbilder*, p. 134, discussed in Wilson, *Holy Faces*, p. 152.

Abgar reigned as toparch of Edessa. To him did the Lord Jesus send [. . .] the most precious linen, wherewith he dried the sweat from his face, and upon which the features of the Savior appear, miraculously reproduced. It showeth to those who behold it the image and proportions of the body of the Lord;[61]

and in Gervase of Tilbury's *Otia Imperialia*, written in 1218, the fact was asserted again:

It has been ascertained, thanks to the story told in ancient documents, that the Lord lay the whole of His body down upon the whitest of linen, and so thanks to divine power there remained impressed on the linen the fairest image not only of the face but also of the body of the Lord.[62]

In 1957, historian Pietro Savio pointed out that a Vatican Library manuscript contained a different testimony, going back to the 12th century, with an "altered" version of the legend of Abgar. Jesus had written to the king: "If thou truly desirest to see my face as it physically is, I shall send thee a piece of cloth; know about it that upon it is divinely transferred, not only the image of my face, but of my whole body."[63]

Around 1190, Pope Celestine III received from Constantinople the gift of a luxurious liturgical canopy for use in solemn processions, a masterpiece of sacred art that represented the *mandylion* as a sheet bearing the image of

---

61   Orderic Vitalis, *Historia Ecclesiastica*, III, lib. IX, 8.
62   Gervasio di Tilbury, *Otia Imperialia*, III, pp. 966-967.
63   Savio, *Ricerche storiche*, p. 340, nota 31.

the dead Christ with his hands joined over his pubis. Gino Zaninotto has recently found in another 10th century Greek codex a further confirmation that the famous Byzantine relic bore the image of the whole body.[64]

From Byzantium to Lirey?

Ian Wilson believes that the Shroud-*mandylion* vanished from Constantinople during the terrible sack suffered by the city in the days of the Fourth Crusade (1204). It remained hidden over long decades, then reappeared in the year 1353 near Lirey, a small town in north central France: In that year, the knight Geoffroy de Charny, bearer of the Oriflamme in the army of King John the Good, and widely popular at court, made a gift of the singular relic to the collegiate church he had just founded in the town. The Shroud started being exhibited for popular veneration as the True Shroud of Jesus with a series of solemn obstentions that drew the enthusiasm of the faithful and the jealousy of the local bishop; in the end, after several events, it passed into the hands of the dukes of Savoy, who had it kept first in their then capital Chambéry, in the sumptuous Sainte-Chapelle of the Ducal Palace, then moved to their new capital, Turin, where it is to this day. The link with the Templar order was first suggested to Ian Wilson by the fact that the man who died at the stake together with Jacques de Molay was named Geoffroy de Charny, the exact same name of the owner of the Shroud in Lirey.[65]

---

64 Wilson, *Le saint suaire*, pp. 207-208; Wilson, *Holy Faces*, pp. 145-148, fig. 17, 26-27; Zaninotto, *L'immagine edessena*, pp. 57-62.
65 Wilson, *Le saint suaire*, pp. 215-253.

Someone might object to this on the ground that the first owner of the Shroud is found named as Geoffroy de Charny, while the surname of the Templar preceptor appears in various documents in different forms, as *Charny*, but also as *Charneyo, Charnayo, Charniaco*. From an objector's viewpoint, there is a big enough difference in spelling to suppose that the two names were different. I take the liberty to reply that in an administration register from the age of King Philip VI of Valois, the surname of the first owner of the Shroud is written as *de Charneyo*, and also *Charni, Charnyo*, and *Charniaco*, just as is found in the case of his kinsman Geoffroy, dead at the stake on March 18, 1314, with Jacques de Molay.[66]

This kind of hair-splitting on the basis of medieval Latin spelling variants can only be fed to someone who has no practice with medieval documents. It would work if our characters had lived in the France of Napoleon or Victor Hugo—a world dominated by printed paper and in a culture that was officially French-speaking.

In medieval society, things were quite different. The acts of the Templars' trial, like a number of other contemporaneous documents, were handwritten, which means that it was easy to make small mistakes. Above all, they were composed in Latin by teams of notaries who translated simultaneously into Latin while they heard the witnesses speak in their native language—in this case, French. All French surnames did not have Latin forms, and yet a way had to be found to render their often peculiar sounds into Latin; adaptations were made, and

---

66   *Les Journaux du Trésor*, for instance p. 156 e p. 195, dated May 31, 1349, in societate domini Gaufridi de Charneyo militis et consiliarii Regis.

they could well have been different from notary to notary.

For this reason, we find the same names quoted in quite different forms, whose variety can seem downright ridiculous to us. Jacques de Molay's surname can also be found written as *Malay, Molaho,* and *Malart,* while the Visitor of the West, Hugues de Pérraud, is also called *Parando, Peraudo, Penrando, Penrado, Peralto, Peraut,* and even *Peraldo, Paurando,* and *Deperando.* In the case of Templar leaders who lived before the trial, the situation was even more curious: Gilbert Erail's surname is also found written as *Roral, Arayl, Herac, Eraclei,* and *Eraclius,* while that of Robert de Sablé turns up as *Sabolio, Sabluillio, Salburis, Sabloel,* and *Sabloil.* And this phenomenon is just as common in the registers of medieval popes: In one and the same letter, written by the same notary, it often happens that the same surname is spelled differently.[67] If we are to assess facts within their historical context, I would say that the notaries transcribed the name of Geoffroy de Charny fairly faithfully, indeed better than in many other cases.

What we can deduce from the records of the trial against the Templars strengthens Wilson's theory. Geoffroy de Charny belonged to the small circle of Jacques de Molay's loyalists, and he was the only *compaignon du Maistre* considered by Nogaret to be powerful enough within the Temple to lock him up in the dungeons of Chinon together with the members of the Templar headquarters. The kind of isolation selected for him, and the attempt to keep him from the

67 Frale, *L'ultima battaglia dei Templari,* pp. 19-20; cf. Archivio Segreto Vaticano. See, for instance, Reg. Lat. 818, ff. 51r (de Cuenca) and 52r (de Cuencha), f. 293r (de Pugdorfila) e 294r (de Purdeifila); Reg. Lat. 819, f. 6r (Palmiero) e f. 7v (Palmerio), etc.

pope when the pope had asked to question him, leads us to suppose that Charny and the others were able to give an important witness. Geoffroy came from a family of knightly rank and had become a Templar in 1269 at the mansion of Étampes, in the diocese of Sens: His ceremony of admission was celebrated by a high Templar officer named Amaury de La Roche, of whom we shall speak later, a front-rank figure in the Temple, but also very close to the Crown of France. It must have been an important ceremony, since even the preceptor of Paris, Jean le Franceys, left his mansion to attend.

Born about 1250, the knight Geoffroy de Charny was put in charge of the mansion of Villemoisson in Bourgogne in 1294, and one year later, at no more than forty-five years old, he received the responsibility for the Templar province of Normandy; he had an outstanding career, but it is not only his hierarchic rank that showed his power and prestige in the Temple. Templar sources show that this man was always very close to the person of Jacques de Molay; in 1303, he was in the mansion of Marseille where he witnessed the admission of a young servant of the grand master, charged with the care of his harness and horses, who was received by Symon de Quincy, the then supervisor of the sea journeys to Outremer. Marseille was France's main port for the East, and both testimonies assert that the monks present at that chapter then left for Cyprus: A norm of the hierarchic statutes forbade preceptors of western provinces from going to Outremer except in obedience to a specific order from the grand master, so it is certain that Geoffroy de

Charny was there, traveling with other brothers to reach Jacques de Molay.[68]

There certainly was a strong tie of personal friendship between the grand master and Geoffroy de Charny: The chronicle known as the *Continuation of Guillaume de Nangis* remembers that it was only the preceptor of Normandy who chose to follow Molay to the stake, shouting to the crowds, during the last appeal they had been granted, that the Temple was innocent and had not betrayed the Christian faith. Geoffroy de Charny seems to have been constantly among the most important dignitaries of the Temple.[69]

There is another detail, too. If we look at the trial documents as a whole, we find that the preceptor of Normandy Geoffroy de Charny was known to his fellow monks by a nickname connected to his area of origin. Just as we would call someone "the Tuscan" or "the Sicilian," Charny was also called *le berruyer*, which in 14th-century French meant "the man from Berry": It is the area known today as *champagne berrichonne*, which lay pressed in the later Middle Ages between two great powers, the count of Champagne and the duke of Bourgogne. This was exactly the area where the de Charnys lived and prospered, always having to cope with difficult situations forced upon them by the presence of these mighty lords.[70]

The Templar preceptor of Normandy, Geoffroy de Charny, and the bearer of the Oriflamme of France who owned the Shroud in the mid-1300s belonged, in all

---

68 Léonard, *Introduction au cartulaire*, p. 160; Michelet, *Le procès*, II, pp. 289-290; I, p. 295; Curzon, *La Règle*, §87.

69 Géraud, *Cronique*, pp. 402-404.

70 Godefroy, *Dictionnaire*, I, p. 628.

likelihood, to the same family, even though the sources don't allow us to check in detail the exact degree of kinship. The de Charnys had connected themselves with the Order of the Temple toward the end of the 12th century: In 1170 Guy de Charny sold a wooded area to the Temple; his sons Haton and Symon, eleven years later, were to donate fifteen *arpent* of land to the Order, while in 1262 another member of the lineage, Adam, would make a gift of the fief of Valbardin to the Order. It is to be noticed that these gifts were often made as "dowries" for a son about to enter the Order. The Templar domain in Charny was only a quarter of a league away from the command. Thanks to the cartulary of Provins, we also know that in 1241 a Templar by the name of Hugues de Charny was alive, and he may well have been an uncle of the future preceptor of Normandy.[71]

The family was also concerned (though indirectly) with another event closely regarding the Shroud—the Fourth Crusade, with the dreadful sack of Constantinople during which the relic vanished. Count Guillaume de Champlitte, one of the leading barons who took part in the storming of Constantinople and later became prince of Achaia, sought the hand of Elisabeth of the lineage of Mont Saint-Jean, lords of Charny. Already by the mid-12th century, the fief of Charny was very closely connected to the de Courtenay family: Peter I de Courtenay, lord of Charny among other fiefs and youngest son of Louis the Fat, king of France, was the father of Peter II de Courtenay, who would become emperor of Constantinople in 1205; one year after the

---

71 Michelet, *Le procès*, I, p. 628; Mannier, *Ordre de Malte*, pp. 181-184; Carrière, *Histoire et cartulaire des Templiers*, pp. 69-70.

conquest of the Greek metropolis, a member of the Courtenay lineage resided in the Charny castle. Later, even after the Greeks had recovered the Eastern Empire, the de Charnys kept significant contact with the fiefs they had built there; early in the 1300s, the knight Dreux de Charny married the noblewoman Agnès, heir of the Greek lordship of Vostzitza.[72]

Known sources suggest, anyway, that the de Charny family did not come into the Shroud's possession immediately after the great sack, but many decades later.

The Tragedy of the Fourth Crusade

On October 10, 1202, the army of the Fourth Crusade sailed from the strand of Venice under the leadership of Marquess Boniface of Montferrat. It was a vast contingent, made up of about 33,000 crusaders, largely of French origin, and about 17,000 Venetians. The strand of this mighty sea power was as far as the French barons with their feudal levies had been able to go; they had been forced to wait far longer than anyone had imagined: Despite sincere intentions to recover Jerusalem and the Holy Sepulchre, the accounts had been very badly drawn up, and organizers had ended up getting heavily in debt to the Republic's dockyards. The shipbuilders had dedicated whole months to the Crusade and now wanted to be paid. So the expedition was born with a grave weakness: Economic interests placed a mighty

---

72 Dijon, Archives Départementales, *Charny* 12-LXIII and H 1169 (Petit Temple de Dijon), quoted by Léonard, *Introduction*, pp. 331-332; Langlois, La Bible Guiot, p. 65; *Anselme de la Vierge Marie*, I, p. 473 A and B, II, p. 481; *Cronique de Morée*, p. 137.

control over religious ideals, a control that would eventually stifle them. In previous months, when it had become known that the Crusade intended to attack Egypt, the Venetians had grown very reluctant to accept it because they saw no advantage in investing in a project that would not have been particularly profitable for their city. The Doge kept the delegates waiting no less than two weeks, then made a counter-proposal: Venice would provide the transport ships for the crusaders and one full year's supplies in exchange for costs covered in advance and the right to half of what would be conquered. The French barons accepted without delay, showing some considerable naïveté.[73]

After stopping in Pola to clear the shore of pirates, the fleet attacked Zadar (Zara) on November 10. It was a grim omen of the future, for the Venetians compelled the army to loot the city, which was Christian but belonged to the Kingdom of Hungary and was a prime target for Venice. The crusaders wintered near Zara, the sea being too stormy to risk travel; then, when the fair seasons returned, the fleet struck a course toward Corfu. Meanwhile, the other half of the Christian army was waiting in the Holy Land; after Pope Innocent III's call, all the forces of the Christian kingdom had mobilized, and the military orders, the Templars and Hospitallers, had worked out a plan of operation: As soon as it reached the coast of Syria, the army from Europe was to organize an expedition to shore up Christian presence in northern Syria up to Armenia. Then Egypt would have to be attacked, because that

---

73 Carile, *Per una storia*, pp. 103-110; Flori, *Culture chevaleresque*, pp. 371-387; Nicol, *Venezia e Bisanzio*, pp. 167-179.

was where the reinforcements to Jerusalem's Muslim masters were coming from.[74]

By the spring of 1203, the army was preparing to sail away from Corfu, but a change had been made: The leaders had decided to alter their route and go through Constantinople, the mighty capital of the Greek Empire that stretched across both sides of the Bosporus. Several reasons were mentioned, but the most popular had to do with the sad fate of the legitimate Greek emperor Isaac II Angelos, who had been blinded and overthrown. His son, Alexius, had escaped to Europe and taken refuge with his sister, who had married Philip of Swabia, the brother of Emperor Henry VI; Philip had then asked that the crusader troops make their way to Constantinople and help his brother-in-law Alexius recover power. It was just a matter of helping the legitimate dynasty, which would then, in gratitude, help the Crusade by placing at its disposal a considerable slice of the Byzantine army. Many lords were not convinced; however, they may have perceived that matters were getting out of hand, and so they abandoned the expedition and made their way to the Holy Land on their own.[75]

Both the goals and the purpose of the Crusade were already compromised. When the Roman Curia heard of the storming of Zara, Pope Innocent III formally excommunicated the Venetians, guilty of the aggression. But the operation was no longer under the pope's control and had not been for months: Apostolic Legate Pietro Capuano had been rejected by the Venetians, who no

---

74   Goldstein, Zara, pp. 359-370; Frale, *La quarta crociata*, pp. 468-470.
75   Tucci, *La spedizione marittima*, pp. 3-18; Nicol, *Venezia e Bisanzio*, pp. 169-171.

longer accepted him as the pope's representative because of the excessive difference between his views and theirs. The cardinal had to go back and eventually reached the Holy Land by himself. On July 18, 1203, the host reached Constantinople. The reasons that had been used for that bizarre detour were no longer valid since the legitimate emperor Isaac Angelos, blinded though he had been by his enemies, had been set back on the throne by his own Greek subjects. A few months of peace and quiet broken by occasional episodes of violence passed. The army had made camp outside the city walls, and the crusaders were inspecting the magnificent capital, greedily looking at all its treasures and thinking of potential loot. Some leading figures were invited by young Alexius, crowned emperor jointly with his father on August 10, 1203, to visit the monumental imperial palace with its inconceivable collection of relics: The French knight Geoffroy de Villehardouin declared in his chronicle that Constantinople contained as many relics as the whole rest of the world put together.[76]

The debts owed to the Venetians hung heavily over the expedition's future. Emperor Alexius tried to bring together what he could but could only cover half the enormous sum for which he had made himself liable; understanding that the situation was out of control, he went as far as to expropriate the patrimonies of noble families and had church vessels of silver and gold melted down. In August, a Greek mob assaulted the Latin quarter, taking advantage of the emperor being out of town, and set fire to the Venetian, Genoese, and Pisan merchant

---

76   Maleczek, *Innocenzo III e la quarta crociata*, pp. 389-422.

stalls. A few days later, a mob of Flemish, Venetians, and Pisans stormed the Muslim quarter and set the mosque on fire. A strong wind drove the flames onward, and a whole quarter of Constantinople was destroyed; about 15,000 Latins who had been stable residents of Constantinople took refuge with the crusaders and swelled their ranks. By the end of 1203, the crusader leaders sent the emperor an ultimatum: If Alexius did not fulfill his obligations soon, their alliance would be considered broken, and they would have the right to wage war against him. In January 1204, the imperial official Alexius Murzuphlos overthrew the emperor in a coup; he then let the crusaders understand that he did not intend to pay his predecessor's debts and that he meant to chase them off Byzantine soil. In March, the French barons and the Venetians met to plan the conquest of Constantinople and the division of the empire they would conquer once the capital had been forced to surrender. Firstly, Venice would be compensated for the expenses she had suffered; then the Doge would have first pick among the loot of up to three-quarters of the total; they also made plans for the election of a new emperor, entrusting it to a commission of six Frenchmen and six Venetians. The defeated party would have the right to nominate the future Latin rite patriarch.[77]

For three days of horror, from April 14 to 16, 1204, Constantinople was subjected to an unprecedented sack that spared nobody; even the churches were desecrated, though the expedition that had taken those men to the Bosporus was supposed to follow the flag of religion.

---

77   Nicol, *Venezia e Bisanzio*, pp. 186-193.

The butchery was atrocious, and even though Byzantine civilization later recovered and still had some periods of splendor, the sack of 1204 left a terrible wound and irreparably compromised that union of the Greek and Latin churches that Innocent III had so longed for.[78]

The violence and looting were followed by a more systematic stripping of all other treasures from the capital, precious objects that the crusaders had been able to study in detail over the previous months; Greek monks had tried to safeguard relics and furniture but all their hideouts were discovered. The conquerors had reached a preliminary agreement: All the booty was to be gathered in the house of Garnier de Traynel, bishop of Troyes, under pain of excommunication, after which it would be properly shared out. It seems that the Doge craftily offered the French barons an efficient guard service for the small sum of ten marks per person, but this time he had overrated French naïveté, and he was politely turned down. Anyway the Venetians were the first to break the pact, taking several precious objects onto their ships on the sly under the cover of darkness—but they weren't the only ones. The official reckoning went on in parallel with a clandestine and wholly autonomous one, which fed a wholly repulsive trade. The notion took hold that to obtain at least one relic would mean to be freed of the vow to go to Jerusalem; they actually thought that once they had a few precious pieces of loot, they would be entitled to turn their backs on the Holy Sepulchre and go home with an easy conscience. Nobody wanted to be left empty-handed, and no sanctuary was spared. The rumor

---

78 Ducellier, *Il sacco di Costantinopoli del 1204*, pp. 368-377.

of these unworthy transactions led the Fourth Lateran Council of 1215 to excommunicate anyone guilty of trafficking in relics.[79]

Individual crusaders found ways to secretly get hold of these eagerly desired objects, intending to take them home to enrich their family churches. In no more than four years, the immense sacred treasury of relics kept in Constantinople was sent to Europe. Crusaders often sent them as gifts to persons from whom they expected favors, or used them as investments: Owning an illustrious relic seemed like an actual guarantee of future earnings, for the faithful were expected to come in crowds to venerate it, bringing fat alms with them. That was the expectation that led the crusader Nivelon de Quierzy, bishop of Soissons, to mortgage the future income of an object he owned to rebuild the cathedral and bridge of the French town of Châlons-sur-Marne; the restorations of the Troyes cathedral were also paid with the income from some relics donated by Bishop Garnier de Traynel, and the same happened in many other cases. When they reached Europe, these relics were expected with great trepidation and were delivered to their addressees in solemn and elaborate religious ceremonies, accompanied by hymns and poems composed for the occasion.[80]

Obviously, the relics from the great imperial collection housed in the chapel of Pharos and in the Blachernae basilica were given special treatment. The whole operation concerning them was carefully recorded in an official report; they were sealed in purpose-made crates

---

79 Riant, *Des dépouilles*, pp. 7, 18-19, 27-35.
80 Ibid., pp. 4-5; Claverie, *Un "illustris amicus Venetorum,"* pp. 506-510.

to prevent thefts and fraudulent substitutions, which were entrusted to the most trustworthy of carriers. They had a general passport and a certificate of authenticity that guaranteed their origin, a certificate bearing the golden seal of the Byzantine emperors.[81]

In 1241, when, after a long decline, the Latin Empire of Constantinople entered into a full-blown economic crisis, the last few priceless relics of the Passion left the capital. They were acquired by an exceptional buyer, the king of France, Louis IX, a man of great and sincere faith, who paid an absolute fortune for them. In the heart of Paris, near the Nôtre-Dame cathedral, an exquisite little church, a jewel in and of itself, had been put up for the express purpose of guarding such treasures—the Sainte-Chapelle. Carefully crated up, sealed, certified, and handed over to trustworthy persons, a fragment of the True Cross, the Spear, the Sponge, the Crown of Thorns, and a number of other relics of Jesus, sealed in their valuable original reliquaries, moved toward France.[82]

If the Templars ever held the Shroud, they cannot have failed to know its history and the fact that it had been stolen during a frightful massacre against which Innocent III had flung curses. The sheet was valuable beyond reckoning, but owning it involved many risks.

More Precious than Rubies

The theory Ian Wilson offered years ago could close the gap between the Byzantine witnesses of the Shroud

---

81   Riant, *Exuviae,* pp. 44-45.
82   Ibid., pp. 48-52; Durand, *Reliquie e reliquiari,* pp. 386-389.

before the sack of April 1204 and those who found it in France about 150 years later. Attractive and based on some credible documentation, it raised some enthusiasm early on, but some scholars also raised serious objections: In effect, the author tended to take as fact certain things that only arose from his own deductions, brilliant and credible though they might have been. Over time, the best-known experts in Templar history have had a wide range of reactions to Wilson's theory, and after an original stage of prevailing skepticism, it seems to have been cautiously but increasingly re-evaluated.

A few years after the publication of Wilson's book, in 1985, Alain Demurger of the Sorbonne declared himself fairly skeptical, while Malcolm Barber of Cambridge showed himself more open to its possibilities. In a 1982 article in the specialist magazine *Catholic Historical Review*, Barber assessed Wilson's theory as weakly supported, since not a single one of these mysterious Templar idols has been preserved. The other evidence Wilson had gathered seemed to him to lack a strong connection, amounting in effect to a sequel of scattered and not very coherent fragments. However, Barber had already had a definite impression, during his own analysis of the trial records, that the Templars were actually worshipping some sort of image of Christ done in the Byzantine manner. He closed by remarking that the idea seemed possible to him, but it still needed a sufficiently strong explanation.[83]

Some time later, Francesco Tommasi of the University of Perugia carried out a broad and extremely detailed

---

83   Barber, *The Templars and the Turin Shroud*, p. 225; Id., *The Trial*, p. 273.

investigation of the relics the Templars had acquired. The Italian historian decided not to study the trial records, which are the most abundant source of evidence about the Templars that have reached us, but in which a great deal of information is vitiated by torture; this left him with a much narrower area of research, but also one that could not be suspected of manipulation. Tommasi discovered that the Order of the Temple had carried out a genuine policy of systematically combing for relics, building up a treasure store of such objects, which in contemporaneous culture were of great economic as well as religious value. More than a thousand years earlier, the acts of the martyrdom of Saint Polycarpus (about 165 AD) stated that the bones of its hero could be much more precious than gems.[84] The author certainly meant only a spiritual value, but that one sentence was to have an incredible career.

The Templar's favorite way to acquire relics was simply to buy them: Either they made a straightforward purchase, or else they took relics pawned against hefty loans made to persons in trouble, loans that were never paid off, leaving the pawn as Temple property. The Temple had money to spend, and in the matter of relics it was quite happy to spend it.

A very interesting fact pointed out by Tommasi is that the sacred treasury of the Templars was full of saints worshipped mainly in the Byzantine East, such as Polycarpus of Smyrna, Plato, Gregory, Anastasia, and Euphemia, but the central place in this collection was obviously taken by direct testimonies of the Passion of

---

84   Tommasi, *I Templari e il culto delle reliquie*, pp. 191-210; *Acta Polycarpi*, Ian. III, p. 319; and Riant, *Exuviae*, p. 2.

Jesus Christ. The Order had owned a great cross-holder in Jerusalem that held a fairly large fragment of the True Cross, from which had been cut several small bits that had then been sent throughout the Templar world; many Templar commands had their own reliquary with a Cross fragment, which must have represented a physical link to Christ and the Holy City to the monks. The Templars seem to have been more devoted to the Cross than other religious orders were and they offered it special liturgies, both in Syria and later in Cyprus.[85]

The Templar collection's centerpiece was a thorn from the Crown of Thorns, which was said to flower miraculously on Good Friday. A curious fact is that when the Hospitallers took over Templar goods after the Order's dissolution, they inherited the Thorn as well, and became used to its annual miracle. On Good Friday of 1497, the Thorn flowered no less than three hours before its usual time at midday, and the grand prior Jacques de Milly immediately called for a public notary to make a legal record of that unusual event. The same wonder was recorded by the last grand master of the Templars, Jacques de Molay, during the trial, as he testified in defense of his order: God would never have granted a similar miracle to unworthy persons or to heretics. Another important relic was a cross inside a little cup that had belonged to Jesus. Kept by the Templars of Jerusalem, it was borne in procession when drought threatened, to beg God for the gift of rain. According to this evidence, it also had the power to heal the sick and free the oppressed.[86]

---

85 Schottmüller, II, pp. 157-158.
86 Michelet, *Le procès*, I, pp. 646-647.

Apart from what they owned themselves, the Templars in general were held to have a particular link to relics and were regarded as among the greatest experts in recognizing true ones; in fact, when great personages had some business to do with relics, it was to the Templars that they turned, as trustworthy and authoritative connoisseurs. In 1164, Louis VII, king of France, charged the Templar knight Geoffroy Foucher, who was about to travel to Syria, with consecrating a ring of his by placing it physically in contact with the sanctuaries he was to meet during his mission. In 1247, the patriarch of Jerusalem wanted to send to Europe an ampoule containing some of the Most Precious Blood to be given to King Henry III of England: Grand Master Guillaume de Sonnac of the Temple and Grand Master of the Hospital Guillaume de Chateaunef were summoned in person to underwrite the certificate of authenticity that went with the relic. Thirty years later, Grand Master of the Temple Thomas Bérard and some faithful from the Holy Land sent some particles of the wood of the True Cross to England, along with relics of saints Philip, Helena, Stephen, Lawrence, Euphemia, and Barbara, along with a fragment from Jesus's table; the archbishop of Tyre was called to sign the certificate of authenticity along with Bishop Hubert of Banyas, who was a Templar. [87]

Before the fall of Jerusalem, this core of sacred goods was almost certainly kept in the mother-house of the Holy City, near the ruins of the Lord's Temple; when Jerusalem fell back into Muslim hands, all

---

87   Tommasi, *I Templari e il culto delle reliquie*, p. 202.

the Templar treasures were transferred to its Acre headquarters, which became the Order's central seat in the East. When Acre, too, fell in 1291, the collection of relics and the most valuable objects found a place in Cyprus in the church of the chief mansion in Nicosia. The never-ending danger, however, had long since made it advisable to send many relics westward, and several such transfers are known to have gone to Italy, to England, and, in all likelihood, to France as well, to the Paris headquarters. The picture reconstructed by Tommasi agrees perfectly with the statements of Jacques de Molay in the trial: The treasury of relics and liturgical furniture that adorned Templar churches was far superior to that of other religious orders and found its equal only in the treasuries of cathedrals. Two of these centerpieces, the body of Saint Euphemia and the Thorn of the Crown, certainly came from that collection that had been the pride of Byzantine emperors where the basin for Jesus's foot wash during the Last Supper was also kept: These are relics that had vanished with many others during the Sack of Constantinople, and as things stand, it is difficult to understand how the Templars managed to gain their possession.[88] I would like to add a curious coincidence: According to the account of Bishop Anthony of Novgorod, who visited Constantinople only a few years before the terrible sack, the cathedral of Hagia Sophia kept two slabs of stone that came from the Holy Sepulchre. During the

---

88   Mention of the presence of the Pelvis, the bowl of the Last
Supper, appears in several descriptions of the sacred treasure of
Constantinople; cfr. Riant, *Exuviae*, for instance, pp. 211, 213, but
according to others, it was a marble basin (cfr. pp. 219, 223).

trial against the Templars of England, an old man was called to testify who had served for twenty years in their Sumford mansion; he described a relic that sounds exactly like one of these small slabs of stone.[89]

He said that he could not find anything bad to say about the Templar monks, except for one oddity he had seen that had greatly surprised him: When the monks of the house had to carry out some important or demanding piece of business, they used to get up very early in the morning and go to the chapel of their church. There, they approached the altar, and from the table of the altar they would draw a smaller stone table, cut so thin that it could be replaced back into the altar so that no outsider would have noticed it was there. Having lifted this stone tablet so that it could stand upright over the altar, everyone knelt and adored it, falling down to the ground before it. Nobody was allowed into that chapel who was not a Templar, or at any rate closely connected to the Order.[90]

We should add that the Templars used to own a precious icon covered in gold and silver, which featured the Face of Christ, something analogous to the images on the verso of the seals of Germany's masters and the face on the Templecombe panel.[91]

It is hardly surprising at the end of this long *excursus* that Francesco Tommasi was decidedly more optimistic than his colleagues from outside Italy about the idea of the Shroud passing into the Temple's possession:

---

89   Ibid, pp. 48, 220.
90   Schottmüller, II, pp. 91-92.
91   Tommasi, *I Templari e il culto delle reliquie*, p. 197.

For it is quite possible that the Templars might have known the image of the man in the Shroud, being the owners of the relic. Besides, there is an undeniable resemblance between the Christ's face (without the traditional aureole) as it appears on a wooden panel discovered in 1951 in Templecombe (Somerset), former home of a Templar community, and the face in the Shroud [...]. Nonetheless there are enough overall elements to not treat Wilson's intuition as groundless, so the hypothesis that iconographies of the Christ of the Shroud type should have a special place in Templar devotional practice seems hardly like it should be rejected.[92]

The new data that has arisen makes Ian Wilson's theory the likeliest one; Tommasi's balanced opinion is very valid, but one might go even further. Certainly not every Templar testimony on the idol referred to this tradition of the Holy Face, and in fact it is legitimate to think that many people confessed because of torture or other forms of violence. It is, however, a fact that within the Order images of the Face of God circulated and were venerated, which were represented in an unusual way— without aureole and not showing the neck—exactly as it appears on the Shroud and in the Byzantine tradition of the *mandylion*.

Most recent Templar research adds confirmation that in some regions of southern France, a full-figure portrait of a man on a linen sheet was offered for the brethren's adoration. The characteristics of this image on cloth that the Templars venerated in southern France (full-scale,

---

92   Ibid., pp. 193-194.

life-sized body, reddish color, ill-defined outline) seem, in effect, to recall nothing so much as the shape of the Turin Shroud. Furthermore, many hints converge to indicate that the Shroud left a very strong imprint on the religious sensitivities of these warrior monks, and this is hardly surprising; according to science, the relic has some decidedly unique features, which it would not be exaggerating to call stunning.

From the Amphoras of Qumran to the Nuns of Chambéry

The Shroud is a linen artifact that, before the restoration of 2002, was made of pieces of material from cloths of different ages, styles, and weaving techniques; to use an effective comparison, it is a patchwork quilt. As a whole, it is fourteen feet, three inches long and three feet, seven inches wide, but this data is by nature an average that can vary by a few inches if the cloth is stretched, for the linen is very yielding due to its great age; it is crossed by the marks—never, at this point, to be removed again—of some folds that tell us how it was stored in certain stages of its history, and in time it has grown so thin as to be almost worn through because of the countless manipulations and even misfortunes it has endured. It has been suggested that whoever cut the material did so on the basis of a definite and commonly used unit of measurement, so that the cloth must have had a length equal to a multiple of this unit. The only such unit known that gives any sort of result is the Syrian cubit, used in the ancient Middle East, in whose terms the cloth is eight cubits long and two cubits wide.[93]

During its frequent obstentions to the faithful, the sheet was opened and hung by pegs; it would hang in this pose for days, remaining stretched, touched by numerous hands, rubbed with many objects that became relics as soon as they touched it, sometimes even kissed. To prevent the linen from tearing under so much mechanical stress, in 1534 the original material was sewn onto another cloth of Dutch linen to make it thicker; then the margin was covered with a border in turquoise silk that allowed it to be handled freely without further touching the ancient material. At various times yet to be determined, there have been several minor repairs with fragments of other linen at points where the weave was broken by holes of various sizes; where the cloth was in danger of tearing, it was mended by the kind of artistic mending once used for precious lace, sewn with the same kind of thread by hands so expert that the most recent repairs are worked into warp and woof to the point of being almost invisible.

The ancient cloth is made of linen fiber worked according to a fairly complex technique that demanded the contemporary use of two spools instead of the more common one; as a result, the fibers show a counterclockwise twisting called "Z-shaped torsion." It was woven on a four-pedal craftsman's frame, using the so-called chevrons or fishbone technique, and a knot called "3-1" because the thread goes three times under the woof and only once over. Each square centimeter of the Shroud has 40 threads and weighs on average 0.8

---

93 On these values cf. Wiseman and Wheaton, "Weights and Measures."

ounces. The short sides have no selvage; the strip of cloth that stands at the start and end of every piece and has a special structure designed to prevent the material from unweaving itself when manhandled: This shows that it was cut from a longer roll of cloth.

Z-shaped torsion, fishbone technique, and 3-1 knots belong to a set of very ancient techniques of cloth-making and can be found in several artifacts of pre-Roman, Roman, and medieval origin. The fishbone style is found in Middle Eastern weaves from the Hellenistic and Roman periods of highly expensive materials meant for decorative purposes (pillow covers and embroidered borders) because this technique creates a material that reflects light differently according to the position from which the eye looks at it. There is a certain innate luminousness to linen cloth, and in the case of this particular work, the superimposition of threads creates a design of repeated V-shapes in relief alternating with V-shapes in depression; the weave has a bright-opaque variation effect that reminds us of certain ancient brocades with simple geometric designs. The German scholar Maria Luisa Rigato has recently confirmed the opinion already stated by other experts in ancient cloths that the Shroud's material belongs to an expensive and not at all commonplace type.[94]

It is a curious feature of the Shroud that it contains no trace whatsoever of wool fiber, a strange fact when you

---

94 Timossi, *Analisi*, pp. 105-111; Pastore Trossello, *La struttura tessile*, pp. 64-73; Jackson, *Jewish Burial*, pp. 309-322; Vial, *Le Linceul*, pp. 11-24; Whanger and Whanger, *A Comparison*, pp. 379-381; Baima Bollone, *Sindone e scienza*, pp. 83-106; Flury-Lemberg, *Sindone* 2002, pp. 25-48; Rigato, *Il titolo della croce*, pp. 198-217.

consider that it was, by a large margin, the most widely used thread and that normally frames were used to weave all kinds of thread; its fibers, however, include traces of cotton from the bush variety *Gossypium herbaceum*, the only one cultivated in the Middle East during antiquity before the discovery of America allowed us to bring in all the other varieties we now know from the New World. The cotton fibers are from other weaves woven on the same frame before the cloth of the Shroud was started, and which remained stuck to the machine and eventually ended up woven into the linen cloth. The total lack of wool suggests that that particular frame, for some special reason, had never used wool at all; now, the Book of Deuteronomy in the Old Testament (22:11) includes a norm that forbids weaving wool and linen together because the mix of the two would produce ritual impurity, so it has reasonably been concluded that the frame had belonged to members of the Jewish religion who did not violate the rule and made what their culture designated as a pure cloth.[95]

Besides the cotton fibers, the oldest weave also contains a large number of diverse materials, traces of objects it must have met with over the course of its long story: pollens from various vegetables, spores, the remains of insect bodies caught in the weave as it was left to weather in the open, wax, traces of aloe and myrrh, dye particles, red and blue silk once used to wrap it, ink, and powders. Traces of pigments found include ocher, Venetian red, and vermilion, along with proteins that once were used to fix and dissolve color dye powders; they are present on

---

95   Raes, *Rapport d'analise*, pp. 79-83; Jackson, *Hasadeen Hakadosh*, pp. 27-33.

the cloth in trace amounts, due to the fact that painted copies were rested on the Shroud to make into relics. In 1973, the criminologist Max Frei carried out a study using the forensic science techniques in use among the scientific squad of the Swiss police, and identified traces of pollen belonging to fifty-eight vegetable species originating from the Middle East, of which some were found in the Dead Sea area and in Jerusalem. Traces have also been found of at least twenty-eight species of flowers laid on the body, most of which grow in Palestine and flower in the spring. The humus includes aragonite, a fairly rare material that can, however, be found in the soil of caves near Jerusalem; the presence of natron, used in Palestine and Egypt to preserve dead bodies, also points to a Middle Eastern origin.[96]

On one of the long sides, someone has sewn on a narrow strip of cloth that is shorter than 18 inches; some experts feel that it had been part of the larger cloth but that it had been unwoven and woven again. The reason is unknown; it was probably cut from the cloth, which was longer than required, to make a long band that could be used to tie the Shroud around the corpse, about the feet, knees, and neck, so that it would stay on tight. It was only later that the band was retrieved and sewn again along the border from which it had previously been cut, for it was seen as a part of the Shroud, and was therefore also preserved. An interesting fact is that the technique by

---

96 Baima Bollone, "La presenza della mirra," pp. 169-174, e Id., *Sindone e scienza*, pp. 5-31; Scannerini, *Mirra, aloe, pollini*; Upinsky, *La démonstration*, pp. 313-334; Curto, *La Sindone*, pp. 59-85; Frei, *Il passato della sindone*, pp. 191-200; Id., *Identificazione e classificazione*, pp. 277-284; Danin, *Pressed Flowers*, pp. 35-37, 69; Kohlbeck and Nitowski, "New Evidence," pp. 23-24.

which it was sewn back on to the Shroud, called the false border, demands great expertise, and it is only found twice in all our knowledge of ancient textiles—on the Shroud and on a linen fragment found in Masada, the fortress where a few Jewish rebels took refuge during the Jewish War and that the Romans destroyed in 73 AD. It is also interesting that the thread used for the sewing is not of the same kind as those that make up the Shroud, with their complex Z-shaped torsion structure, but belongs to a simpler and more ordinary kind (S-type torsion); it may be that the person who sewed it back on was no longer able to obtain the same kind of thread, which was surely of uncommon quality, and had to be satisfied with what she or he found.[97]

The upper left-hand side shows another glaring lacuna: It is the part that was destroyed in the radiocarbon test. Near this lost rectangle of material we can see clear traces of a double strip of burnt material that runs along the entire length of the Shroud. In fact, these show the position of a fold from when the cloth was stored in the 16th century, in Chambéry, then the capital of the Duchy of Savoy, now a French provincial town. In 1532 a fire burst out in the ducal palace's chapel, heating the invaluable silver casing where the Shroud was kept almost to melting point, and a few droplets of metal—or possibly a sharp and heated object—burned the cloth. The Poor Clare nuns then repaired it, adding many patches of linen in those parts where no material had been left at all; the accident also left four holes in a rhomboid shape near the middle of the cloth, as well as a quantity

---

97 Baima Bollone, *La sindone e la scienza*, pp. 60-61, 83-86.

of stains more or less everywhere due to the impurities in the large amounts of water used to extinguish the fire. It may, however, be that someone had accidentally water-stained the Shroud much earlier.

In April 2008, Aldo Guerreschi and Michele Salcito published the results of a research they had carried out on the water stains left on the Shroud in the specialist magazine *Arch*. Until then, it had always been thought that they were the result of the water used in Chambéry to extinguish the fire, but analysis showed a different truth. The very shape of the Chambéry scorch marks allows us to reconstruct the way that the Shroud was put away in the 1500s: It was a most careful and precise folding, with the edges accurately lined up with each other, done by first laying the Shroud down on a long table. The water stains, however, speak of a wholly different folding, the kind called concertina, but above all one that was far less precise: The edges did not match, and the central fold did not fall in the exact center of the cloth. This is more reminiscent of a housewife snatching a sheet from the rain and folding it in a hurry to run back inside before the storm reaches its height; that is, it leaves the feeling of a rushed, provisional arrangement. Turned in on itself in a concertina shape, and then closed, the cloth was not under even tension, the forward part sagging under its own weight. Based on the way the Shroud was arranged, it is also possible to deduce the shape of the container where it had been placed—a cylindrical object, narrow, long, and not very large. It was not a case like its Chambéry silver reliquary and neither did it resemble the lovely Byzantine container decorated in lozenges that we see in the representations of the *mandylion*. Rather, it was a container designed for other purposes, where the Shroud was perhaps only provisionally housed. The shape of the object is exactly like that of the terra-cotta amphoras found in Qumran, which held the 800 or more manuscripts of the Essene library. In effect, amphoras were very versatile containers in which anything could and would be stored, from oil to grain to books. At the very bottom of that container there must have been some water, a small amount but enough to dampen the lower part of the cloth.[98]

This reconstruction seems to open a new and promising path of research. No doubt that kind of earthenware container was a highly commonplace object, made all over the Middle East and certainly not only in Qumran, but the community that lived in isolation on the Dead Sea shore had several features that might have made it a safe refuge for the earliest Christians, persecuted by the Jerusalem authorities almost from the time of Jesus's death. At any rate, if Salcito and Guerreschi's reconstruction is correct, it argues for a phase in the Shroud's history in which this object was not exhibited to the veneration of the faithful, but, on the contrary, hidden: Whoever raised the lid would not have seen anything but a featureless mass of cloth, too tightly turned in on itself to show even the abundant marks of blood. As is known, Jewish tradition held blood in horror and saw it as necessary to destroy anything that had come into contact with corpses, being in the highest degree impure and able to pollute people, things, and places.[99]

---

98 Guerreschi and Salcito, *Tra le pieghe*, pp. 62-71.
99 Lipinski, *Sangue*, p. 1161; Sacchi, *Storia del Secondo Tempio*, pp. 417-421.

Between the 12th and 13th centuries, the Templars held dozens of establishments in the Syro-Palestinian territories, but there is no evidence that they ever had any direct contact with Qumran: What archaeology currently tells us is that the Essene citadel was abandoned in 68 AD and never reopened until almost twenty centuries had passed. On the other hand, that the Shroud may have spent some time in Qumran over a thousand years before it ended up in the Templars' hands—this does seem possible.

III

Against All Heresies

A Map of Butchery

Because of its unique properties, the Shroud of Turin was an object that could have left an indelible mark on the spirituality of a religious order such as the Templars, which is exactly what happened.

The cloth's most singular feature is that on one of its faces can be seen the image and the imprint of an individual; corresponding and practically fused together, they show the outline of a man as if he had been wrapped in the cloth. This was an adult but still youthful person, drawn up in the rigor mortis that is typical of cadaveric muscles in the first few hours after death, bearing the marks of severe trauma and violence everywhere. This man wrapped in the cloth, whoever he was, had been slaughtered. Besides the numerous wounds that covered his whole body surface, we know that his face was struck repeatedly and with great violence: His nose was broken to the extent of showing a decomposed fracture, and streaks of blood flowed from the wound and soaked the linen. The right side of the face was completely swollen.[1]

---

1   Baima Bollone, *Sindone e scienza*, p. 99.

The print on the Shroud is made mainly of blood, sweat, a mixture of aromatic oils, the traces of earth we already mentioned, and probably also bits of skin torn off during the tortures: All these substances have been left on the sheet through direct contact when the body was shrouded. The blood is human, type AB, as shown by a team of forensic medicinal experts led by Pier Luigi Baima Bollone, professor of Legal Medicine at the University of Turin; it contains a large amount of bilirubin, as happens in subjects who have suffered a violent death. The blood imprint near the face seems connected to the unusual phenomenon of "sweating blood"; it is a rare process that is found when a person suffers a tremendous emotional shock that causes the skin's blood vessels to dilate and hemorrhage in the sweat glands. Near the cranium can be seen the marks of thirteen wounds inflicted by sharp objects of the same kind, arranged over the upper part of the head to form a kind of helm or head cover, which caused several lines of coagulated blood. They are also present in the face area, where a curious flow stands out where the blood has soaked through; it shows an abundant flow, for it comes from a break in the frontal vein, while the unusual shape results from its coagulation over a forehead already contracted in furrows from atrocious suffering. Several analyses have found that the hemorrhages, which the sheet touched, came in part from wounds inflicted when the man was alive, and in part from when he was already dead. The rivulets of blood described took place mainly while the victim was still in a vertical position. Examination of the blood flow and of its characteristics seems to have proven that the man was placed in the sheet no more than two and a half hours after death.[2]

When ultraviolet light is shone on the cloth, it shows an entire body covered with a large number of lacerated and contused wounds (save the ones to the face and to the area of the heart) inflicted while the subject was naked; these wounds were placed with a certain symmetry in groups of six, as if an object with six spikes had been used to strike the man a great many times, possibly up to 120. In the shoulder-blade area, these wounds, after having been inflicted, had been further expanded and scratched as if a large and rigid object had been viciously rubbed over the back, causing lacerations of the skin near bone protrusions. All these wounds and excoriations drew many stains of blood, as did the hole in the left wrist, placed to cover the right one which is unseen, and the same for the wounds in the feet.

The holes near the wrists and feet, the contracted posture of the chest and of the thigh muscles, and the rips left by a large and stiff support on the back, indicate that the man was executed by crucifixion, a form of capital punishment practiced in antiquity by several peoples including the Assyrians, Celts, and Romans.

It amounted to fastening a man to a pole by various means and waiting for him to die over a long time and after indescribable suffering; the tears on the back

---

2 Baima Bollone and Gaglio, *Applicazioni di tecniche*, pp. 169-174; Baima Bollone, Jorio, and Massaro, *La determinazione del gruppo*, pp. 175-178 and Id., *Ulteriori ricerche*, pp. 9-13; Id., *Gli ultimi giorni*, pp. 95-97; Heller and Adler, *Blood on the Shroud*, pp. 2742-2744; Adler, *Aspetti chimico-fisici*, pp. 165-184.

suggest that the condemned man had to bear for some time an object shaped like a *patibulum*, a large wooden beam that was anchored to the pole and served to fix the body so as to make it impossible for the victim to move. In the time of the Persian king Darius (522–485 BC), people were executed by impaling, but later it became common to nail the condemned man's hands and feet to the wood: A passage of the Book of Isaiah, who lived between the 8th and 7th centuries BC, and above all a verse in Psalm 22 ("They have pierced my hands and my feet") already seem to point to this practice of nailing, which was later (3rd century BC to 1st century AD) to become a sadly common affair, as shown by fragments from the excavations of Qumran,[3] among other things.

In June 1968, north of Jerusalem in the area called Giv'at ha-Mivtar, a family grave of impressive dimensions was found, holding the bones of nearly twenty persons; an ossuary held the remains of a man crucified at about thirty years of age. A nail was still driven into the bone of the heel, and it had not been possible to draw it out as he was taken down from the cross, because it had bent inward.[4]

Under the reign of King Antiochus IV Epiphanes (175–164 BC), crucifixion became tragically commonplace, falling briefly into disuse during the reign of Herod the Great (39–4 BC) only to then be brought back by the Roman legate Publius Quintilius Varus. Romans practiced this kind of execution very early on, reserving

---

3 Ps. 22, 17-19; Puech, *Notes*, pp. 103-124.

4 Naveh, *The Ossuary Inscriptions*, pp. 33-37; Tzaferis, *Jewish Tombs*, pp. 18-32; Puech, *Notes*, p. 120 and note 33.

it for public or solemn executions of persons who did not enjoy the protection of Roman citizenship—major public enemies who had committed extremely serious crimes or had placed public order at risk. The case of the revolt of slaves led by Spartacus became famous: After the revolt, it was decided to inflict an exemplary punishment on the rebels, and the crosses on which they had died lined miles upon miles of Via Appia. According to the Greek historians Polybius and Plutarch, it was reserved for those convicted of crimes against the state; Cicero and Livy said that Romans regarded it as the most cruel and disgraceful of penalties. The enormous agonies suffered by the condemned excited the same ugly pleasure that drove the Roman people to gladiator games, and when these public shows also featured crucifixions, advertisements mentioned them as if they were a special treat to get the public in, no different from distributions of fruit and money. Crucifixion was chosen when political enemies had to be gotten rid of, because it added appalling suffering to the insult of an infamous death, and the history of the Jewish people includes many cases of this kind, cases in which it was desired to make punishment spectacular by turning it into a ghastly mass display. In 162 BC, High Priest Alkimos had sixty devout Jews who had opposed him crucified in a single day, while King Alexander Iannaeus in 88 BC had as many as 800 Pharisees killed. No more than thirteen years later, eighty other people suffered the same fate under charges of sorcery.[5]

---

5 Radermakers, *Croce*, pp. 378-379; de Fraine and Haudebert,
   Crocifissione, col. 379; Sabbatini Tumolesi, *Gladiatorum Paria*, for
   instance, p. 107, note 79.

In crucifixion by nailing of limbs, the condemned man tended to die of asphyxia, for the body weight pushed the ribcage downward and only allowed him to breathe in, while breathing out demanded motions that caused intolerable pain. The presence of several secondary wounds informs us that it was a crucifixion carried out in the Roman fashion, that is by having the actual execution follow an additional form of torture, flagellation: The victim was struck with the *flagrum*, a whip with a wooden handle and leather strips at whose ends were sticks of bone or wood with points at both ends. Handled violently enough, these stings were literally able to rip off skin. No known description of Roman usage, on the other hand, can be connected with the two other outrages suffered by this individual—whatever it was that caused the multiple wounds over the cranium, and the wound between the fifth and sixth rib on the right side of the chest that was inflicted by a pointed, cutting weapon. That wound may be connected to the fact that the condemned man did not have his legs broken, a Jewish practice meant to hasten the convict's death and allow burial before the end of the day, according to a precept in Deuteronomy. Such alterations to normal practice could be explained by the Gospel account: The trial of Jesus of Nazareth took place in a unique sociopolitical context, and for that reason his burial, too, did not follow the usual practice.[6]

---

6   Blinzler, *Il processo di Gesù*; Brown, *La morte del Messia*, pp.1354-
     1357; Martini, *La condanna a morte di Gesù*, pp. 543-557; Miglietta, *Il
     processo a Gesù*, pp. 767-784; Id., *Riflessioni*, pp. 147-184; Fabbrini, *La
     deposizione di Gesù*, pp. 97-178.

The "Belt of Blood" and the "Sign of Jonas"

The most glaring of all the blood marks can be found on the right side of the chest, near the fifth space between the ribs. It was caused by a large wound, 1.77 inches long and 0.6 inches wide, with straight and slightly spread margins, typical of a wound inflicted by a pointed weapon used for cutting. The big blood flow that followed it and soaked the cloth went down the side and ended up coloring the whole breadth of the back, creating a horizontal stripe; this glaring red-brown streak is even more visible to the eye when the back imprint of the Shroud is looked at; because of its shape and impression, specialists call it "the belt of blood." The abundance of the blood flow suggests that the wound caused a break in the lung or in the upper right ventricle of the heart; furthermore, it was found that this blood had broken down into its two components, that is the serum and the blood particles (red blood cells), which never happens except after death. The wound that ripped the chest open had been made when the man was already a corpse.[7]

Modern historians are in the habit of looking at the Shroud with the eyes of science, that is, in light of the countless chemical and physical analyses carried out more or less ceaselessly on it since the early 1900s, but we have to take a step back and try to understand how men from the Middle Ages saw it. From the tear in the ribs, just where the spear had struck Jesus, according to the Gospel of John, the signs of a huge hemorrhage were visible. The blood had flowed down the side, drenching

---

7   Baima Bollone, *Sindone e scienza*, pp. 99-100.

the cloth the entire breadth of the thorax, from side to side. The deep red on the ivory white of the linen would have leapt to the eye, glaring, awesome.

To those who used to listen to the story of the Passion, as the Templars did, the belt of blood must have held an immense fascination. Could this "belt," red with blood, be something that the Templars tried to represent with the little strand they bore on their bodies every day? Their belts had once been consecrated by touching the stone of the Sepulchre that had received the body of Jesus and seen his resurrection. And the Shroud, too, according to tradition, had covered Jesus's body and had "experienced" his rise from death, but with something extra: A bit of his blood still rested on the material. For a medieval man, this was priceless: Later on, the Franciscan theologian Francesco della Rovere, later to be Pope Sixtus IV (1471–1484), pointed to the Shroud of Turin in his treatise *De Corpore et Sanguine Christi,* as a relic of the Lord's true blood.[8]

As we mentioned, in St. Bernard's time, the Templars' belt had a merely symbolic value, representing the vow of chastity; then, during the 1200s, this meaning was forgotten and replaced with a loftier, almost theological one: The belt was consecrated through contact with relics and material places that had witnessed the earthly life of Jesus. It was therefore impregnated with a special sacred power and gave the monks who wore it a material contact with the human dimension of Christ. I am certain (as I have already said) that the special night ceremonies the Templars carried out by

---

8   Savio, *Pellegrinaggio di san Carlo,* p. 436.

the Holy Sepulchre were vigils of prayer during which the dignitaries consecrated the linen strands that would then be given to all future Order members, a guarantee of protection against the enemies of body and soul. I would not be surprised at all if one day new documents were to show that the great reputation enjoyed by the Templar dignitaries in their time as profound experts on relics also depended on the fact that benefactors of the Order often asked them to consecrate certain objects—rings, handkerchiefs, and so on—during those same liturgies at the Sepulchre, to make them relics as precious as Templar strands. We know for certain that the king of France, Louis IX the Saint, had done exactly that—and who knows how many others did the same.[9]

By coming into contact with stone that had been present at the resurrection of Christ, the belt somehow absorbed its potency, and was itself a guarantee of resurrection for the Templar willing to live and die according to the spirit of the Order. In 1187, Jerusalem was lost, and we can only guess what a terrible blow this was to Templar morale. Then, one day, along came this unbelievable piece of cloth, with the marks of a man who had literally been butchered exactly as Jesus had been, according to the Gospels. The most authoritative tradition describes it as the true winding sheet of Christ. What can be seen on that sheet is not only terribly realistic, it is even embarrassing: Indeed, it forces Christians to reflect.

Medieval man interpreted some things in a much clearer way than we can today. The corpse that was

---

9 Tommasi, *I Templari e il culto delle reliquie*, p. 202.

wrapped in the Shroud was wholly stiff, its neck collapsed on its chest, the fingers extended, the muscles at full tension. Such rigor mortis occurs between one to three hours following death, becomes complete by about ten to twelve, and fades away after thirty-six to forty-eight when natural decomposition begins to set in.[10]

Medieval men were aware of such matters as it was part of their lives. The corpses of their beloved were often exhibited on a bed in the house and stayed there, surrounded by lit candles for many hours under the eyes of relatives who honored the dead with long vigils of prayer, which neighbors also attended. Bodies of popes and other important figures were exhibited in churches for several days so that everyone would be able to give them a last farewell. And then there was the sad and ghastly sight of battlefields where unburied corpses could lie for indeterminate amounts of time, touched by jackal thieves and by the poor in search of anything however useful before some merciful passersby saw to it that they were somehow buried. Medieval man would know at first sight that a man had been inside the Shroud for only a definite amount of time, that is, no more than two or three days; for the mark had been made before rigor mortis had begun to set and flesh to naturally dissolve. Their minds must have gone straight to the words of the Gospels: "For it is written that the Christ was to suffer first, and be raised from the dead on the third day."[11]

In the language of Scripture, this was called the "sign of Jonah," a reference to the episode of Jonah who had spent three days inside the belly of a whale. Jesus had

---

10   Baima Bollone, *Sindone e scienza*, pp. 101-103.
11   Luke 24:46 (Nestle-Aland, p. 753).

used this comparison to announce his death and coming resurrection, and in Christian art the symbolic tale of Jonah coming out of the mouth of the sea monster had always been widely popular, since it allowed the artist's imagination to run wild. It was also an excellent way of inculcating the mystery of the resurrection among simple and unlettered people.[12]

The Templars belonged to a religious order and followed the liturgies of the Canons of the Holy Sepulchre: Their daily lives were timed by a fixed cycle of hours during which they listened to readings of the Old Testament and the Gospels. They knew perfectly what the "sign of Jonah" was, and its exact meaning; if they saw the image on the Shroud, the unbelievable realism of that tense and tormented body must have roused emotions beyond what we can guess. Even in Constantinople, the sight of the ribs must have roused profound emotion and astonishment, as shown by the words of Gregory the Referendarius, who first saw the image in 944 when the *mandylion* was taken from its holder and subjected to an in-depth investigation to ensure it was the right item to take to the capital; to the Templars, if anything, the shock was even stronger because the Order had been established for the armed defense of Christians, and in its own specific ideology lay the idea that the Templar who died to save the weak was imitating the sufferings of Christ. During the Cyprus trial, a layman appeared in defense of the Templars and explained it all with exemplary clarity to the commissioner bishops, remembering the sacrifice made by Grand Master Guillaume de Beaujeu who had

---

12   John 2:1-11; Mt 12:38-42; Dulaey, *I simboli cristiani*, pp. 70-91.

practically let himself be killed to cover the retreat of others: "He preferred to die to defend the Catholic faith, and chose to pour his blood for Christ against the enemies of the faith just as Christ did for our redemption."[13]

At about one-quarter of the length of the Shroud, there is another series of holes that also seem arranged to mirror each other on both sides, because they also come from a burn that took place while the sheet was folded. There are four holes, three in a row and one farther to the side. In the past, it had already been noticed that a shroud with these exact kinds of holes was represented in a miniature of the striking Pray Manuscript, a codex made between 1192 and 1195 in a Benedictine abbey, well known among scholars for containing the first written testimonies of the Hungarian language. A recent study by Marcel Alonso, Éric de Bazelaire, and Thierry Castex has brought out the fact that the miniature of the three Marys visiting the Sepulchre tells the story rather oddly: The angel shows the women the shroud that had covered Jesus's face, fallen to one side, while a larger shroud is still found stretched out on the stone where the body had lain. In typical 7th-century fashion, the artist shows the front of the shroud in fishbone weave, on which can be noticed four holes in the very same shape borne on the Turin cloth; on the back, there is a white lining decorated with many red Greek crosses like those that were the badge and pride of the Templars.[14] It's an interesting clue that suggests that in Constantinople, too, they attached a lining to the Shroud to increase its thickness as they were to do in the 1500s in Chambéry, but nobody said that motif of closely

---

13   Schottmüller, II, p. 156.
14   Villanueva, *Viage literario*, V, pp. 207-221.

drawn red crosses necessarily connected it to the Order of the Temple. In fact, it was a symbolic decoration widely used in Constantinople: A lovely icon from the 1300s that represented Christ as Supreme Pontiff shows his sumptuous liturgical dress studded with crosses just like those in the Pray Codex miniature, and many other saint figures in Byzantine icons are depicted with that typical design of many closely drawn crosses. More than any direct contact with the Templars, what these ornamental motifs in the Pray Codex confirm is that in 1192–1195 the Shroud was still in the possession of the emperor of Byzantium, but that does not make the idea of any connection with the Templar order wholly absurd. The Templars had a special funerary custom that allowed the monk who had lived honorably the privilege of being buried in a linen shroud on which was woven a red woollen cloth cross—the Greek cross patent that was the badge and honor of the Order. It was a local and uncommon habit, since in Western monasticism, monks were generally buried in the usual habit of their order.[15]

We don't know at present whether the abbey where the Pray Codex was made had any special link with the Temple, but it is certain that the Templars had several establishments in the area; furthermore, they were familiar with the Byzantine court, since some of their dignitaries had been employed by Byzantine emperors in delicate diplomatic missions.[16]

---

15 Archivio Segreto Vaticano, Reg. Aven. 48, c. 441v, edited by Schottmüller, II, pp. 57-58; Curzon, *Règle*, § 469; Tréffort, *L'Eglise carolingienne et la mort*, pp. 67-70, 74.

16 Barber, *The New Knighthood*, pp. 244-245.

At any rate, the miniatures of the Pray Codex represent a first-rate avenue of research of the early history of the Shroud. They represent the burial of Christ with unusual realism for the period: Joseph of Arimathea takes an already stiff corpse down from the Cross, places it naked on a shroud, and cannot compose the hands over the pubis properly because they were still spread out in the cross posture. This corresponds exactly to what may be seen of the man of the Shroud; considering the stiffness of the muscles in order to place one hand over the other, in all likelihood they must have bound the wrists together.[17]

Another major fact is that the Jesus of the Pray Codex has hands whose thumbs cannot be seen. This is alien to the whole tradition of Christian iconography, and can only be derived from the Shroud, in which the thumb is folded inward—hence invisible—by the damage caused by the nail to the median nerve. This surprising detail, along with the fishbone weave and the four holes in a pattern, shows that the author of the miniatures did not mean to draw just any kind of shroud, but he specifically intended to make an exact depiction of the Shroud of Turin, an individual and extremely famous object, unique with unmistakable details. The Pray miniature, in short, contains a replicate of the Shroud as it appeared in the 11th century to pilgrims— one of whom was probably the ancient miniaturist—who had the privilege to see it exhibited in Constantinople on the occasion of very solemn ceremonies, decorated with a precious lining bearing the signs of high priesthood according to Byzantine religious culture. It should be noted

---

17   Berkovits, *Illuminierte Handschriften*, pp. 19-20; Bazelaire, Alonso, and Castex, *Nouvelle interpretation*, pp. 8-23.

that the king of Hungary, Béla III, had married the daughter of the Byzantine emperor Manuel I Komnenos (1143–1180). These are facts of overwhelming historical importance: The Pray Codex is much older than the age suggested by the 1988 radiocarbon test of the Shroud. It seems clear that something went wrong with that test, possibly a simple lack of essential data.

To conclude, we do not currently have any certain information about the moment that the Templars took possession of the Shroud, nor do we know precisely when it passed into other hands; most likely, the politically demanded dissolution of the Order in 1312, and then the death of the last grand master at the stake, forced it into the hands of other guardians. There is, on the other hand, no doubt that the Shroud, thanks to its unique properties, left ineffaceable traces on the Templars' spiritual and liturgical practices—traces already pointed out by Ian Wilson in 1978 that led to similar arguments by Malcolm Barber and Francesco Tommasi, two great scholars of Templar history. Systematic investigations into the Templar trial in recent years have done nothing but confirm their intuitions. And maybe they allow us to say a little more still.

Images

The Shroud's cloth carries traces of aloe and myrrh, substances used in antiquity to help preserve dead bodies: They were mixed together to form an oily anointing substance or used as powders to spread over the corpse. According to some investigators, these substances had a basic role in the mechanism that allowed the forming of the strange image. The traces of humus already mentioned can be found near the heels, typical of a body that had walked without shoes, and near the right knee, where the image also shows a noticeable swelling as if the person had fallen and hit the ground viciously; since the same humus has also been found near the tip of the nose, it has been deduced that the victim must have tumbled down without a chance to cover his face with his hands.[18] This is a detail that calls for historians to reflect. None of the four Gospels mentions Jesus falling during the climb to Golgotha, but in the special liturgy of the *Via Crucis*, celebrated during Holy Week, it is remembered that Jesus fell to earth under the weight of the Cross no less than three times. The glaring swelling visible on the man in the Shroud's knee and face could give great credibility to the notion of several falls to the ground, and this might even suggest that the Holy Week liturgy had been affected by the examination of this astonishing object, taken in the past for an undoubtedly genuine relic. From what we know, the *Via Crucis* was born in Syria-Palestine from a very ancient local tradition first given a fixed shape by St. Petronius in the 5th century. Later, during the Crusades, the Christian kingdom of Jerusalem played a major part in popular devotion with a special staged pilgrimage to the places in Jerusalem where the Passion had taken place. Later still, toward the end of the Middle Ages, this liturgy was greatly encouraged by Franciscan and Carmelite friars. All its "stations" recall facts mentioned in the Gospels, except for three: Jesus's meeting with his mother, the merciful

---

18   Pellicori and Evans, *The Shroud*, pp. 34–43.

gesture of Veronica in drying his bleeding face, and the three falls. These are believed to actually come from the popular religious tradition of Jerusalem, a wealth of traditions probably handed down in the local Christian community from father to son.[19]

The two images—front and back—present on the Shroud, are found exactly above a big mark left by blood, sweat, and other substances such as myrrh and aloe; it was formed after all these compounds had entered and soaked the cloth. As pointed out earlier, it has the singular feature of being visible only if the observer stands at a distance of about six to thirty feet from the unfolded sheet: Any closer or farther away, and the human eye can only see featureless bloodstains. What is seen is the outline of a tall adult male, presumably 5' 7" to 5' 11", with a long lean figure and well-defined muscles, possibly in part because of the cadaveric rigidity already discussed. The subject must have been between 30 and 40; to judge from the lack of fat in his physique, he did not eat much and was used to manual labor. His neck was wholly collapsed forward, with his chin touching his sternum, his chest had stiffened while being flexed forward, and his legs also seem slightly folded; his arms were stretched along his sides, while forearms and hands, one over the other, were joined to cover the pubis. Neither hand's imprint shows the thumb, and this (as I mentioned) probably has to do with the wound in the center of the wrist: The object that pierced it also damaged the median nerve, and the finger reflexively bent completely toward the inside of the hand. The feet are also slightly superimposed, and

---

19   Brandys, *Via Crucis*, coll. 1348-1350; Berre, *Via Crucis*, pp. 1310-1311.

the right foot seems almost crushed against the cloth, as if cadaveric rigidity had set in as the man found himself with this foot attached along the whole of its length to a hard and vertical surface. The man wore a mustache and a middle-length beard that seems to be parted in the middle and was in part torn off; his long hair reached his shoulders and joined along the axis of his back in a sort of pigtail, while on the side of the face it appears slightly lifted rather than falling straight down, just as if it had been held up by some support.[20]

In May 1898, Secondo Pia, a Turin lawyer, took some photographs of the Shroud, and the result was an absolute shock: It became evident, for the first time, that the sheet acted like a photographic negative. That pale, indistinct, yellowish image perceived by the naked eye was changed by photography into a clear, hyper-realistic picture, full of striking detail. The image is indelible: It had not been painted on and it is not due to any kind of dye. There is no trace of brushstrokes. The sepia color is due to the fact that thin surface linen fibers have yellowed thanks to a process of oxidation, dehydration, and conjugation of the cellulose molecules that make up linen threads; the phenomenon only affected the fibers themselves at an infinitesimal depth (125 micron), leaving the rest untouched so that the image cannot be seen from the back of the cloth. Over about a century of studies, hundreds of analyses and experiments have been carried out, among them many intended to duplicate the image through various techniques. Scientists started very early to try and

---

20   Baima Bollone, *Sindone e scienza*, pp. 94-96.

produce new "Shrouds" through various devices, managing only to produce copies that have, at most, a few of the original's very strange properties. These attempts are praiseworthy and indeed very useful as long as they are carried out scientifically, for they allow us to discard fruitless procedures and channel energies toward more profitable directions; alas, it often happens that they are exploited for cheap and tawdry commercial ends, nothing less than swindles at the expense of a passionate public without the scientific education to defend itself against frauds. From time to time, some occasional writer will emerge out of nowhere, fabricate a dirty rag, and write a book of sensational revelations accompanied by lots of advertising.[21]

One of these mystifications even claimed to prove that the Shroud bore the image of the last grand master of the Templars, Jacques de Molay. This barely deserves a mention as the reader's intelligence can judge for itself. Jacques de Molay was burned at the stake on a small island on the Seine, in Paris, at sunset on March 18, 1314. His body was reduced to ashes, and we know from an eyewitness that the commoners of Paris fought to take away some of the ashes from that pyre, which they regarded as mighty relics of a saint. And another thing: When he died, Jacques de Molay was about 64, at a time when old age began at 60, and had spent his last

---

21 I chose not to quote this sort of book by name, because their science fiction taste is out of keeping with the guiding principles of this text. Broad and scholarly treatments of the issue include Baima Bollone, *Sindone e scienza*; Barberis-Savarino, *Sindone, radiodatazione*; Marinelli and Petrosillo, *La sindone, storia di un enigma*; Zaccone, *Sulle tracce della sindone*.

seven years in the horrors of Philip the Fair's dungeons. The man whose imprint was left on the Shroud was indubitably young and strong, no more than 40.[22]

The advances of imaging technology have recently allowed new directions in such studies, letting us see certain kinds of images that had once seemed impossible. It has been discovered that the Shroud is like a photograph. Unlike photographs, the image contains three-dimensional information within itself. It is a kind of optical projection, reminiscent of holography in some ways. It is certain that the image was formed after the flow of blood stopped because the Shroud carries no image beneath the bloodstains. The new frontier of research points in the direction of certain theories that seem particularly probable. The most studied concerns the effect of a very strong and very short (a few hundredths of a second) burst of radiation, capable of leaving an impression on the cloth and oxidizing its fibers without, however, burning them; this model would explain many things that are otherwise inexplicable—for instance, that the intensity of the image was derived from the distance it was from the body. Many hypotheses have been made over time about the formation of the very strange image of that man; the fact remains, however, that no scientist has thus far managed to reproduce an object with the same features as the Shroud. The phenomenon remains unknown. The various attempts to explain, though scientifically very important, remain purely theoretical models.

New hypotheses have also recently been put forth concerning the controversial radiocarbon dating.

---

22 Demurger, *Jacques de Molay*, pp. 19-24.

The physicist Christopher Bronk Ramsey, director of the Oxford Radiocarbon Accelerator Unit—one of the three labs that had been given the task of dating the Shroud—has said the carbon dating test should be re-evaluated. In an interesting recent interview with the BBC, he has clarified how far technology has progressed since the original test of the Shroud, and today the method seems far more trustworthy than before. The procedure is based on measuring the amount of carbon left on an archaeological find to be dated. Carbon is an element found in every organic matter, and diverse varieties of it exist; the most widespread in living matter (equal to 98.89 percent) is made of atoms whose nucleus consists of six protons and six neutrons, but there are also other types such as carbon-13 (whose nucleus bears six protons and seven neutrons) and carbon-14, whose nucleus is made of six protons and eight neutrons. Both carbon-13 and carbon-14 are isotopes of the most widespread kind, and C-14 is unstable and naturally radioactive: As time goes on, it slowly disintegrates, and during this process it emits an electron and a neutral particle (neutrino). C-14 is found in the atmosphere, and all living beings continuously absorb it; when the organism dies, absorption ceases and its remains start slowly losing the radiocarbon that is no longer being reintegrated. Looking at the speed of decay of C-14 over time, and measuring how much C-14 is left in a certain find, it is possible to work out how long ago the organism from which that find comes from died: For instance, it is theoretically possible to identify the period when the fiber used to make a cotton cloth was harvested. Although understanding radiocarbon is quite simple in and of itself, measuring it turns out to be extremely complex. With the old method, we had to measure the atoms decayed over a given period of time, making sure not to include the measurement of other atomic decays that are present but have nothing to do with the test (for instance, background radiation in the environment). There is another method but neither is wholly foolproof; indeed, every measurement has a built-in margin of error, and many possible interferences can alter the result.[23] It is very rare that an archaeological find remains free of contact with the world after it has been made; in general, objects come into contact with people or substances through everyday use. Our ancestors had an excellent habit of recycling objects several times over, practically until they wore out. Even the very rich never threw anything away: A medieval lady's dress would be inherited by her daughter, and eventually perhaps presented to a church that got a priest's liturgical vestments out of it. When it really was too worn for any use, it was cut up for household rags, and when the rags were beyond use, they were still used to make paper.

That cotton cloth we used as an example may have passed through any number of incarnations—worn, dyed with vegetable or animal dyes, used to clean a household or make the stopper of an amphora of oil impervious to leaks, maybe even as swaddling cloths for a newborn baby—each of which brought it into contact with other living beings or other organic material, and each time absorbing C-14 of alien origin. In fact, radiocarbon is only one of many scientific

---

23   Marion and Courage, *La sacra sindone*, pp. 104-108.

methods used to try and date a find; it is neither better nor worse than the others, and indeed in some situations it proves wholly unsuitable. Experts in the field know famous tales of C-14 dating with absurd, even ludicrous results; for instance, the prehistoric site at Jarmo was tested four times and had four different results, starting with 4,700 BC, then 10,000 BC, then 7,000 BC, and finally 6,000 BC. Some primitive caribou bone tools from Old Crown, Alaska, were carbon-dated to 27,000 years ago; the experts, unhappy with the result because the archaeological exam suggested a much more recent date, went into the matter in more depth and found that the dating came from material from the external part of the bone, and upon testing the internal, possibly less contaminated, part, the result was a much more modest 1,350 years earlier. No doubt the most amusing case was the one that occurred at a laboratory in Tucson, Arizona: A helmet from a Viking tomb—a well-researched site whose dating and typology can generally be guessed with some accuracy—whose every other aspect indicated it dated to the 10th century AD, had a radiocarbon test result that informed the scientists that the cow whose horns decorated the helmet was yet to be born! These are, of course, paradoxical cases that are, however, very useful to scientists because they show how easy it is to go monumentally off trail even when using the finest technology available. You may carry out the test in the most textbook fashion, but an absence of essential data can totally compromise the result.[24]

---

24   Ibid, pp. 108-123.

Doubts had been gathering over the Shroud's C-14 dating almost from the moment the results were published. Some denounced the whole procedure as approximate and lacking scientific rigor. Even scientists outside the fray had noticed that the approach had been, to say the least, unusual: No notes or minutes had been taken during the collection of samples, which laboratories always do because all kinds of unexpected things can happen during the process that must later be taken into consideration; the specific weight of the samples taken (300 mg) was nearly double the Shroud's average specific weight for that surface (161 mg), whereas, being from the same cloth, it should have been more or less identical; finally, more samples had been taken behind closed doors without notifying the scientific community, and in the following years, results of exams carried out on threads and fragments of the Shroud, which according to the agreements should not even have existed, kept popping up here and there. Besides the genuine professional rivalries between the concerned laboratories, who were keen to be awarded the examination, other interests appear to have come into play. The controversy surrounding the tests eventually turned into something akin to a thriller rather than a scientific test; it is therefore not surprising that several books were written about this incredible story.[25]

Today the international scientific community is inclined to believe that if there were any errors, they were due to a technology still too unripe to hope to date such a complex object. Much of the Shroud's history is

25 Among the most up-to-date are Emanuela Marinelli, *La Sindone*, and Marco Tosatti, *Inchiesta sulla sindone*, both published in 2009.

still unknown, so we have no idea what contaminations it may have suffered; to know the manipulations suffered by a find proves vitally important to carrying out a reliable test. It is not a hard concept to understand: An analysis of urine that uses a contaminated test tube is not valid. We only know the details of the Shroud's history for the last 650 years or so: So many imponderables lurk in its past that radiocarbon testing still seems inappropriate, and we seriously risk cutting the Shroud away piece by piece before any truly reliable test is developed. A significant example of contamination is the presence of a bioplastic coating on the linen fibers, due to the activity of a bacterium, which contaminated the sample and might well have "rejuvenated" the linen with extra helpings of C-14 that have nothing to do with the age of the Shroud. The bioplastic coating was only discovered years after the 1988 test, and obviously that test had not taken its presence and the contamination into account.[26]

How many other contaminating agents could be present in the cloth, even today, with us still in the dark?

The continuous progress of science leads us to hope that in a few years new dating techniques may be developed that are more refined and, above all, less destructive. They are badly needed: Every square millimeter of Shroud that is destroyed is a loss of great value as it cannot be examined by our successors, who will surely have measuring tools far more advanced than ours.

Meanwhile, the hair area is being investigated with particular care: Thanks to it, it is thought that the idea that the image was formed by contact should be

---

26 Adler, *Updating*, pp. 223-228; Gove et al., *A Problematic Source*, pp. 504-507.

excluded. The hair would then have looked crushed, whereas it is soft and flowing, as if free from any pressure.

Mysterious Traces of Writing

In 1978, the chemist Piero Ugolotti was examining a negative of the Shroud drawn from some photos taken about ten years earlier when he noticed some marks that leapt decidedly to his eye: They were not like stains, or if they were, they seemed to have a curiously neat geometry, all oriented the same way, closely reminiscent of alphabetical characters, and, what's more, they appeared to be arranged into groups. In short, they looked very much like written words.

The history of writings on the Shroud began that day thirty years ago, and is still taking place: In this book, I shall only give it brief notice, otherwise the argument would take us too far along the paths of Syria-Palestine into the days of the Second Temple, within Roman-age Judaism, and we shall be forced to deal with issues too distant from the story of the Templars. At any rate, the presence of this writing, and, in particular, some of them in Hebrew, is not without importance even for the purposes of our argument, since it may help us understand why the Templars chose to keep the Shroud secret at the crucial historical moment when it reached them.

Piero Ugolotti had managed to clearly distinguish the outlines of some Greek and Latin letters, but even though he was an educated person, he did not want to risk trying to read them alone and preferred to entrust them to a specialist: Aldo Marastoni, professor of ancient literature at the Catholic University of the Sacred Heart in Milan, who had edited important editions by Seneca and other Latin authors for the prestigious *Bibliotheca Teubneriana* of the Deutsche Akademie der Wissenschaften in Berlin.[27] Marastoni identified the letters at once, but he also saw other things that captured his interest, so he asked for new negatives from the Centro Internazionale di Sindonologia di Torino, the most illustrious and respected institute of Shroud studies. Having obtained the negatives, the two set to work: These traces of writing can only be seen thanks to the contrast of clear and dark tones in the photos, so it was necessary to develop them several times and make several photocopies to delineate the letters as much as possible. The result was electrifying: On the Shroud were traces of Greek, Latin, and even Hebraic writing. These are not characters written directly on the sheet, but on a different object that had been partially transferred to the cloth: Looking directly at the Shroud—which, we remember, behaves like a negative—almost nothing could be distinguished, while on the negatives (which show the realistic image of a man as if they were the positives or photographs themselves), the characters become recognizable.

As was natural, considering the context, their minds went straight to the words of the Gospels: Pilate had had a placard placed on the cross of Jesus that spelled out the reason for his conviction, the famous *titulus crucis*.

---

27 Marastoni, *P. Papini Stati Silvae.*

The three synoptic texts (Mark, Matthew, and Luke) mention the fact briefly, quoting only the actual cause of why the heads of the Sanhedrin and the scribes had denounced Jesus to the Roman procurator, presenting him as a rebel leader who had proclaimed himself "the king of the Jews"; the Gospel of John, on the other hand, gives a longer and more detailed account:

> And Pilate wrote a title, and put it on the cross. And the writing was JESUS OF NAZARETH THE KING OF THE JEWS. This title then read many of the Jews: for the place where Jesus was crucified was nigh to the city: and it was written in Hebrew, and Greek, and Latin. (John 19:19-20).

But immediately after the understandable early rush of enthusiasm, the situation struck Marastoni as very strange, maybe even disappointing: In effect, what can be read on the Shroud does not correspond to the Gospel description, because essential details reported by the Gospel of John are missing, while alien items with nothing to do with the Gospels are present. Above the right eyebrow (left in the negative), Marastoni noted the presence of at least three characters in square Hebraic writing: a *taw*, a *waw* or *iod*, then a mark that seemed to him like a *zade* (corresponding to the sound *ds*) in the form used only at the end of a word, then another rather confusing character that appeared as if it could be the *soph pasu*, a punctuation comparable to a modern period. He took them as parts of some word in Hebrew or Aramaic that, however, does not coincide with the description of the writings stuck on Jesus's cross according to the Gospels. On the center of the forehead, he read the sequence of Greek characters IBEP, and in particular the group IB, which seemed to him repeated immediately close by, parallel, but slightly shifted right. Marastoni immediately thought that the sequence might be the remnant of the name TIBEPIOS written in Greek, a name popular among Romans since the Etruscan Age and used by several emperors, of whom the first, the adopted son of Augustus, reigned in the years the Gospels place the death of Jesus (14–37 BC). Another discovery took place in 1979 thanks to Francis L. Filas, S. J., a theologian from the St. Ignatius University of Loyola, Chicago: Within the print of the right eye socket, a small circle can be noticed, and within that, a few tiny letters. The sequence identified after a series of enlargements is UCAI, and forms an arch around a curious form not unlike the shepherd's crook carried by bishops. Filas carried out patient research and found that those marks correspond to a particular coin coined by Pontius Pilate during his governorship of Judea, from 26 to 36 AD. The writing on this coin bears a strange grammatical error, which is anything but unusual in Roman provinces; there, Greek was the universal language spoken by the people, but it was full of incorrect grammar and dialect forms that made it quite unlike the language spoken in Athens.[28] The Greek text TIBEPIOU KAICAPOS ("Tiberius Caesar") came out wrong, written as TIBEPIOU CAICAPOS.

---

28   See, for instance, Teodorsson, *The Phonology,* pp. 197-199; Milani, pp. 221-229.

The sequence UCAI corresponds to the central part of this phrase.[29]

Marastoni felt that these signs were written on some object placed on the convict's head. It may have been a *mitra infamiae*, a kind of crude and light hood, made of a material like papyrus, on which outrageous sentences were written for the exact purpose of humiliating the convict; the slight shifts of this hood might have caused the double imprint of the characters IB on the forehead, which otherwise needs explaining. The professor also saw two more Latin texts that ran vertically along the left cheek (right on the negative) parallel to each other. The bigger one showed a series of letters that seemed to him to form the sequence NEAZARE, with the Z written in reverse, and the other, written in smaller characters, INNECE, what is left of the Latin expression *in necem* ("to death"); even further down, in the lower quarter, he saw again a Latin capital T and, just under the chin, a strange sign that seems to be made of two capital Ns joined together. Meanwhile an imaging technology expert, Aldo Tamburelli, tried to subject the Shroud to a recently designed test, thus discovering another surprising feature of the picture—the fact that it is three-dimensional: Even though it behaves like a photograph, the image does not come from a procedure like that of photography, because photographs are two-dimensional.

Marastoni got in touch with Tamburelli and asked him to verify whether the writing was still visible on the three-dimensional elaboration of the Shroud: The result

---

29   Baima Bollone, *Sindone e scienza*, pp. 132-137.

was not only positive, but thanks to imaging technology applications, the characters could be read much better.[30]

The term NEAZARE seems right away a very likely deformation of the original NAZAPENOS found both in Mark and in Luke; it is the adjective for Jesus's geographical origin, "inhabitant of Nazareth."[31] The group INNECE also seems highly pertinent in this context—it is Latin, and means "to death"—and it is clear that the Shroud covered just that, a victim of the death penalty. Finally, Marastoni noticed another piece of writing in the negatives of some photographs taken in 1931, quite clear and articulate this time: A little above the knee, it was written around a cross, and to judge by its lines it seems to have been traced with a quill and ink on some different support (such as papyrus or parchment) that touched the linen. The fragments of the words it was made of (ISSIE, ESY, SNCT, I SERE, STR) were immediately identified by the professor of the Catholic University of the Sacred Heart with a Latin prayer (*Iesu sanctissime Miserere nostri*, "Most Holy Jesus, have mercy on us"): The letters are rudimentary Gothic, and their presence corresponds quite well with the widespread medieval usage of placing notes written on paper or parchment of prayer formulas over relics, to turn them into relics as well by virtue of the belief that they would soak up the same spiritual power via contact. Considering the age suggested by the shape of the letters, as far as they

---

30 Tamburelli, *La sindone e l'informatica*, pp. 240-254; Id., *Studio della sindone*, pp. 1135-1149; Marastoni, *Le scritte*, fig. 4.

31 Schaeder, *Nazarhnó*, coll. 833-848; Eusebio di Cesarea, *Onomasticon*, 138, 24 ss.

can be estimated, this prayer-bearing paper might well have been made by none other than the Templars.

Captions?

In 1994, Marcel Alonso and Éric de Bazelaire, two members of the Centre International d'Études sur le Linceul de Turin in Paris, decided to start over again on the matter of the writings, and see whether the technologies developed in the meantime could offer any new contributions. They also decided to go to specialists, taking the problem to the scientists of the Institut d'Optique Théorique d'Orsay, near Paris, a greatly respected research center where some physicists who specialize in treating images work on, among other things, the identification of writing on palimpsests and other unreadable texts.[32]

A team of experts in signal analysis was assembled, led by André Marion, a CNRS researcher and professor at the Institut d'Optique; over seven months, between May and December 1994, they studied the most suitable procedures to deal with the problem. Then in January 1995, André Marion and his colleague Anne-Laure Courage presented the results of their long investigation to a conference. All around the face of the executed man who had left his image on the linen of the Shroud there were at least five separate words in Greek and Latin, to which must be added at least three series of single

---

32 Marion and Courage, *Nouvelles découvertes*, foreword by Christian Imbert (director in chief, Institut d'Optique and of l'École Superieure d'Optique d'Orsay), pp. 7-10.

characters.[33] Along the left side of the face (right on the negative), two parallel vertical sequences were identified, one in Latin characters INNECE (inside and near the cheekbone) and the other in Greek, NAZAPENOS (toward the outside). These are the same words seen by Marastoni, but the second is corrected: The computer does not make it NEAZARE but NAZAPENOS, and both its N's seem made in the same funny way—as two Ns bound together—which Marastoni had already identified in INNECE and as an isolated mark beneath the chin, which was also confirmed. But there was more: Still in the same area, a little farther down beneath the isolated sign of the two joint Ns, a sentence could be read that Marastoni had not seen and seemed utterly to the point: It is the group HSOY, immediately recognized as the central part of the word (I)HSOY(S). It is the Greek name of Jesus, and together with the other Greek word, says "Jesus of Nazareth."

Vertically along the left cheekbone, two more words, also in parallel, could be read, the one outside in larger characters, the other inside in smaller but in fine relief: The first showed a group of Greek characters: S, separated by some blank space as if it were the ending of a word, then a sequence of three signs of which KI seem quite clear, while the last is dubious and might make one think of an A. The smaller writing, still in Greek, said PEZ, and had the singular quality of appearing clear in the negative while the others appeared dark, so it must have been made with a different ink or material. As for the isolated clusters, Marion and Courage picked out above

---

33   Marion, *Discovery of Inscriptions*, pp. 2308-2313; Marion and
Courage, *Nouvelles découvertes*, pp. 218-226.

the head, nearly at the center but shifted somewhat to the right side, a sequence that seemed to them to be formed by the characters IC (which in Latin stand for *i* and *k*, in Greek *i* and *s*); near NAZAPENOS they could see the cluster ARE a second time, and the two items of writing are one on top of the other, as if the same text had been attached twice to the linen at different times, leaving two distinct marks at almost the same point. Further outside and in the same orientation, they also read a cluster of four signs, of which the first three (in Greek characters) were clear, while the last (which seemed to the French scientists like a U or maybe a rounded M) was covered by some sort of stain; finally, still near the word NAZAPENOS, but farther below and upside-down, the letters SB appeared.

At this point, we have to attempt to interpret. Marion and Courage submitted the writings to some experts in ancient and medieval history, a real roster of famous names working at the Sorbonne and other prestigious institutions.[34] The two parallel writings, HSOY(S) and NAZAPENOS hardly seemed problematic: They were Greek for the name *Jesus of Nazareth*, with a small variant compared to the standard Gospel spelling, that is the vowel *Eta* (H) instead of *Epsilon* (E), and thus became NAZAPHNOS. The confusion between these two vowels was a very common feature of the Roman-age Middle East, and was so widespread in written Greek of that period that epigraphic catalogs hardly even mention it as a peculiarity. The sequence INNECE offers no difficulties either, given that the context involves an executed man,

---

34 Marion and Courage, *Nouvelles découvertes*, pp. 11-12.

while the identification of the remaining clusters (several fragments of words) seemed tougher and less obvious. As for the purpose these words were meant to serve, on the other hand, the two physicists received no consensus opinion, for there were many theories. One of the most interesting suggests that these words were written on a reliquary or on some kind of container: They were a kind of caption, whose traces were inadvertently transferred onto the sheet. Most recently, another signals analysis expert, the Frenchman Thierry Castex, applied the same method perfected by Marion and Courage, and managed to identify new traces of Hebraic characters in the area under the chin, which he was kind enough to send to me for a second opinion; this is the first time that, with his permission, they are mentioned in print. Among the visible marks, it seems possible to distinguish the characters *mem*, *sade*, and *aleph*, corresponding to the root *ms*, which is found in both Hebraic and Aramaic and means "to find"; there is also a second sequence of two marks that might be *nw* or *ky*, given their similar shapes and the objective difficulties in reading. The whole might then be *nw ms'* ("we have found") or else *ky ms'*, "because found."[35] It seems a rather

---

35 I am grateful to Émile Puech and to Simone Venturini for helping me with this reading. To be correct, I wish to underline that both scholars received photographs of simple Hebraic writings and identified them without having any idea that they were signs found on the Turin Shroud. This procedure was required in order to obtain unpolluted views, free from any conditioning that might have arisen from the history of this famous object: During my research, I found out personally that the radiocarbon affair has had a disastrously polluting effect on the cultural landscape, creating a prejudice so powerful as to darken the finest, most objective scholarly minds.

interesting issue: Those words, torn off from a longer sentence, correspond exactly to a passage of the Gospel according to Luke on the trial of Jesus. To be precise, it is Luke 23:2, when the High Priest and the Sanhedrin deliver Jesus to Pontius Pilate, with a precise charge: "We found this man subverting the nation, forbidding to pay tax to Caesar, and saying that he himself was Christ, a king." Besides, a 1989 study by Roberto Messina and Carlo Orecchia had pointed out more Hebraic characters in the forehead area.[36]

Byzantine tradition has no trace of these strange scattered writings on the Shroud, and to the question of whether or not they might be the Templars' work, the answer must be, No: Only the small area with the inscribed prayer, *Most holy Jesus, have mercy on us,* corresponds to their time. The experts consulted by Marion and Courage agree that nearly all the Greek and Latin passages were carried out long before the foundation of the Order of the Temple, indeed that they seem to go back to the early Christian age, to about the 1st to 3rd centuries AD. These were devotional writings made by some believer to clarify who that man was whose image was left behind, or maybe scrolls of some legal value, as a hypothesis of Grégoire Kaplan once suggested.[37]

The traces of Hebraic writing leads us to think that they were carried out in Syria-Palestine (or Qumran?) very early on. Everything rejects the suggestion that they might have anything to do with the Templars. It may

---

36   Messina and Orecchia, *La scritta in caratteri ebraici*, pp. 83-88.
37   Kaplan, *Le Linceul de Turin*, pp. 19-22.

be that the Temple brothers noticed their existence, as will be said below: If so, that would have encouraged them to keep the Shroud strictly to themselves.

The Trail of the "Jewish Question"

In the view of many experts who have long studied the Shroud of Turin, the image is growing less vivid as time goes on, on account of the natural degradation due to the effects of light, and in past centuries it could be seen more neatly; in effect, some ancient representations of the Shroud show the imprint in a much more intense tint of sepia, although we cannot exclude that the painters may have reinforced their color to make the image stand out better. When starting its research, André Marion's team of physicists chose to work from certain negatives shot by Enrie in 1931, both because the analog photographs of that time carried an enormous amount of information, and because there is a suspicion that the image may have been noticeably more intense then than today, and so much richer in detail. The hints of writing may be recognized just because of the contrast of tone against tone, because they are like so many ivory-colored stains, except in the shape of letters, against the light sepia background of the image. In order to see them today, we have to make use of photographic negatives, which play up contrasts greatly, but if the scientists are right and the image was once darker, maybe some writings could have been seen by the naked eye, too. This is not a matter of small importance, if we take into account the social history of the Middle Ages; the words in Greek and Latin would not have been an issue, but the same could absolutely not be said for the Jewish characters.

Relationships between the Jews and political power during the Late Antiquity and the early Middle Ages were variable. After the Edict of Milan in 313 AD, Constantine vigorously promoted the growth of Christianity and certainly did not favor the Jews, but decades later, when the whole empire was essentially Christian, Theodosius I (379–395 AD) issued a series of decrees for the protection of this minority, which was by then no threat to his religious policy. In the West, the popes often protected them, especially Gregory I the Great, who designed a clear and permanent strategy to defend them from their enemies—essentially the local authorities and the local populace. We have no less than six letters from this pontiff condemning acts of violence and chicanery against Jews, and we know that the communities scattered in the countries of the Christian world would often turn to the rabbi who led the Roman community to intercede with the pope so that the latter could help as a political mediator with kings and emperors. The most famous of these letters, titled *Sicut Judaeis*, was later repeated in following centuries by many popes: Its basic concept had already been stated by Emperor Theodosius I, and yet it was extremely difficult for it to enter the minds of the commoners: "There is no law forbidding the Jewish religion."[38]

From the beginning to the end of the Middle Ages, Europe was shaken by frequent bouts of anti-Semitism,

---

38   Simonsohn, *The Apostolic See*, pp. 39-40.

acts of hard-to-imagine violence arising spontaneously among the public because of a widespread hostility born from intolerance, which rulers, be they popes, emperors or kings, always tried to uproot, for it was a threat to public order. It was, however, during the Low Middle Ages that the question took alarming proportions. Starting about 1150, and even more so in the 1200s and 1300s, waves of anti-Semitism followed each other, causing slaughter. A specter rose from the dim past, the specter of a very ancient popular tale: Jews kept a Christian boy hostage for one whole year, feeding him abundantly to fatten him up; then, when he was properly plump and ready, they killed him and ate his flesh during one of their sacrilegious ritual banquets. This macabre fable was already doing the rounds throughout the Roman Empire in the days of the pagan philosopher Celsus (2nd century AD). It was used indifferently against Christians and Jews by the pagan populace, who felt disgust at certain traditions of theirs such as circumcision. When the tale came back into fashion a thousand years later, it found particularly fertile ground and spread with devastating effect. In 1144, the body of a boy murdered by an unknown person was found in Norwich; the local Jews were immediately blamed and wiped out. Some twenty years later, a rumor swept Gloucester that a youth named Harald had been first barbarously tortured and then even crucified by Jews. From then on, cases multiplied like an epidemic—in Bury St. Edmunds, Bristol, and Winchester during the last years of the 12th century, then during the early 1200s in Lincoln, Stanford, and London. From England, the legend crossed over to France, spreading its vicious spell everywhere: It was as if any tragic and unclear event necessarily had to be because of the Jews. As early as 1171, the evidence of one of these "ritual murders" had supposedly been found in Pontoise. The victim was buried in Paris, in the church of the Holy Innocents; rumors spread that the young man had performed many miracles, and many people took to making pilgrimages to the tomb of this boy, seen as a martyr of "Jewish perfidy." A special rite was even written to honor him. In the same year, Thibaut, count of Blois, had no less than thirty-two Jews burned at the stake on account of this legend and pressure from the local community; while on the other hand, his neighbor Thibaut IV, count of Flanders, like King Louis VII of France and Emperor Henry VI, officially proclaimed that the tale had no real basis, and tried to uproot it—alas, with no success. During the 1200s, the dark legend spread the length and breadth of Europe, and was easily believed by a credulous populace. Its hold on the imagination was so strong that it developed a new and hideous feature: Jews needed human blood to make the unleavened bread they ate during their Paschal rites.[39]

In 1235, there was a notorious case in the German city of Fulda. The Jews were charged with the murder of a miller's five sons, and were subjected to torture so horrendous as to force them to "confess" that the unleavened Easter bread was really made with human blood. The result was another mass murder. The episode resonated so widely that it reached, and concerned, Emperor Frederick II. A man of immense learning, and amazingly broad-minded for his age, Frederick was very familiar with Eastern customs. Having been

---

39   Ibid., pp. 48-50.

brought up in Sicily, where Muslims still lived, he had spent time incognito as a child with a Muslim family who had taken and hidden him to protect him from his enemies. The emperor was very skeptical of the matter; however, since the legend had such a firm hold on the minds of the commoners, he decided to nominate an expert commission made up of Jews who had converted to Catholicism to make an accurate and in-depth study of the problem. Obviously the experts proved that the Old Testament absolutely forbids the eating of blood, even that of animals killed for food. Frederick II thought he would solve the problem for good by associating the persecutors of Jews with those guilty of lèse-majesté, the most serious and most terribly punished of all crimes. And yet in the same year, the communities of Lauda and Pforzheim carried out more slaughters; Pope Gregory IX had to issue a new version of the bull *Sicut Judaeis* in which he ordered the bishops of France to severely punish Christians who made themselves guilty of violence against the Jewish population or their property.

Just in those years, one of the most violent persecutions burst out, and it is thought that as many as 2,500–3,000 Jewish persons were murdered, including women and children, by the crusaders who took part in the Sixth Crusade, while hundreds more were baptized by force. This may have been the moment of highest tension: Exacerbated by the spread of heresy and religious contestation, the Church started to condemn traditional Jewish books such as the Talmud, which was not properly a sacred text but contained some disrespectful passages about Jesus that had come from popular literature. Hate of Jews fed on the notion that

Jews deliberately profaned the Eucharist. The rumor had spread that Christian wet nurses hired by rich Jews to feed their babies, who took Communion on Easter day, were forced to throw their milk away for three days afterward to stop the Eucharist from contaminating the newborn through their milk. There were more than fifty accounts of profaning Jews who had taken consecrated hosts by deceit and had suddenly seen them turn to flesh and blood in their hands.

By the mid-1200s, Pope Innocent IV allowed himself to be conditioned enough by these notions to approve the decree of expulsion passed by the archbishop of Vienne against the Jews in his diocese; this was in fact a very rare case since the popes kept publishing bulls in defense of the Jewish population, which the public regularly ignored because prejudice was so rooted in the popular mind that it was invincible. By the end of the century, expulsions became mass phenomena: In 1290, it was the turn of the Jews of England, then in 1306 those of France, by order of Philip the Fair. Between 1298 and 1337, Germany saw a simply monstrous wave of anti-Jewish mania: One hundred and fifty local communities were destroyed because of these rumors about desecrated Hosts, and historians calculate that these horrors resulted in the murder of between 20,000 and 100,000 Jews.[40]

This was the climate in which the Templars, in all likelihood, gained possession of the Shroud. Most Templar monks were rather on the ignorant side, but some of the leaders were well educated. Traces of writing surely would not have been noticed by pilgrims

---

40   Ibid., pp. 51-60.

rushing by in front of the relic and kept at a safe distance, but maybe a careful, precise, and prolonged exam could still have perceived them. If any of the brothers had realized that the sheet carried Jewish writing, as is not at all impossible, it would have been an even better reason for the Temple leadership to keep utterly silent about the relic. And the Order simply could not afford to lose it; for certain reasons, it regarded it as a necessary bulwark against an evil that was affecting the whole of Christianity. An evil with ancient roots that had been finding a few victims even within the Temple.

Keep the Path of Peter

In 1143, abbot Erwin of Steinfeld informed St. Bernard of Clairvaux that members of a peculiar heretical sect had been arrested in the neighborhood of Cologne: They declared themselves members of an ancient Church that had remained hidden since the days of the martyrs and had survived in Greece and other countries under the leadership of some "apostles" and bishops. From the second half of the 12th century to the end of the 13th, Christian society was shaken to its foundations by the unprecedented proliferation of a movement of religious dissent that not only challenged a number of fundamental dogmas and the Church's tradition, but associated theological protest with forceful accusations against the corruption of the clergy and vigorous political demands.[41] In this shaky climate, relics and objects of Jesus's earthly life were to the Church something like a saving anchor, something that could help Christians not

41 Vauchez, *Contestazioni*, pp. 442-455 and pp. 447-448.

drift off toward the latest faddish doctrine. It was a matter of staying on the beaten track, the track that had once been opened by the apostles.

Shortly before his death, the old fisherman from Bethsaida in Galilee, Shimon, a.k.a. Peter, had dictated to his disciples a letter, which they then composed and dispatched to every Christian community that could be reached, like an actual encyclical. The letter expressed certain serious concerns of his and recommended that Christians stay away from some recent theories that gave a merely intellectual and spiritual portrayal of Jesus, as if he were no more than a symbol of the complete renewal of mankind at large. Modern historians call this religious current docetism, from Greek *dokèin* ("to seem"), because their teaching was based on the idea that Jesus had no more than the external appearance of a man. Their fault was placing too much emphasis on personal interpretation. Peter was not widely read, but he did not like at all those novel and sophisticated interpretations that were becoming so fashionable in Christian thought. For a start, they had their roots not in Jewish religion but in neo-Platonic philosophy, from the pagan Greeks; what is more, they left the impression of extolling the spiritual face of Jesus to try to hide the human face, as if being human were a weakness, something to be ashamed of. Above all, they were myths. Having followed him for three years, having seen in person the trial, the death, and the events that had followed, Peter had very concrete memories of Jesus, and would not let the new generations imagine him as an abstract concept. His reaction against these new directions, as far as we know, was immediate and unreserved condemnation: Christianity meant to recognize that the Messiah of Israel and the historical person Jesus of Nazareth were one and the same, and since the Docetists refused the human being Jesus, in Peter's eyes, they were simply not Christian. To place a modern label on it, the religion of Peter, like that of Paul and John, was a historical religion, in the sense that everything was born from certain fundamental facts precisely located in time and space. There had been one strong man who had done certain things, and the soles of his feet had left their prints on the earth in Jerusalem.

In the writing that Christian tradition handed down as the Second Epistle of Peter, the old fisherman warned against the dangers that could arise when the claim was made to interpret the Gospels in too free and personal a manner. Against all personal constructs in the matter of Jesus, Peter raised a simple and immediate truth—what he had seen:

> For we have not followed cunningly devised fables, when we made known unto you the power and coming of our Lord Jesus Christ, but were eyewitnesses of his majesty [. . .] knowing this first, that no prophecy of the Scripture is of private interpretation.[42]

Eighty years after his death, things had gone further and many independent churches had spread, to which the human part of Jesus, his body, was not just secondary but a negative to be discarded. They

---

42   Second Epistle of Peter, 1:20-3:17..

tended to feel that it was impossible for the Spirit of God, from which the celestial Christ had been forged, could remain caged in a human body that fell sick and died; Christian thinking tended to suppose that the Spirit had at some point taken possession of this mortal detritus purely in order to communicate with human beings, teach them the way of knowledge, only to then rid himself as soon as possible of this embarrassing physical carrier before it was undone by crucifixion. These churches called themselves Gnostic, from the Greek word *gnosis*, knowledge, because according to their religious views, the salvation of man depended not on Jesus's sacrifice, which had never really taken place, but on his preaching alone, thanks to which men came to the knowledge of God. Docetic and Gnostic currents strongly separated the earthly Jesus from the heavenly Christ, as if they were two separate and irreconcilable entities. The mortal Jesus, the Jesus of Nazareth, was an empty and irrelevant container of no importance, the temporary abode of the spiritual Christ; to some sects, he was just another man and to others not even a man of flesh and bone, but some sort of ectoplasm. According to both, at any rate, the Resurrection had never happened, because the heavenly Christ could neither suffer nor die; there had been no sacrifice to redeem mankind, and the Eucharist was a meaningless ritual and so should not be celebrated. God had sent this celestial Messenger of His among men under the false appearance of a mortal man, a commonplace individual, so that he could preach to mankind and thus deliver it from false opinions; the physical baggage of the Messenger was nothing but a kind of visual illusion needed so that people could see him, but of no real consequence. Certain extremist Gnostic groups went as far as to say that it had actually been Simon of Cyrene who had been crucified: For at the right moment, God had dazzled the soldiers to force them to get the wrong man.[43]

Apart from these exaggerations, the Gnostic movement had its own fascinating theology which exalted the spiritual greatness of the Christ and celebrated the way in which the human soul, through his mediation, can carry out a great path of ascesis till it comes to contemplate the Face of God. From the end of the 1st century till the age of Constantine, even Catholic Christianity was more than once attracted to this intellectual and spiritual vision of Jesus, which underplayed the value of his human nature and interpreted every bit of the Gospels allegorically. Several representatives of these views moved constantly on the edge of orthodoxy, such as the theologian Valentinus, who had lived in Rome during the reign of Hadrian, of whom we are left a fragment of great religious poetry:

> When the Father, the sole good being, turns to it his glance, the heart is sanctified and shines with light; and so he is made blessed who has such a heart, for he will see God.[44]

At the end of the 1st century, Christians already felt this kind of idea very keenly, and their attraction was reinforced by the fact that Gnostics lived exemplary

---

43   Simonetti, "Note di cristologia gnostica," pp. 529-553; See extensively *Testi gnostici in lingua greca e latina*.

44   Clemente Alessandrino, *Stromata*, II 114, 3-6.

ascetic lives. Valentinus had a special intuition, and he seemed to somehow have set into motion that theological debate which was later to ripen into the dogma of the Trinity. The beauty of his religious thought, joined as it was with an overwhelming power of eloquence, had let much of the clergy of Rome propose him as a future pope; something, however, went wrong, and in the end another candidate, of no great theological gift but who had given an impressive witness of faith in his daily life, had been elected instead. The reasons for this choice must be found in a peculiarity of Gnostic thought already denounced by St. Ignatius of Antioch, who had a major role in the Christian community during the reign of Trajan (98–117 AD): Gnostics neglected to help the poor, the sick, widows, and orphans. That was the inevitable result of their theological apparatus: If flesh was nothing but sin and corruption, why cure the sick? If life was nothing but incarceration and exile, why help the poor live longer? In short, their exaggerated ascetic ideal made Gnostics pretty nearly inhuman. Jesus, on the other hand, had been very clear: Following his path meant helping anyone who needed help, whatever the cost. The primitive Church had been, before anything else, a group of religious volunteers made up of people who held their goods in common to feed the poor and care for the sick; there was no doubt that this was the will of Jesus, since this had happened when he was still with the apostles and had guided them. These sects interpreted the message of Christ as if it were pretty much a school of philosophy, and ignored charity to the needy. Even if they were pure of any stain, Gnostics ended up betraying the essence of Christianity.[45]

Disappointment at missing the papacy caused the theologian Valentinus to develop a violent resentment against the Roman clergy; it seems that he left the capital for the East, and that he started to write works widely different from what he had previously published, aggressively expounding Gnostic theories against the human body of Christ, which he had perhaps already worked out without ever making them public before. Peter's vision, which had handed down a cult of Jesus as the Christ announced by the prophets and still a man of flesh and bone, ended up prevailing, and Gnostic doctrines were refuted; Gnosticism, however, did not altogether vanish, for its roots were deep both in the East and in the West. Modern historians have trouble seeing the differences between sects, because notices are few and as often as not, they come from contemporaneous Christian intellectuals, who had it in for those doctrines because of the confusion they sowed among the public: Some leaders of major Gnostic schools had circulated heavily edited versions of the Gospels, or even gospels of their own writing and devising. The text of John, peculiarly full as it is of symbolic expressions, was their favorite target.[46]

---

45   Luke 8:2-3; At 6:1-6; Ignatius of Antioch, *Letter to the Christians of Smyrna*, VI, 1-2.

46   Dubois, *Valentin*, coll. 146-156; Mercati, *Anthimi Nicomediensis,* pp. 87-98; Janssens, *Héracléon,* pp. 101-151; Blanc, *Le Commentaire d'Héracléon,* pp. 81-124; Brown, *Giovanni,* pp. LXVII-LXXI; Peretto, *L'inno cristologico,* pp. 257-274.

There were great differences between Gnostic schools of thought, although in the end they all went back to a common idea that basically denied the humanity of Christ. To the writers of the early Church, Gnosticism was like the hundred-headed hydra, a monster with ancient roots and yet everlastingly capable of turning up again with a new face.[47]

Survivals

Constantine had decided to legalize the Christian cult both out of personal sympathy and out of political calculation, but obviously he wished for a united and peaceful church, a solid organism that could serve his projects; he therefore outlawed dissident sects. Gnosticism survived; especially in north Africa and some areas of the Middle East, it came back into favor in the time of the Manichees, one of whose members, in his youth, had been none other than St. Augustine of Hippo. During the Byzantine age, enclaves survived in various patches of the Empire's vast hinterlands; then the current picked up strength again inside the larger iconoclast movement that intended to destroy icons because they bore the human image of Christ and wished instead to worship only the Gospels, which bore his words. In the 8th and 9th centuries, several Byzantine emperors found themselves having to fight the Paulicians, so called because they followed the Gnostic doctrines of Paul of Samosata: Michael

---

47 Grossi, *Lo gnosticismo e i Padri della Chiesa*, pp. 69-80; Segalla, *Vangeli canonici e vangeli gnostici*, pp. 47-68; Gianotto, *Gli scritti di Nag Hammadi*, pp. 36-46; Filoramo, *La gnosi ieri e oggi*, pp. 21-35.

I (811–813), Leo V (813–820), Theodora (842–856), who outlawed iconoclasm, and finally Basilius I, who defeated them in the year 871. Because these dissenters were excellent soldiers, they had been settled in Thrace and Macedonia as a border shield to protect the imperial territories; there the movement grew again and spread widely into Bulgaria, the Balkans, and certain regions of Russia. By the middle of the 10th century, they had taken the name of *Bogomils*, from the name of their spiritual leader Bogumil, which meant "Dear to God."

Like a returning wave, this stream of thought, in which religious dissent tended to be coupled with political protest during the 11th century, had reached the capital once again: During the time of the imperial house of the Komnenoi, Gnostic-derived heresy grew powerful, and merciless measures of repression were adopted. Anna Komnena, daughter of Emperor Alexius I and author of a famous chronicle, tells that in the year 1117 a kind of conspiracy was discovered, organized by the leaders of these Gnostic churches, whose reach had come as far as the edge of the imperial throne and lurked among the most trusted officials. To deliver a really exemplary lesson, Alexius condemned them to be burned at the stake, but he had two different burning pits prepared: one overlooked by a cross, the other not. The Cross was the mark of true faith, and to accept it meant to accept the real humanity of Jesus, his real and freely willed sacrifice, and all its beneficent effects on the salvation of humankind. Some of the heretics chose to die under the cross; the emperor took this as a sign of conversion at the point of death and granted them amnesty.[48]

In the 11th century, some members of the Gnostic Bogomil movement crossed over into Western Europe, bringing their teachings with them. Their ideas took hold very swiftly, especially in southern France, northern Italy, and Germany. The Midi—the whole central and southern area of modern France—became the home of a swiftly growing Gnostic church. In the year 1167, the Gnostics even held a general council of this new independent church at Saint-Félix-de-Caraman in Languedoc; they called themselves the Cathars, from the Greek *katharòs*, meaning "pure." Several Catholic bishops adhered to Gnosticism, going over to its particular creed and taking all their faithful with them, and a kind of union was agreed upon between the Western and Eastern Cathars; the leader of a Greek church, named Niketas and who wore the significant title of *papas*, took part in the council.[49] A dangerous doctrinal confusion had also infiltrated the hierarchies of the Catholic Church; it was such that Pope Innocent III found himself forced to write a crop of letters and treatises addressed, not to ordinary people, but to bishops whose ideas seemed to be tottering on matters as central and basic as sacraments. At the same time, Innocent III expended a great deal of energy on underlining the significance of the cult of relics, especially those that related to the life of Christ. Just as with the Byzantine emperors Romanus I and Constantine VII when they had found themselves up against the heretics, the pope understood an important point: These objects may

---

48   Mayer, *Pauliciani*, coll. 996-997; Di Fonzo, *Bogomili*, coll. 1759-1760; Carile, *Potere e simbologia*, pp. 432-433; Kazhdan, *Bisanzio e la sua civiltà*, pp. 97-99; Patlagean, *Contestazioni*, pp. 434-442.

49   Patlagean, *Contestazioni*, p. 436; Vauchez, *Contestazioni*, pp. 449–450.

well have been poor things tied to popular devotion, but to tradition they represented concrete evidence that Jesus had really lived as a human being, had suffered the Passion, and had died. In the face of those who preached that the Celestial Christ had been a pure spirit, a concept, an abstract being, even relics of the most everyday things, such as the milk of the Virgin, served as fundamental evidence to ordinary people, evidence that heretics considered false.

As already explained, the truth of a relic is something our mental attitude cannot take in as the Old World used to: The men of the Middle Ages, from professors at the Sorbonne to the last beggar, perceived it with very great strength, and that cannot simply be ascribed to their stupidity. It is true that any number of fakes circulated, and we know the famous quotation ascribed to Erasmus or Calvin, that one could load a whole ship with the wood from the relics of the True Cross of Christ scattered around Christendom. No doubt they were right, mostly about the shocking abuse made of these objects in their time, to collect alms from pilgrims; something of the kind was also violently denounced by a 12th-century churchman, the Cistercian abbot Guibert de Nogent. Both Guibert and Calvin or Erasmus were, however, neglecting a matter of some relevance to modern historians: For instance, if the emperor of Constantinople wished to make a gift to some church of a piece of the True Cross, he would not hack off a large chunk, but rather shave off a minute part, often a bare sliver. The value of relics was spiritual and did not depend on weight. The only thing that mattered was whether that wood had been drenched in the blood of Christ; whether it was a tiny fragment or the whole *patibulum* arm, it was still a witness of the Passion. Of course one could not exhibit some thin wooden fiber, impossible to see once it was sealed within a reliquary, to the faithful, so the holy fiber would be placed within a larger piece of wood, selected from the same kind of material from which the original fragment had been taken. The more recent wood carrier became itself sacred by contact, and the sliver, once inserted, would be lost and become all but impossible to distinguish. But in all this, there was no intent to deceive or defraud. Most relics of the Cross circulating in the Middle Ages were at least authentic in this sense, derived from an authentic lift of material from the greater relic that tradition said St. Helena had retrieved from Jerusalem.

The study of relics is a very fascinating chapter in the history of culture, so long as it is done with sufficient respect. For it is a matter of cultural processes that today's historian must be able to record without claiming to eviscerate them in light of a realism that is both too recent in origin and too distant in context to properly judge. Besides, the modern world may well be said to have something that looks very much like the ancient hunger for relics: It is the curiosity toward the so-called "historical Jesus" that drives the research aimed at reconstructing the human and terrestrial figure of Jesus of Nazareth in the most realistic manner possible. Born of positivism, relativism, and also of a certain 1900s faddish skepticism, the culture of the early third millennium claims to be able to separate the historical man, a Galilean subject of Herod Antipas and of Tiberius Caesar, from the mysteries bound to his person which have made him the center of a religion. To do so, the Gospels are sometimes sliced like hams, dismantled and recomposed in different ways in the hopes that we will be able to get at the "actual words" spoken by Jesus.[50] I am not able to assess the sense of this on a theological level, but certainly as a historical method it has none. A man who goes to a conference on Dante and proposes to move the Paolo and Francesca episode from Canto V of *Hell* to Canto V of *Paradise* would be met with obloquy. A historian finds such an idea unacceptable: It is like a crazed restorer intending to destroy a painting by Giulio Romano with acid because he is certain he shall find, hidden behind it, a sketch by Giulio's master, Raphael. At any rate, even if it shows itself in paradoxical and laughable forms, the modern desire to reach the Jesus of history so as to be able to nearly look him in the face is actually very similar to medieval man's morbid affection for all the remains of Jesus's terrestrial passage.

Himself a lover of relics and certain that they were a mighty weapon against heresies, Innocent III wrote a hymn to celebrate the Veronica, a famous image of the Face of Jesus kept in Rome. Its tradition was tied up with the *mandylion's*: The Veronica was also an *acheropita* image—a miraculous portrait not made by man. It was said to have been made when a compassionate woman had approached Jesus on the way to Golgotha, to clean his face dripping with blood and sweat.[51] The Templars knew that this pontiff loved collecting, or rather coveted, Christ's relics because of their meaning, and

---

50 Further reading on these tendencies: Brown, *Giovanni*, pp. XXII-XLIII; Segalla, *La verità storica dei Vangeli*, pp. 195-234.

51 Mattheu Paris, *Historia maior*, c. 290, in Potthast, *Regesta Pontificum*, I, p. 450; Spadafora, Veronica, coll. 1044-1048; Pfeiffer, *Le voile de sainte Véronique*, pp. 127-131; Paschalis Schlömer, *Le «sindon» et la «Véronique»*, pp. 151-164.

popes who followed were just as eager. A famous case that may give a feeling for the times was that of the miracle in the Bolsena cathedral, in 1263. A German priest who was going on pilgrimage to Rome was saying Mass on the altar of St. Christina, but at the back of his mind (like many priests of his time, perhaps), he felt a doubt about the Host really being the body of Christ. Suddenly he saw blood coming out of the bread, dripping down to stain the corporal. The event, of course, made an enormous amount of noise, and Pope Urbanus IV ordered its memory to be celebrated with the Feast of Corpus Domini.[52]

The Order of the Temple owed everything to papal favor; what is more, as we already mentioned, its own statutes said in so many words that the Roman pontiff was its lord and master. Once he had learned that the Templars kept such a relic, there is every likelihood that the reigning pope would have let the grand master understand that he wanted it in the Roman Curia. The Templars could not have said no, and it was probably to ward off such a prospect that it was decided that it was best to keep silent.

In southern France at the same time, a lethal association was arising between the Cathar religious ideas—followed by many with sincerity—and political opposition to the king. Philip II Augustus was working to unify the territory of his kingdom politically so as to make it a stronger monarchy, and this obviously implied that the great southern fief-holders would lose their autonomy.[53] Besides, the north, the *langue d'Oïl* had a

---

52 Pesci, *Bolsena*, coll. 1817-1819.
53 Meschini, *Note sull'assegnazione della viscontea*, pp. 635-655 (with a rich and well up-to-date bibliography).

very different culture from the south. The connection between ecclesiastic and political autonomy was very strongly felt, and was amplified by the unworthy lifestyle often enjoyed by Catholic hierarchs, as opposed to the exemplary austerity of Cathar bishops. The idea itself of heresy was recklessly broadened: To protest a bishop's authority, or to refuse to pay tithe, was counted as disobedience of the Catholic Church and evidence of supporting the heretics.[54]

The opposition was thus animated by a certain reforming spirit that gave it a potent moral charisma and drove many people to Cathar churches. At first, the king attempted ending the conflict with religious weapons alone, thanks in part to the fervid preaching of St. Dominic de Guzman, but this did not ward off disaster. On January 5, 1208, the papal legate Peter of Castelnau was murdered by a subject of the count of Toulouse and his murder went unpunished: The murderer was tied to the Cathars, his lord seemed to be protecting him, and the whole matter was very suspicious. Whatever the truth, this crime was the spark that exploded the gunpowder store. Philip II Augustus prompted a true civil war that caused the massacre of thousands upon thousands of Frenchmen and the military conquest of Provence and, above all, of Languedoc. It was called the Albigensian Crusade because one of the most tragic events of repression took place in a town called Albi, and because political propaganda demanded that this butchery be misrepresented as a crusade. The operation achieved its political goal, but did not manage at all to uproot the Cathar church of the Midi, which went on existing

---

54 Chiffoleau, *Vie et mort de l'hérésie,* pp. 73-99; Griffe, *Le catharisme,* pp. 215-236; Becamel, *Le catharisme,* pp. 237-251.

for over a century there and elsewhere: According to Raniero Sacconi, born and raised in a Cathar family but who later converted and joined the the Dominicans in 1251, the spread of this parallel church was stunning. It was still flourishing in the late 1200s; the last leader we know of, by the name of Guillaume Bélibaste, died at the stake in 1321.[55]

Curiously and surely not by chance, the area of Catharism's highest popularity coincides with where we find the most numerous testimonies of these simulacra of the Face of Christ among the Templars.

Between Provence and Languedoc

We know that at the time of the Sack of Constantinople, when the Shroud vanished from the imperial collection, a small group of Templars was present in the Byzantine capital. Their leader was Jacopo Barozzi, a knight from one of Venice's most prominent families, who at the time held the important office of preceptor of the Temple for the province of Lombardy (meaning most of northern Italy). What they were doing there is not quite clear, and the only certain thing is that they were there under orders from the grand master. In fact, these Templars took no part in the sacking of the city, nor would they have been allowed to; not only did Innocent III excommunicate all those who had been guilty of aggression against other Christians, but the Templar regulations themselves ordered that anyone who

---

55   Da Milano, *Albigesi*, coll. 708-712; D'Amato, *Sacconi, Raniero*, coll. 1530-1531; Duvernoy, *Le catharisme en Languedoc*, pp. 27-56; Henriet, *Du nouveau sur l'Inquisition*, pp. 159-173; Dossat, *Les cathares d'après les documents*, pp. 72-77.

had been guilty of violence against other Christians was to be expelled from the Order, immediately and irrevocably.[56]

The Temple units were in fact already in the Holy Land, and had already committed themselves to the military operations which, according to the agreed plans, were to precede the re-taking of Jerusalem— strengthening the Christian positions in northern Syria. This little group, led by the preceptor of Lombardy, left Venice together with the remaining crusader army because, in all likelihood, the Venetian Templar house had given the French barons a massive cash loan to help them finally leave, since the debt they had made with the Republic prevented the host from moving out. Immediately after the conquest of Constantinople, the new Latin emperor, Baudouin de Courtenay, was to charge Barozzi with the most delicate and serious of diplomatic missions: go to the pope and beg him to remove the sentence of excommunication from the leaders of the Crusade. On this occasion, the new emperor gifted the Temple with a small fortune in money, precious objects shining with gems, and even two fragments of the True Cross: wealth that was to repay the Order for the expenditure it had previously suffered.[57]

Was it Preceptor Jacopo Barozzi who brought the Shroud from the imperial Byzantine collection to the Temple? The idea does not seem acceptable, because known sources do not support it; if anything, the horror of the sack and the indignity of the trade in relics that followed were what allowed the Templars to see the relic up close and assess its awe-inspiring peculiarities.

---

56 Curzon, *La Règle*, § 226.
57 Frale, *La quarta crociata e il ruolo dei Templari*, pp. 447-484.

The evidence that has come down to us does not place the Holy Face in the hands of the Order any earlier than several decades later, in 1266, near the tower of Saphed in Palestine, when Sultan Baibars snatched it from the Order and was greatly astonished to find a bas-relief of a man's face in the grand hall of the mansion where the Knights used to hold their chapter, and obviously could not guess at the man's identity.[58] More or less at the same time, these simulacra started appearing in the mansions of southern France, especially in Provence; for some particular reason, the cult there spread earlier and faster than anywhere else.[59] The following decades witnessed a kind of explosion of copies, which meant that by the last quarter of the 13th century they could be found practically in every country where the Temple was present.[60] In Paris, the presence of the "idol" is continuously documented from 1298 to 1307, which was the year of the last general chapter that the Templars were able to hold only a few months before their arrest. In Cyprus, too, it seems to appear somewhat late.[61]

Mentions of the relic may have spread earlier in Provence, as compared with the rest of France, on account

---

58   Defremery, *Mémoires d'Histoire Orientale*, pp. 363-364; Riant, *Études sur les derniers temps*, pp. 388-389; Barber, *The Templars and the Turin Shroud*, p. 222.

59   Among the earliest mentions, it appears in Saint-Gilles in 1266, in Valence in 1268, in Richarenches in 1272, in Albon in 1278, in Avignon in 1280, and so on; cf. Frale, *L'interrogatorio ai Templari*, pp. 250, 251, 255, etc.

60   In Germany in 1271, on the German preceptors' seals, in Bulst-Thiele, *Sacrae Domus*, pp. 272-274; in Portugal in 1274; and in Puglia in 1292 (Frale, *L'interrogatorio ai Templari*, pp. 256 and 254).

61   In Gastina (Frale, *L'interrogatorio ai Templari*, p. 259) and in Limassol (Michelet, *Le procès* II, 290).

of its strategic position, since Marseille was the main port of embarkation to Outremer, but there may also have been other reasons, issues connected with specific persons. A rumor that went around the Order said that the unworthy acts practiced in the Order's rituals (*errores*) had been introduced in the days when Thomas Bérard had been grand master and Roncelin de Fos had been preceptor of Provence.[62] The masters of this province seem to have had a privileged role in the spread of the cult; there are in fact no less than nineteen witness statements that tie the idol continuously to the preceptors of Provence and to their lieutenants[63] in the second half of the 8th century: Roncelin de Fos,[64] Pons de Brozet,[65] Guy Audémar,[66] and Bernard de La Roche.[67]

The sources ascribe the introduction of the cult specifically to Roncelin de Fos and a significant date: It was 1266, the year when the fortress of Saphed was taken from the Templars, and when the sultan found that curious image of the Face carved into the chapterhouse wall. It is not hard to imagine that that same hall might also have kept another simulacrum of that same Face,

---

62 Michelet, *Le procès*, II, pp. 398-400.

63 Ripert du Puy: 1290 and 1291 (Frale, *L'interrogatorio ai Templari*, pp. 246 and 249).

64 In 1266 (ibid. p. 250) and 1271 (p. 1251); before 1268 (p.262); undated (Finke, II, p. 324).

65 1288: Schottmüller, II, p. 29, and Frale, *L'interrogatorio ai Templari*, p. 270; 1289: Finke, II, p. 321; undated, Finke, II, p. 319 and Schottmüller, II, p. 50; 1290 or 1291: Schottmüller, II, p. 67.

66 1288 (Schottmüller, II, p. 28); 1298 (Schottmüller, II, p. 70); 1300 or 1301 (Frale, *L'interrogatorio ai Templari*, p. 245); undated (Finke, II, p. 323); 1300 (Frale, *L'interrogatorio ai Templari*, p. 253).

67 1291: Frale, *L'interrogatorio ai Templari*, p. 265; 1305: ibid., p. 247.

taken to the West when the fortress had fallen into Muslim hands.

On Roncelin de Fos, unfortunately, we currently have very little information. Following Anne Marie Bulst-Thiele's very valuable study of the Templar grand masters, we find that Roncelin de Fos had a long career in the Order, which coincides with the period in which Thomas Bérard became grand master. From 1252–1255 and 1262–1266, Roncelin held the office of master of England to which he added, during the periods 1248–1250, 1254–1256, and 1260–1278, that of master of Provence.[68] The man may, however, have been more important in the Order than even his list of offices seem to warrant; a document dated 1252 makes him, along with his kinsman Geoffroy de Fos, a member of the private company of Grand Master Thomas Bérard—a narrow roster of dignitaries chosen by the leader as his most trusted collaborators.[69]

The grand master's companions, who had to be of noble birth, helped him closely in all delicate situations and in important matters, such as lending Order funds, that could not be tackled by the grand master without their agreement.[70] In general, the rules describe these persons as always close to the person of the grand master, so close indeed that in some cases it became necessary to specify which kinds of honors and privileges were

---

68 Bulst-Thiele, *Sacrae domus*, p. 235, note 11.
69 Delaville Le Roulx, *Documents concernant les Templiers*, pp. 26–30: The source suggests that the bond between the two de Fos and the grand master was close (*frere Recelins de Fox, frere Jofroiz de Foz compagnon dou Maistre*).
70 Curzon, *La Règle*, § 82.

an exclusive prerogative that the grand master was not allowed to share with his companions.[71] Belonging to the narrow circle of the grand master's companions, and the full confidence from the latter that this honor implied, surely allowed Roncelin de Fos the opportunity of taking part in most confidential matters, and it seems that de Fos was the first to take the cult of the Shroud-type Face to the West. As a companion of the grand master, he certainly had access to plenty of information unknown to ordinary brothers. In his dossier of charges, Philip the Fair specified that knowledge of the mysterious "idol" was an elite matter open only to the very highest ranks. If we remove what is only there to support basically groundless charges, we must notice that something of this statement is true.

From the sources, it seems that the cult did not cross the geographical boundaries of Templar Provence, at least in its early times. Outside Provence, we must go as far as 1270 for a sporadic apparition in Paris, and 1271 to see it represented on the seals of German preceptors; on the other hand, documents show that the area under the command of Roncelin de Fos knew of these simulacra earlier and more widely. Three statements that refer directly to de Fos cover a long chronological arch, reaching probably to the end of his life; after him, his successor Pons de Brozet "inherited" the cult and forced its transmission to some brothers, as did the last Templar to hold this post. Concerning the physical presence of the figure, there is no evidence that it was ever kept in a single place: On the contrary, some witnesses said

---

71   Ibid., §§ 86, 152, 368.

that it was entrusted to certain individuals, rather than being tied to one or more mansions. One of the persons mentioned as having a personal guardianship of the "idol" is none other than the Provencal officer Pons de Brozet.[72]

There is an important clue in the first of the three statements that refers to the central mansion of the Paris Temple.[73] As already mentioned, the sergeant who had been shown the "idol" wondered at the fact that he had never seen it again after his ceremony of admission. Now, considering that he had been admitted a long time before (1270) and that the presence of the "idol" is only proven in Paris for the continuous period of 1298 to 1307, it seems that showings depended not on the place but on the people— those who celebrated the ceremony of admission. It may have been mostly a matter of confidence, of trust in the man's moral fiber. The brothers were shown the idol at the start of their lives as Templars during the ceremony that made them Order members; it is as if the purpose was to place the new Templar forthwith under the protection of the Order's great patron, who would then perpetuate his protection through the power of the strand consecrated through contact.

Amaury de La Roche

The last person we hear of having a personal connection with the "idol" is a figure of primary importance in the Temple of the mid-1200s; in some ways, at least on

---

72   Finke, II, p. 319.
73   Michelet, *Le procès,* II, 191.

the international stage, he may have had more influence than the grand master himself. Amaury de La Roche belonged to a senior family of the French nobility, which had already given the Temple a preceptor of France in the first half of the 13th century[74]; in 1261, older by a generation than the Templar dignitaries tried by Philip the Fair, he had reached a very prestigious rank among the Templars—commander of Outremer, commander-in-chief of the whole Eastern sector. It was the third hierarchic rank in the whole order, and entitled him to counter-sign decrees issued by the grand master. The following year, he still had that rank, but had added another of greater delicacy and importance: Just like Roncelin de Fos exactly ten years earlier, in a decree from 1261, Amaury de La Roche is mentioned as *compaignon* of the master, Thomas Bérard.[75]

In 1264, the grand master summoned him back to France, saying in so many words that the situation in the West called for his presence; the following year, the king of France set out on a kind of diplomatic campaign because he saw Amaury as a valuable man and absolutely did not want to lose the opportunity to have him as an ally. From the popes' generosity, the Order of the Temple had always been free to select its own leaders through a vote and without any kind of outside interference. Templar

---

74 Olivier de La Roche (1226-1227): Paris, Archives Nationales, *Layettes du Trésor des Chartes, II*, p. 117, n. 1914, quoted in Trudon des Ormes, *Liste des maisons*, p. 57. I thank Luigi Boneschi for the suggestions and materials he has offered me on the subject of this dignitary.

75 Platelle, *Luigi IX*, coll. 320-338; Curzon, *Le Régle*, §§ 77-119; Bulst-Thiele, *Sacrae domus*, p. 245, act of May 31, 1261; Delaville Le Roulx, *Documents concernant les Templiers*, p. 34.

statutes only allowed one exception—when a pope, for reasons of higher necessity, might interfere and make his desires felt. Louis IX made use of this exception, and strongly pressured Pope Urbanus IV to favor Amaury de La Roche's candidacy as preceptor of France, a role that would have involved a great deal of cooperation with the Crown in many ways. The pope had a hard time imposing his interference on the Templar assembly, which did not view this interference from the king of France as fair; on the other hand, the sovereign would not yield. He kept insisting, extolling Amaury and underlining that that man was bound to him by a very old friendship. The pope did not wish to displease a man of Louis IX's caliber: a just king and a faithful husband of exemplary devotion. It certainly was not easy to say no. Besides, considering his wisdom, it is not hard to imagine that the choice of Amaury would have been a very sound step. In the end, Urbanus IV thought to seek help from the patriarch of Jerusalem, a religious and moral authority to whom the Templars were closely bound. Grand Master Thomas may well not have wanted to lose that man because he felt his need in the East, but in the end, the greatest powers in contemporary Christian society had aligned around the request to make Amaury de La Roche preceptor of France, so he was forced to yield. The situation was to repeat itself later: Pope Urbanus' successor, Clemens IV, pressured the grand master no less than twice to place Amaury at Charles of Anjou's disposal, by giving him oversight of the Templar houses of the Kingdom of Naples.[76]

---

76   Guiraud, *Registres d'Urbain IV*, t. II, nn. 760, 761, 773; *Registres de Clément IV*, nn. 855, 1253, 1263; Runciman, *Storia delle crociate*, II, pp. 902-933.

Although his specific duties were from then on focused on Western territories, Amaury de La Roche seems to have had, thanks to Louis IX's confidence, a role above his rank. Sources show him taking personal charge of Eastern issues—above all, the new crusade that dominated the king's thoughts: In 1267 the patriarch of Jerusalem turned to him, rather than to the grand master, to lament the persecution of the Palestine Christians at the hands of the sultan of Egypt, and asked him to intercede with the pope, King Louis, and Charles of Anjou, for a swift intervention.[77] Amaury went on the Eighth Crusade with the French king, and took part in the siege of Tunis[78]; it seems likely that the king's death in 1270 interrupted his rise in the Temple, for according to the last notice that still mentions him alive, of a reception he held in Paris in 1287, he was still Master of France.[79]

This man's life intersects at many points with the story of the Shroud as it has been reconstructed thus far. He had the full confidence of Louis IX, who set up a whole policy of searching for the most important relics of Jesus left in Constantinople to take to France, and had a container of fantastic value, the sublime jewel that is the Sainte-Chapelle of Paris, built especially for them: the True Cross, the Spear, the Sponge used to give drink to the crucified Jesus, and other priceless objects. They were solemnly transported to France in a transit intended to have every confirmation of legality through appropriate

---

77   Servois, *Emprunts de Saint Louis*, pp. 290-293.
78   Duchesne, *Historiae Francorum scriptores coaetanei*, V, pp. 390-391.
79   Michelet, *Les procès* II, pp. 401.

written documents.[80] Considering his functions, there is no doubt Amaury assisted Louis IX at some crucial moments, supervising the examinations to ascertain that the right relics were being sent, and then organizing the security measures during transport.

The sources of the Templar trials alone do not allow us to establish this important Templar's parentage with certainty, and we have to be content with knowing that he was of the house of La Roche, a noble family that had taken part in the Fourth Crusade and established its own fiefdom near Athens. And it was near Athens, according to a document dated in 1205, which reached us thanks to a copy made by the archbishop of Monreale (Sicily), Monsignor Benedetto D'Acquisto, that the nobleman Othon de La Roche decided to keep the most precious object of the booty he had taken during the Sack of Constantinople—the Shroud of Jesus Christ. The document is a letter written to Pope Innocent III by Theodoros Angelos, a brother of Michael, despot of Epirus and member of the deposed and exiled Byzantine imperial family, demanding from the pope the return, at least, of the most sacred objects. [81]

The diplomatic form of the letter certainly seems to be genuine, a Latin translation of a Greek original: The Byzantine imperial chancellery produced their official documents in Greek, but attached to them Latin translations, and the unknown scribe probably only copied out the latter. No expert until now has challenged its authenticity, and it seems to agree in form with other Byzantine documents of the time, at least to judge by

---

80   Riant, *Exuviae*, pp. 22-23, 52.
81   Rinaldi, *Un documento*, pp. 109-113.

such formulas as calling the Roman pontiff "Pope of Old Rome," or the heading scheme that specialists call *illi-ille*.[82] In this context, I would like to mention an interesting fact that might have to do with the presence of the Shroud in the region of Athens. The accurate catalog of churches in the Empire of Constantinople drawn up by Raymond Janin states that in the neighborhood of Daphni, on the ancient sacred way that once took pilgrims to the famous temple of Apollo, stood an abbey dedicated to the Mother of God. In a letter from 1209, Pope Innocent III strangely calls this "the church of the Blachernae," the very same name of the famous basilica in Constantinople where the crusader Robert de Clari saw the Shroud exhibited just before the sack. The abbey was settled by Cistercian monks from the French town of Bellevaux, which had ties to the La Roche family; Janin, who has made a detailed study of the history of many Byzantine religious foundations, could find no explanation for this novel naming of Blachernae, which had nothing whatsoever to do with the history of that monastery and seemed to appear out of nowhere on the morrow after the great sack.[83] It would not be surprising if the church of Daphni had been so renamed just by virtue of the unique object it came to hold, which made it somehow a new basilica of the Blachernae

---

82 Pieralli, *La corrispondenza diplomatica*, for instance pp. 41, 43, 45-46. It must be borne in mind that this is a private letter, and thus much freer in form than one would expect from an official document of the imperial chancellery.

83 Janin, *Les Églises*, pp. 310-311; Fedalto, *La Chiesa latina in Oriente*, I, p. 299.

The last La Roche duke of Athens, also named Othon, died without an heir on October 5, 1308, and was buried in the monastery of Daphni; in all likelihood, the Shroud had long since left his family's possession.[84]

In 1261 the Latin Empire of Constantinople ceased to exist, Greek emperors recovered the throne, and the establishment of fiefdoms also had to be reorganized. In those years—to be precise, from 1260 to 1265—Amaury was the commander of the Temple throughout the whole East, and therefore had great military, political, and economic powers. The Fourth Lateran Council had forbidden the trade of relics under pains of excommunication, so the Shroud could never have been sold. After the Sack of Constantinople, several precious reliquaries containing tiny fragments of the Shroud of Christ had been sold across Europe, and even King Louis IX the Saint had procured one for his treasury at the Sainte-Chapelle; although these were only fragments, they were objects that mightily drew people's devotion and curiosity. It is easy to imagine what would have happened if the existence of the sheet—one of the most famous and celebrated relics in all Christendom—had been made widely known. Excommunication could have been avoided by making it a free-will gift or some kind of disguised purchase, but at any rate the conveyance had to be carried out as discreetly as possible.[85] There would have been nothing strange about it if the Order of the Temple, as greedy for relics of Jesus Christ as anyone, had come forward to make an offer to the troubled La Roche family through one of its own kinsmen, offering

---

84   Rodd, *The Princes of Achaia*, II, p. 119.

85   Riant, *Exuviae*, p. 7.

to take this object as a pawn for a monumental sum of money—a sum the La Roche family would never have been able to return.

The Templars never exhibited the Shroud to the faithful, never got alms from it, and never used it to profit from indulgences; indeed they kept it hidden from most of their own members.

Why, then, did they wish to hold and keep this strange object?

A New Sepulchre

As I explained earlier, there is reason to believe, from the complex information at our disposal, that the Templars may have endowed their little linen strings with a new, spiritual meaning when the Order came into contact with the Shroud and discovered its singular properties, especially the awe-inspiring "belt of blood." The little belts worn by every member of the Order, which had been consecrated in the past thanks to contact with the stone of the Holy Sepulchre, were now consecrated by contact with the Shroud after Jerusalem was lost. The Shroud came to be, in a sense, a "new Sepulchre," but as compared with the grave inside the magnificent basilica of Anastasis, it had a much greater power over the imagination; this power seemed to the Templars to be of vital importance in a truly difficult historical time.

Between 1198 and 1202, as the French barons were working on the organization of the new crusade, Innocent III set up a series of reforming policies to raise the fortunes of the Temple and Hospital: After the catastrophic defeat at Hattin by Saladin, the two

243

military orders were on their knees, both because of the loss of fighting men and goods, and because of the immense blow to their image in the eyes of the West that saw them as the bulwark of Christianity in the Holy Land. The pope intended to make it easier to join the two orders, and thus encourage many lay knights to replenish the ranks of the Templars and Hospitallers. His first step was to broaden certain privileges already granted by Innocent II in 1139, especially allowing Templar cemeteries to bury such faithful as wished to be laid to rest there; then came the permission to admit excommunicates into the Temple, a very bold decision that wholly reversed the clearly stated purpose of St. Bernard of Clairvaux from the start. Bernard had long fought to stem the spread of Cathar heresy in the Midi, and his preaching had resulted in many conversions, which, however, had not lasted long. When drafting the Templar rules, the abbot of Clairvaux was stern: Admission to the Temple was totally forbidden to excommunicates, and Templars had no right to even accept alms from such persons that had been placed outside the Catholic community.[86]

In 1206, this rule was abrogated, and the Temple was opened to these knights, who made up a kind of reserve of energies that could not be exploited because they had been placed outside Christian society. Innocent III had decided that the emergency of the times was enough to justify such an alteration of St. Bernard's precepts, and that in the end one could follow the same rationale seen in his time by Pope Urbanus II when

---

86 Curzon, *La Règle*, § 13.

he had called for the First Crusade in 1095: In many countries in Europe, these excommunicated knights lived at the margins of society, eking out a living by enlisting as mercenaries with some mighty lord who employed them to raid his enemies, or indeed by turning into true bandits, bloodily assaulting peasants and churches. Offering them absolution if they took vows as Templar or Hospitaller brothers meant giving them a second chance: They could save their souls by serving God and the defense of Jerusalem, and, what is more, they could be turned into a strong resource for the Christian army.

This is a typical instance of a reform carried out with the best intentions and yet ending up doing serious damage. Innocent III was fully within his rights to rewrite Templar statutes; a principle contained precisely in their statutes declared that the pope was the master of the Order and their lord after Jesus Christ.[87] Pontiffs did not, in actual fact, ever meddle in Order affairs, and the interference mentioned a few pages ago to have Amaury de La Roche made preceptor of France is probably the only notable case of this kind; at any rate, and to judge by the tone of the papal missive, it seems that it had been the Templars themselves who had suggested this reform. The move was completed when another pontifical letter was issued, sanctioning the automatic extension of privileges bestowed on knights intending to become Templars to their whole family. In 1213, Innocent III was to complain about excessively broad interpretations of the papal will, but it is a fact that the

---

87   Ibid., § 475.

way his letter had been drafted all but encouraged that kind of reading.[88]

Within certain limits, the Temple had become a kind of free port, a privileged pathway to redemption, as well as a means of sheltering from persecution. When you consider how widespread the Cathar heresy was in southern France and the climate that was created early in the Albigensian Crusade, it is obvious that many families with Cathar connections could not take the opportunity offered by this amnesty fast enough; to be legally protected against the Inquisition, but also against the hard men from the North who were taking advantage of theological conflicts to strike at their political and economic enemies. Many passages in ancient sources show that the atmosphere had become nightmarish, and had brought about absurd situations. For instance, it had become quite dangerous to call on the Holy Spirit, for it was known that Cathars recognized only one sacrament, the transmission of the Holy Spirit by the laying-on of hands. In the Gospels, Jesus repeatedly underlines the power and sacredness of the Spirit for Christians, but still they preferred not to so much as mention it at all, as if it did not exist; even during the most intimate moments there might be someone who listened, made guesses, and then laid information before the authorities. A knight's wife from Cestayrols near Albi was declared a suspect because, in the agony of childbirth, she had cried out: "Holy Spirit of God, help me!" In 1254, a man from Montgey in Tarn, gravely ill, called on the Holy Spirit

---

88   Frale, *La quarta crociata e il ruolo dei Templari*, pp. 454-466.

to be healed, but his brother made him shut up lest he attract the interest of inquisitors.[89]

We cannot currently make firm estimates, but it seems more than likely that some sons from aristocratic families with Cathar connections were made Templars, thus extending the mantle of papal protection, and it may be that not every one of these men changed their religious ideas, when you consider that they had entered the Temple to stay alive. Unorthodox talk or behavior from this or that Templar leader may have roused some scandal among the laity and in any case did not do the Order's public image, already damaged by widespread envy of their many privileges, any good.

The file of Philip the Fair's charges against the arrested Templars of France included an accusation that the priests of the Order would not consecrate the Host during Mass: a charge that makes no sense if taken in a general manner, for many ordinary folks went to Mass in Templar churches and such an oddity in the liturgy would never have gone unnoticed. It is, however, possible that Nogaret's hired spies had picked up sporadic evidence—isolated and very rare rumors that must have looked, however, like manna from Heaven from the prosecution's viewpoint.

Cathars, in fact, did not celebrate the Eucharist, because according to their doctrine the body of Christ was not important (it was simply a kind of empty shell), nor had there ever been a real sacrifice of Christ to renew or to commemorate by celebrating a sacrament. The Christ, the heavenly messenger of God, could not, in

---

89 See, for instance, Mt 12:28; Mc 3:29, etc; Dossat, *Les cathares d'après l'Inquisition*, pp. 81-82.

their view, die at all, for his nature was not compounded of the vile, useless mortal detritus that forms men; death may have welcomed the man Jesus, the physical carrier in which the Christ had dwelled for a while, and who to the Cathars had no importance at all. In effect, during the trial some testimonies were collected that pointed in that direction: During a ceremony of admission, a preceptor said to the newly made Templar that God had never died.

It is probably these kinds of broken-up reports of hearsay that led an Oriental scholar such as Hammer-Purgstall to write things like *Baphometus Revelatus*. Reading the few sources then available on the trial, he may have guessed at the connection between the charges made against the Templars and those against the Cathars. Then the cultural fashions of his time, the deforming pressure of Metternich's interests, and, for that matter, a highly questionable method of research, led him to exercise his imagination till he fantasized a whole Templar order turning its back en masse on Catholicism and secretly reviving dark and extremely ancient rites.

Today, an overall examination of all the sources on the trial allows us to know that this was at best a tiny phenomenon, limited in time and restricted to the French Midi where repression against heresy was most intense and above all most bitterly political. The Templars of Italy, of Spain, of Germany, of Scotland and England, of the Slavic countries, of Syria-Palestine and Armenia, as far as we can tell, were wholly untouched. It was only southern France that saw a momentary and extremely limited spread of heterodox ideas of the Christ, tied to a precise historical moment and to Innocent III's amnesty: a negligible phenomenon, a tiny spark that, however, Nogaret was to use to start a forest fire over time.

Thomas and the Wound

Curiously, the area where the heretical contamination was broadest was also the one where the cult of Christ's Shroud was most strongly rooted in the Temple. If the Templars had the opportunity to keep the precious object, it is clear that they wished to keep it for the same reasons that had led Constantine VII to make it the most venerated relic in Constantinople: It was a deadly weapon against the spread of heresies, a far stronger antidote than preachers' sermons or even the fires of the Inquisition. No learned debates could have controlled medieval men, often illiterate but endowed with an intuition we cannot fully understand today. The Cathars said that the Christ had no true human body or blood; once properly unfolded, the sheet of the Shroud shows the tormented body of the Passion just as the Gospels describe it. Above all, one can see blood, a lot of blood, scattered everywhere. Near the tear among the ribs, the flow is indeed of stunning size, and the mind cannot but go back to the words of the Gospels. During the Last Supper, Jesus had said: "This is my blood for the new and everlasting Covenant, poured out for many for the forgiveness of sins."[90]

---

90   Mt 26:27-28.

That outpoured blood was still there for everyone to see, soaked through the linen of the Shroud. It could be seen, touched, kissed. It was the best remedy against all heresies. Two centuries later, Martin Luther would write: "The Cross alone is our theology." It is a sentence distant in time, but it embodies excellently what the Shroud meant for the Templars. One testimony given in the Poitiers trial before the pope seems to show exactly this dynamic: Brother Pons de Brozet, preceptor of Provence, welcomed a young recruit into the Temple in 1288, and after the obligatory liturgy of the admission ceremony, showed him first the face above the altar, then a cross. Then he told him that he should not believe in the Cross but in that Face, because God never died, and made him adore and kiss the Face "as relics are kissed." Pons de Brozet was one of the dignitaries charged with the personal keeping of the Shroud; if we visualize the scene with the Shroud folded in the container-reliquary that only showed the face, then everything starts to make sense: the miraculous image that shows how Jesus was not in the Sepulchre for more than three days, the image that bears the sign of Jonas, that shows the Resurrection. Heretics preached that the man Jesus had died, that that was the natural end of man, and that flesh could not rise again. But a Templar did not have to listen to such false alternative doctrines, must never believe that everything ended with the crucifixion. The crucifixion was only the beginning: The idol, the mysterious image that bore the marks of Resurrection, was proof.[91]

---

91   Archivio Segreto Vaticano, Reg. Aven. 48, f. 441r; Schottmüller, II, p. 29.

Another important fact must be noted. The bloodstains left on the Shroud correspond to dense flows, some of which—especially those of the face, the nail wounds, and the hit to the ribs—came from broken veins and are the remains of a very abundant flow. Today, however, nothing is left of the large, solid coagulations that the linen once bore, as if the stuff had lost, after unknown events, most of that thickened, solidified blood that originally stood in solid masses in relief on the sheet, like the crusts of so many wounds. In Constantinople, dispersed among over 1,000 of the capital's churches, there were many reliquaries claiming to contain a part of the Holy Blood of Jesus, and many of them were taken to Europe by crusaders after the sack of 1204. This vast movement of relics of the Blood intensely excited the imaginative faculties of medieval man, because they were intimately connected with the mystery of the Eucharist. It could have influenced the transformation of the legends of the Holy Grail, which in the most ancient versions is nothing more than a miraculous dish described in some Celtic sagas. However, just in the years that followed the Fourth Crusade, it began to be celebrated as the Cup of the Last Supper, or as the cup in which Joseph of Arimathea was supposed to have collected the blood coming from the side of the crucified Jesus.[92] In any case, these reliquaries of the Blood were small ampoules made of crystal or rock crystal that contained minute amounts of dried blood. Considering their Byzantine origin, everything suggests that this dried blood had been scraped from the crusts once present on the Shroud; in that sense, those relics

---

92 About the legend's development, see Scavone, *British King Lucius,* pp. 101-142; Loomis, *The Grail,* pp. 165-248.

were true, that is, they contained the blood from an object believed to be the True Shroud of Christ, certified by the authority of the emperor of Constantinople. If that was the case, it is not surprising to hear that people spent astronomical sums to have them.[93]

If the Order of the Temple suffered a certain contamination of heretics, it is not strange that it should think of gaining a powerful antidote of faith to fight its war in a quiet, private, invisible way. The Order's high dignitaries carried out delicate diplomatic missions for the emperors of Byzantium, and they knew the imperial palace of Constantinople, with its hall of wonders, well. Concerned about the spread of Cathar thought, which had shot through a large part of Christian society and the Catholic Church, the Order of the Temple thought that the disbelief of some of its own members could be cured in the simple, effective way that had once conquered St. Thomas. The apostle had declared that he would not believe Jesus had risen from the dead until he had first seen and touched the open wound in his side; so too, Templars fallen into doubt would have been saved by the ability to see with their own eyes the signs of Christ's humanity imprinted on that amazing relic. To see and also to touch, as according to the sources the Templars used to worship the Shroud with a liturgy that included kissing the wounds on the feet.[94]

In light of these thoughts, it no longer seems so strange that the investigators who led the Languedoc Inquiry came down so hard on issues of heresy and sorcery,

---

93 Riant, *Exuviae*, for example X, 48, 61, 96, 107, 113, 124, 149, etc.

94 Paris, Archives Nationales, J 413 n. 25, unnumbered folios (f. 9); Finke, II, pp. 323-324.

in such an excessive way as to have no comparison elsewhere: Maybe in those territories, there had been whispers of scandal, hearsay, or even only unorthodox behaviors that had roused a shadow of suspicion. Even if it had been only one case or two, one or two cases would have been enough in that territory.

It is curious that many modern believers tend to look on the Shroud of Turin as evidence that Jesus actually did rise; the Templars, on the other hand, if they kept it at all as the evidence suggests, sought in it an utterly different truth. That Jesus had risen they had never doubted; what they needed was the evidence that the Christ had indeed died. The Templar leaders' choice to keep the existence and cult of the Shroud secret proved in time a tragic mistake. Although it is unfair to write history from the point of view of 20/20 hindsight and to start imagining what might have happened if-if-if, some facts are absolutely evident: The Shroud's identity and its charisma were more than enough to protect the Order of the Temple from any attempt to charge them with crimes against religion. Had the world known with certainty what the mysterious Templar idol really was, had they seen it and seen the veneration with which it was treated, the black legend of Baphomet would never have been born and all of Philip the Fair's other charges would have shrunk to the level of backstairs courtier chit-chat.

At present, the sources we have do not allow us to understand when exactly the Shroud came into the Temple's possession, and when it left it to pass to other guardians: The one thing we do know is that it stayed within the Order for some time and that it left indelible traces on its spirituality. Some authors, such as Dubarle, Zaccone, Raffard de Brienne, and Alessandro Piana, believe that after the Sack of Constantinople the sheet passed directly into the hands of the house of La Roche, and I also share this idea as far as the available sources are concerned; historian Willy Müller, on the other hand, believes that the Shroud was kept in Germany for some time and had something to do with Emperor Frederick II, and on his side it must be said that the Shroud's face has left very clear traces on the German Templar tradition, which placed it on the verso of the seal of the preceptors of Germany. All these reconstructions cannot really be said to contradict each other; they are only the distinct stages in a long journey of which, in the end, we still know very little.[95]

In fact, the history of the Shroud remains open to hypotheses until the mid-14th century, when it became the object of so many written accounts as to leave no space for doubt; for the previous centuries, Ian Wilson's reconstruction is indubitably the one that shows the highest degree of likelihood and probability. At any rate, whether or not it was the same as the celebrated *mandylion*, the presence of the Shroud in the imperial collection in Constantinople is certified by various sources. In 1200–1201, the city was in chaos due to the coup that had overthrown Emperor Isaac II Angelos; a riot shook the imperial palace, and the custodian of relics, the historian Nicholas Mesarites, had to face down the rioters to prevent the profanation of the chapel of Pharos. He managed to calm the soldiers

---

95 Raffard de Brienne, *Les duc d'Athènes et le Linceul*, pp. 171-176; Dubarle, *Le Linceul de Turín*, pp. 173-176; Zaccone, *Le manuscrit 826*, pp. 214-216. Müller, *Festliche Begegnungen*, I, pp. 2-241.

down by appealing to the extreme sacredness of the place: The objects collected within made up a new Jerusalem, something that kept the earth in touch with the heavens, and had to stay outside any political issue. Nicholas describes the Shroud unmistakably as a funeral sheet on which the image of Jesus was imprinted as a shape without border lines. "It is made of linen, a humble and simple material, and still has the smell of myrrh. It cannot perish, because it covered the dead body, with ill-defined borders, naked, covered with myrrh after the Passion."[96]

That the linen could still carry the smell of funeral perfumes in the 12th century is not as surprising as it sounds: In the 1500s, some excavations in Rome opened up imperial-age graves, more than 1,000 years old, and found several mummified corpses. The excavators' accounts remark on the clearly perceivable smell of funeral perfumes.[97]

That was the last description of the Shroud in the imperial chapel at Byzantium.

---

96   Nikolaos Mesarites, *Die Palast-revolution*, p. 30, cit. in Wilson, *Holy Faces*, pp. 154-155, note 30.

97   Chioffi, *Mummificazione e imbalsamazione*, p. 63.

Abbreviations for Series and Periodicals

AC   Archaeological Chemistry, American Chemical Society Symposium Series

AOL   *Archives de l'Orient Latin*

Apocripha   *Apocrypha. Revue Internationale des Littératures Apocryphes*

ARAL   *Atti della Reale Accademia Lucchese*

BAR   Biblical Archaeology Review

BCIELT   *Bulletin du Centre International d'Études sur le Linceul de Turin*

BÉFAR   *Bibliothèque de l'École Française d'Athènes et de Rome*

Bib   *Biblica*

Bible   *La Bibbia.* Latest version from the original texts, with introductions and notes from. A. Ghirlanda, P. Gironi, F. Pasquero, G. Ravasi, P. Rossano, and S. Virgulin; Cinisello Balsamo 1987 [Translator's note: Biblical passages have been copied from the King James Version]

Bib Sacr   *Biblioteca Sacra*

Biblio   *Bibliologia*

BS   *Bibliotheca Sanctorum,* ed. F. Caraffa, 12 vols., Rome 1961–1969, fourth reprint 1998

CA   *Cahiers Archéologiques*

CA.AMA   *Cahiers Archéologiques. Fouilles de l'Antiquité et Moyen Age*

Catholicisme	*Catholicisme hier, aujourd'hui, demain,* edited by G. Jacquemet, 7 vol. I, Paris 1948–2000
CAV	*Collectanea Archivi Vaticani*
CdF	*Cahiers de Fanjeaux*
CHR	Catholic Historical Review
Co	*Credere oggi*
DACL	*Dictionnaire d'Archéologie chrétienne et de Liturgie,* published under F. Cabrol, volume VI, Paris 1822
DBE	*Deutsche Biographische Enzyklopädie*
DDC	*Dictionnaire de droit canonique,* published under R. Naz, volume 7, Paris 1935–1965
DEB	*Dizionario Enciclopedico della Bibbia,* published under R. Penna, Rome 2000
DHGÉ	*Dictionnaire d'histoire et de géografie écclesiastique,* published under A. Baudrillart, vol. I–XXVIII, Paris 1912–2003
DIP	*Dizionario degli Istituti di Perfezione,* published under G. Pelliccia and G. Rocca, vol. 10, Rome 1974–2003
DS	*Dictionnaire de spiritualité ascétique et de mystique: doctrine et histoire,* published under M. Viller, vol. 17, Paris 1937–1994
DTC	*Dictionnaire de Théologie Catholique,* published under A. Vacant, E. Mangenot, and E. Amann, Paris 1923–1940
EAM	*Enciclopedia dell'Arte Medievale,* Istituto della Enciclopedia Italiana, Rome 1991–2002

	EC : Enciclopedia Cattolica, published under P. Paschini, 12 volumes, Firenze 1948–1954.
	EP : Enciclopedia dei Papi, edited by the Istituto dell'Enciclopedia Italiana, 3 volumes, Rome 2000
Finke	Finke, H., *Papsttum und Untergang des Templerordens,* 2 vol., Münster 1907
GEIB	*Grande Enciclopedia illustrata della Bibbia,* Casale Monferrato 1997
GLNT	*Grande Lessico del Nuovo Testamento,* Italian edition by F. Montagnini, G. Scarpat and O. Soffritti, 11 volumes, Brescia 1977
GLS	*Il Grande Libro dei Santi,* encyclopedic dictionary directed by C. Leonardi, A. Riccardi and G. Zarri, edited by E. Guerriero and D. Tuniz, 3 volumes, Cinisello Balsamo 1998
HTR	*Harvard Theological Review*
IEJ	*Israel Exploration Journal*
JE	*The Jewish Encyclopedia,* directed by I. Singer, 2 vols., London 1901–1906
JMH	*The Journal of Medieval History*
JSNT	*Journal for the Study of the New Testament*
JTS	*Journal of Theological Studies*
LM	*Le Muséon*
LTK	*Lexikon für Theologie und Kirche,* founded by M. Buchberger, Freiburg 1993–2001
MÉFR	*Mélanges de l'École Française de Rome*
MSR	*Mélanges de science religieuse*

Nestle-Aland	*Vangeli e Atti degli apostoli. Greco, latino, italiano, testo greco di Nestle-Aland, traduzione interlineare di A. Bigarelli, testo latino della Vulgata Clementina, testo italiano della Nuovissima versione della Bibbia, a cura di P. Beretta, Cinisello Balsamo 2005.* [Translator's note: Greek, Vulgate Latin and Italian versions of the Gospels]
NIMPR	Nuclear Instruments and Methods in Physics Research B
NTS	New Testament Studies
ÖAW	*Österreichische Akademie des Wissenschaftes*
OE	Optical engineering
OM	Written in honor of Orsolina Montevecchi, edited by E. Bresciani, G. Geraci, S. Pernigotti and G. Susini, Bologna 1981
Op. Epigr.	*Opuscula Epigraphica*
PEQ	Palestine Exploration Quarterly
PG	*Patrologia Graeca*
PL	*Patrologia Latina*
RA	*Recherches Augustiniennes*
RB	*Revue Biblique*
RÉB	*Revue des Études Bibliques*
RÉJ	*Revue des Études Juives*
RFIC	*Rivista di filologia e di istruzione classica*
RHR	*Revue de l'Histoire des Religions*
RILT	*Revue Internationale du Linceul de Turin*
Riv Bib	*Rivista Biblica*

RJK	*Römische Jahrbuch für Kunstgeschichte*
RQ	*Revue de Qumran*
RSLR	*Rivista di storia e di letteratura religiosa*
RSR	*Recherches de Sciences Religieuses*
SBE	*Studia Biblica et Ecclesiastica*
SBF	*Studium Biblicum Franciscanum*
Schottmüller	Schottmüller K., *Der Untergang des Templerordens*, 2 vols., Berlin 1887
SDB	*Supplément au dictionnaire de la Bible*
SDHI	*Studia et documenta historiae et iuris*
SEG	*Supplementum Epigraphicum Graecum*
SM	*Studia Monastica*
SP	*Studia Patavina*
SRDT	*Supplemento alla Rivista Diocesana Torinese*
SSI	Shroud Spectrum International
ST	*Studi e testi*
VC	*Vetera Christianorum*
ZKG	*Zeitschrift für Kirchengeschichte*

Sources and Bibliography

Acta Polycarpi, in PG 5, columns. 1029–1046, see col. 1043.

Adler, A., *Updating Recent Studies on the Shroud of Turin*, in "AC," 625 (1996), pp. 223–228.

—*Concerning the Side Strip of the Shroud of Turin*, in ΑΧΕΙΡΟΠΟΙΗΤΟΣ, pp. 103–111.

—*Aspetti chimico-fisici delle immagini della Sindone*, in *Sindone. Cento anni di ricerca*, pp. 165–184.

Aguirre Monasterio, R. and Rodríguez Carmona, A., *Vangeli sinottici e Atti degli Apostoli*, ed. it. a cura di A. Zani, Brescia (*Introduzione allo studio della Bibbia*, 6) 1995.

Albright, W. F., *L'archéologie de la Palestine*, Paris 1956.

Alonso, M., *Approches et méthodologies de décryptage du Suaire*, in Nouveaux regards, pp. 23–33.

Amarelli, F. and Lucrezi, F., *Il processo contro Gesù*, Natpoli (*Quaestiones*, 2) 1999.

Anne Comnène, *Alexiade* (Règne de l'empereur Alexis I Comnène. 1081–1118), ed. B. Leib, 3 voll., Paris (*Collection Byzantine*) 1937–1945.

Anselme de la Vierge Marie, *Histoire génealogique et chronologique de la Maison Royale de France, des Pairs, Grands Officiers de la Couronne et Royaume*, vol. IX, Paris 1726–1733.

Apocrifi dell'Antico testamento, ed. P. Sacchi with the help of F. Franco, L. Fusella, A. Loprieno, F. Pennacchietti e L. Rosso Uhigli, Turin 1981.

Apogeo del papato ed espansione della cristianità (1054–1274),
in *Storia del cristianesimo. Religione politica cultura*,
vol. V, ed. A. Vauchez, Rome 1997.

L'arte paleocristiana. Visione e spazio dalle origini a Bisanzio, ed. M.A. Crippa and M. Zibawi, Milano 1998.

Aubert, R., *Jérusalem*, in DHGÉ, vol. XXVII, Paris 1999, coll. 1074–1090.

Auzépy, M.F., *L'iconodulie: defense de l'image ou de la dévotion a l'image?*, in *Nicée II*, pp. 157–165.

ΑΧΕΙΡΟΠΟΙΗΤΟΣ-Acheiropoietos. "Non fait de main

d'homme," Actes du IIIème Symposium scientifique
international du Ciélt, Nice, 12–13 mai 1997, Paris 1998.

Bacci, M., *Relics of the Pharos Chapel: A View from the Latin West*, in *Eastern Christian Relics*, pp. 234–246.

Bacher, W., *Hillel*, in JE, vol. VI, pp. 397–400.

Bagatti, B., *Palestina*, in EC, vol. IX, coll. 611–626.

—*Alle origini della Chiesa. I: La comunità giudaico-cristiana*, Città del Vaticano 1981.

Bagatti, B. and Testa, E., *Il Golgota e la Croce. Ricerche storicoarcheologiche*, Jerusalem 1978.

Baima Bollone, P., *La presenza della mirra, dell'aloe e del sangue sulla sindone*, in *La sindone. Scienza e fede*, pp. 169–174.

—*Ulteriori ricerche sul gruppo delle tracce di sangue umano sulla Sindone*, "Sindon", 33 (dic. 1984), pp. 9–13.

—*Sindone o no*, Turin 1990.

—*Gli ultimi giorni di Gesù*, Milano 1999.

—*Sindone e scienza all'inizio del terzo millennio*, Turin 2000.

Baima Bollone, P. and Coppini, L., *Rilievi anatomici per la valutazione delle lesioni da corona di spine*, in *La sindone. Scienza e fede*, pp. 179–193.

Baima Bollone, P. and Gaglio, A., *Applicazioni di tecniche immunoenzimatiche ai prelievi della Sindone: la dimostrazione di elementi epidermici*, in *La Sindone, nuovi studi e ricerche, Atti del III Congresso Nazionale di studi sulla Sindone, Trani 1984*, Cinisello Balsamo 1986, pp. 169–174.

Baima Bollone, P., Jorio, M. and Massaro, A.L., *La dimostrazione della presenza di sangue umano sulla Sindone*, in "Sindon", XXIII (1981), 30, 5.

—*La determinazione del gruppo di sangue identificato sulla sindone*, in *La sindone. Scienza e fede*, pp. 175–178.

Balossino, N., *L'immagine della Sindone*, Turin 1997.

—*Vent'anni di elaborazione dell'Immagine della Sindone mediante computer*, in *AXEIPOΠOIHTOΣ*, pp. 225–230.

Balzanò, A., *Il cristianesimo nelle leggi di Rome imperiale*, Milano 1996.

Baphometica. Quelques aperçus sur l'ésotérisme du Graal et de l'Ordre du Temple, par *A. de Dánann*, Milano 2005.

Barbaglio, G., *Gesù ha affermato di essere Messia?*, in *Gesù e i messia di Israele*, pp. 107–120.

Barber, M. C., *James de Molay, the Last Grand Master of the Temple*, in SM, XIV (1972), pp. 91–124.

—*The Trial of the Templars*, Cambridge 1978.

—*The Templars and the Turin Shroud*, in CHR, 68 (1982).

—*The New Knighthood. A History of the Order of the Temple*, Cambridge University Press 1994.

Barberis, B. and Savarino, P., *Sindone, radiodatazione e calcolo delle probabilità*, Turin 1997.

Barbero, A., *L'aristocrazia nella società francese del medioevo. Analisi delle fonti letterarie (secoli XI–XIII)*, Bologna 1987.

Bazelaire, E. de, Alonso, M., and Castex, T., *Nouvelle interprétation de l'image du Linceul de Turin è la lumière du codex Pray*, in RICT, 30 (Dec. 2007), pp. 8–27.

Becamel, M., *Le catharisme dans le diocèse d'Albi*, in *Cathares en Languedoc*, pp. 237–251.

Beckwith, J., *Early Christian and Byzantine Art*, in *Pelican History of Art*, London 1970.

Belting, H., *Il culto delle immagini. Storia dell'icona dall'età imperiale al tardo medioevo*, it. trans. B. Maj, Rome 2004.

Benvenuti, A., *Reliquie e soprannaturale al tempo delle crociate*, in *Le crociate*, pp. 355–361.

Berkovits, I., *Illuminierte Handschriften aus Ungarn vom 11.–16.Jahrhundert*, Budapest 1968.

Bernard Gui et son monde, in CdF 16, Toulouse 1981.

Berre, L., *Via Crucis*, in *Dizionario Ecclesiastico*, chief editors A. Mercati and A. Pelzer, III, Turin 1958, pp. 1310–1311.

Bersolt, J.E., *Sanctuaires de Byzance. Recherches sur les anciens trésors des églises de Constantinople*, Paris 1921.

Bini, T., *Dei Tempieri e del loro processo in Toscana*, in ARAL, XIII (1845), pp. 400–506.

Blanc, C., *Le Commentaire d'Héracléon sur Jean 4 et 8*, in *Augustinianum*, 15 (1975), pp. 81–124.

Blinzer, J., *Il processo di Gesù*, it.trans. M. A. Colao Pellizzari, Brescia 1966.

Bottini, G. C., *Introduzione all'opera di Luca. Aspetti teologici,*

Jerusalem 1992.

Brandone, A., *L'analisi per attivazione neutronica di fibre tessili prelevate dalla sindone di Torino*, in *La Sindone. Scienza e fede*, pp. 293–298.

Brandys, M., Via Crucis, in EC, vol. XII, coll. 1348–1350.

Braunn, J., *Die Reliquiare des Christlichen Kultes und Ihre Entwicklung*, Freiburg im Breisgau 1940.

Brezzi, P., *Catari*, in EC, vol. III, coll. 1087–1090.

Brown, R. E., *La morte del Messia. Un commentario ai Racconti della Passione nei quattro Vangeli*, Brescia (*Biblioteca di Teologia contemporanea*, 108) 2003.

—*Giovanni. Commento al vangelo spirituale*, it. trans. A. Sorsajas and M. T. Petrozzi, Assisi 2005.

Buchler, A., *L'enterrement des criminels d'après le Talmud et le Midrash*, in RÉJ, 46 (1903), pp. 74–88.

Buchon, J. A., *Histoire de la domination franque dans l'empire grec*, 2 voll., Paris 1881.

Bugnini, A., *La croce nella liturgia*, in EC, vol. IV, Vatican City 1950, coll. 960–963.

Bulst-Thiele, M.L., *Sacrae Domus Militiae Templi Hyerosolimitani Magistri*, Göttingen 1974.

Bultmann, R., *Cristianesimo primitivo e religioni antiche*, it. trans. P. Severi, Genova 2005.

Calderone, S., *Costantinopoli: la seconda Roma*, in *Storia di Roma*, III, Turin 1993, pp. 723–749.

Camelot, P. Th., *Ophites*, in *Catholicisme*, vol. X, coll. 100–101.

Capitani, O., *Gregorio VII*, in EP, vol. II, pp. 188–212.

Caravita, R., *Rinaldo da Concorezzo, arcivescovo di Ravenna (1303–1321) al tempo di Dante*, Firenze 1964.

Cardini, F., *Alle radici della cavalleria medievale*, Florence 1981.

—*Francesco d'Assisi*, Milan 1991.

—*I poveri commilitoni del Cristo. Bernardo di Clairvaux e la fondazione dell'ordine templare*, Rimini 1992.

—*Il pellegrinaggio. Una dimensione della vita medievale*, Manziana 1996.

Cardona, G. R., Storia universale della scrittura, Milan 1986.

Carile, A., *Per una storia dell'impero latino di Costantinopoli (1204–1261)*, Bologna 1978.

—*Potere e simbologia del potere nella nuova Roma*, in *Comunicare e significare nell'Alto Medioevo, LII settimana di studio del Centro di studi sull'Alto Medioevo di Spoleto, Spoleto, 15–20 aprile 2004*, 2 voll., Spoleto 2005, vol. I, pp. 395–440.

Carriére, V., *Histoire et cartulaire des Templiers de Provins, avec une introduction sur les débuts du Temple en France*, Paris 1919.

Casalegno, A., *Le opinioni degli anonimi circa l'identità messianica di Gesù nel Vangelo di Giovanni*, in *Gesù e i messia di Israele*, pp. 159–173.

Casey, P. M., *Idiom and Translation: Some Aspects of the Son of Man Problem*, in NTS, 41 (1995), pp. 164–182.

Cathares en Languedoc in CdF, 3 (1968).

Cavalcanti, C., *Croce*, in EAM, vol. V, pp. 529–535.

Cencetti, G., *Lineamenti di storia della scrittura latina*, reprint edited by G. Guerrini Ferri, Bologna 1997.

Cerrini, S., *Une expérience neuve au sein de la spiritualité médiévale: l'ordre du Temple (1120–1314). Etude et édition des règles latine et française, Thèse de doctorat sous la direction de Mme G. Hasenohr, Université de Paris-Sorbonne* (Paris IV) 1997.

—*La rivoluzione dei Templari. Una storia perduta del dodicesimo secolo*, Milano 2008.

Chiffoleau, J., *Vie et mort de l'hérésie en Provence et dans la vallée du Rhône du début du XIIIe au début du XIVe s.*, in *Cathares en Languedoc*, pp. 73–99.

Chioffi, L., *Mummificazione e imbalsamazione a Roma ed in altri luoghi del mondo romano*, in Op. Epigr., 8 (1998), pp. 8–95.

Cirillo, L., *Correnti giudeo-cristiane*, in *Il nuovo popolo*, pp. 265–316.

Claverie, P. V., *Un «illustris amicus Venetorum» du début du XIIIe siècle: l'évêque Nivelon de Quierzy et son temps*, in *Quarta crociata*, vol. I, pp. 485–523.

Clemente Alessandrino, *Stromata*, in PG 8, coll. 685–1382 e coll. 9–602.

Coarelli, F., *L'ellenismo e la civiltà di Roma*, Milano 1970.

Collin de Plancy, J. A. C., *Dictionnaire critique des reliques et des images miraculeuses*, Paris 1821–1822.

Collins, J. J., *The Son of Man in First-Century Judaism*, in NTS, 38 (1992), pp. 448–466.

—*The Scepter and the Star. The Messiahs in the Dead Sea Scrolls and Other Ancient Literature*, New York-London-Toronto 1996.

Combes, L., *Études sur les sources de la Passion. La vraie Croix perdue et retrouvée, recherche historique*, Paris 1902.

Les Conciles OEcuméniques. Les Décrets, 2 voll., Paris 1994.

Coppens, J., *Le messianisme et sa relève prophétique. Les anticipations vétérotestamentaires. Leur accomplissement en Jésus*, Leuven 1989.

Coppini, L., *Le lesioni da punta e il colpo di lancia visibili sulla Sindone. Rilievi di anatomia topografica e radiologica*, in *La sindone. Indagini scientifiche*, a cura di S. Rodante, Turin 1988, pp. 74–91.

Coste, J., *Boniface VIII en procès, publication de l'École Française à Rome*, 1995.

Coüasnon, Ch., *Le Golgotha. Maquette du sol naturel*, in BTS, 149 (1973), pp. 10–15.

—*La fouille d'août 1974 à l'Anastasis de Jérusalem, Atti del IX Congresso Internazionale di Archeologia Cristiana*, Vatican City, 1978, II, pp. 163–166.

Couilleau, G., *Esseni*, in DIP, vol. III, Rome 1976, coll. 1318–1323.

Cox, H., *Rabbi Yeshua Ben Yoseph: Reflections on Jesus' Jewishness and the Interfaith Dialogue*, in *Jesus' Jewishness*, pp. 27–62.

Craig, W. L., *The Historicity of the Empty Tomb of Jesus*, in "NTS," 31 (1985), pp. 39–67.

Crippa, M. A. and Zibawi, M., *L'arte paleocristiana. Visione e spazio dalle origini a Bisanzio*, Milan 1998.

Le crociate. L'Oriente e l'Occidente da Urbano II a san Luigi (1096–1270), catalogo della mostra, Rome, Palazzo Venezia, 14 febbraio-30 aprile 1997, ed. M. Rey-Delqué, Rome 1997.

Currer-Briggs, N., *The Shroud and the Grail*, New York 1987.

Curto, S., *La Sindone di Torino: osservazioni archeologiche circa il tessuto e l'immagine*, in *La S. Sindone*, pp. 59–85.

Curzon, H., *La Règle du Temple*, Société de l'Histoire de France, Paris 1886.

—*La maison du Temple à Paris*, Paris 1888.

Dagron, G., *Naissance d'une capitale. Constantinople et ses institutions de 330 à 451*, Paris 1974.

D'Albon, G., *Cartulaire général de l'Ordre du Temple*, voll. II, Paris 1913–1922.

Dalla Riforma della Chiesa alla Riforma protestante (1450–1530), in *Storia del cristianesimo. Religione-politica-cultura*, vol. VII, ed. M. Venard, Italian ed. M. Marcocchi, Rome 2001.

D'Amato, A., Sacconi, *Raniero*, in EC, vol. X, coll. 1530–1531.

Da Milano, I., *Albigesi*, in EC, vol. I, coll. 708–712.

Danielou, J., *Les symboles chrétiens primitifs*, Paris 1961.

Daniel-Rops, H., *La vita quotidiana in Palestina al tempo di Gesù*, Cles 1986.

Danin, A., *Pressed Flowers*, Eretz Magazine, nov.-dic. 1997, pp. 35–37 e 69.

De Ambroggi, P., *Anna*, in EC, vol. I, col. 1362.

De Bazelaire, E. and Alonso, M., *Réflexions sur l'encodage de l'image et propositions de recherches à effectuer*, in *AXEIPO.OIHTOS*, pp. 7–11.

De Bazelaire, E., Alonso, M. e Castex, Th., *Nouvelle interprétation de l'image du Linceul de Turin à la lumière du codex Pray*, in "RILT", 30 (December 2007), pp. 8–25.

De Fraine, J. and Haudebert, P., *Crocifissione*, in DEB, p. 379.

De Fraine, J. and Saulnier, C., *Sadducei*, in DEB, pp. 1144–1145.

De Francovich, G., *L'origine e la diffusione del crocifisso gotico doloroso*, in "RJK", 2 (1938), pp. 143–261.

Defremery, C. F., *Mémoires d'Histoire Orientale*, Paris 1862.

Delaville Le Roulx, J., *Documents concernant les Templiers extraits des Archives de Malte*, Paris 1882.

—*Un nouveau Manuscrit de la Règle du Temple* in "*Annuaire-Bulletin de la Société de l'Histoire de France*", 26 (2), 1889.

Delisle, L., "*Mémoire sur les opérations financières des*

Templiers, in *"Mémoires de l'Académie des Inscriptions et Belles-Lettres"*, t. XXXIII, IIe pars, 1889.

Demurger, A., *Vita e morte dell'ordine dei Templari*, It.trans. M. Sozzi, Milan 1987.

—*Trésor des templiers, trésor du roi. Mise au point sur les opérations financières des templiers*, in *"Pouvoir et Gestion"*, 5 (1997), pp. 73–85.

—*Chevaliers du Christ. Les ordres religieux-militaires au Moyen Âge (XIe-XVIe siècle)*, Paris 2002.

—*Jacques de Molay. Le crépuscule des templiers*, Paris 2002.

De Saint-Laurent, G., *Iconographie de la croix et du crucifix*, in *"AA"*, 26 (1869), pp. 4–25.

De Vaux, R., *Histoire ancienne d'Israël*, I, Paris 1971.

—*L'archéologie et les manuscrits de la mer Morte*, London 1976.

Di Fazio, L., *Lombardi e Templari nella realtà socio-economia durante il regno di Filippo il Bello, 1285–1314*, Milano 1986.

Di Fonzo, L., *Bogomili*, in EC, vol. II, coll. 1759–1760.

Dizionario degli Istituti di perfezione, ed. G. Pelliccia and G. Rocca, vol. IX, Rome 1974–1997.

Dobschütz, E. von, *Christusbilder. Untersuchungen zur christlichen Legende*, Leipzig 1899.

—*Joseph von Arimathia*, in ZKG, 23 (1902), pp. 1–17.

Dölger, F.J., T.C. II: *Der heilige Fisch in den Antiken Religionen und in Christentum*, Münster 1922.

Doré, D., *Apocrifi del Nuovo Testamento*, in DEB, pp. 164–171.

Dossat, Y., *Les cathares dans les documents de l'Inquisition*, in *Cathares en Languedoc*, pp. 71–104.

Dubarle, A. M., *Storia antica della Sindone di Torino,* Rome, 1989.

—*Le Linceul de Turín passe incognito par la Sainte Chapelle*, in *ΑΧΕΙΡΟΠΟΙΗΤΟΣ*, pp. 173–176.

—*L'homélie de Grégoire le Référendaire pour la réception de l'image d'Édesse*, in *Révue des Études Byzantines*, 55 (1997), pp. 5–51.

Dubois, J. D., *Valentin, école valentinienne*, in *Dictionnaire de spiritualité ascétique et mystique, doctrine et histoire*, vol.XVI, Paris 1994, coll. 146–156.

Du Buit, M., *Archéologie du Peuple d'Israël*, Paris 1958.

Ducellier, A., *Le drame de Bysance*, 1976, it. trans.
A. Masturzo, Naples 1980.

—*Il sacco di Costantinopoli del 1204 e la posterità*, in *Le crociate*, pp. 368–377.

Ducellier, A. and Kaplan, M., *L'Impero cristiano compimento dell'Impero Romano, in Bisanzio*, ed. A. Ducellier, Turin 1988, pp. 21–53.

Duchesne, A., *Historiae Francorum scriptores coaetanei*, 5 voll., Lutatiae Parisiorum 1636–1649, t. V, pp. 390–391.

Dufournet, J., *Villehardouin et les Champenois dans la quatrième croisade, in Les Champenois et la croisade. Actes des 4e journée rémoises (27–28 novembre 1987)*, Paris 1989, pp. 55–59.

Du Fresne Du Cange, C., *Glossarium mediae et infimae latinitatis*, Graz 1954.

Dukan, M., *La Bible Hébraïque. Les codices copiés en Orient et dans la zone séfarade avant 1280*, in *Biblio*, 22 (2006).

Dulaey, M., *I simboli cristiani. Catechesi e Bibbia (I–VI secolo)*, Cinisello Balsamo 2004.

Dunn, J.D.G., *Jesus-Flesh and Spirit. An Exposition of Romans 1:3–4*, in JTS, 24 (1973), pp. 40–68.

Dupont-Sommer, A., *Un hymne syriaque sur la cathédrale d'Édesse*, in CA, 2 (1947), pp. 29–39.

Dupuy, P., *Histoire de l'Ordre Militaire des Templiers*, Bruxelles 1751.

Durand, J., *Reliquie e reliquiari depredati in Oriente e a Bisanzio al tempo delle crociate*, in *Le crociate*, pp. 378–389

Durante Mangoni, M. B., *La polemica contro i giudei nel Vangelo di Matteo*, in *Giudei e cristiani*, pp. 127–161.

Duvernoy, J., Le catharisme en Languedoc au début du XIVe siècle, in *Cathares en Languedoc*, pp. 27–56.

Dyonisii Sandelli seu P. Vincentii Fassinii *De Singularibus Eucharistiae usibus apud Graecos commentarius*, Vindobonae 1776.

Eastern Christian Relics, ed. A. Lidov, Moscow 2003.

Edbury, P., *The Templars in Cyprus*, in *The Military Orders*, I, pp. 189–195.

Efod, in GEIB, vol. III, p. 453 (collective entry).

Egeria, *Diario di viaggio*, ed and comm. E. Giannarelli (intro. A. Clerici), Milan 2006.

Eisenman, R. H. and Wise, M., *Manoscritti segreti di Qumran*, It.ed E. Jucci, Casale Monferrato 1994.

Emmanuel, M., *The Holy Mandylion in the Iconographic Programmes of the Churches at Mystras*, in *Eastern christian Relics*, pp. 291–304.

Epiphanius of Salamis, *Letter to Bishop John of Jerusalem*, PG 43, coll. 390–391.

Eshel, H. and Greenhut, Z., *IAM EL-SAGHA, a Cemetery of the Qumran Type, Judaean Desert*, in RB, 100/2 (1993), pp. 252–259.

Evagrius Scholasticus, *Historia ecclesiastica*, IV, 27, in PG 86, coll.2415–2866.

Fabbrini, B., *La deposizione di Gesù nel sepolcro e il problema del divieto di sepoltura per i condannati*, in SDHI, 61 (1995), to the memory of G. Lombardi, pp. 97–178.

Fanti, G., *A Proposal for High Resolution Colorimetric Mapping of the Turin Shroud*, in *AXEIPO.OIHTOS*, pp. 39–43.

Fanti, G. and Marinelli, E., *Cento prove sulla sindone. Un giudizio probabilistico sull'autenticità*, Padova 1999.

Farina, R., *L'Impero e l'imperatore cristiano in Eusebio di Cesarea. La prima teologia politica del Cristianesimo*, Zürich (*Bibliotheca theologica salesiana. Fontes*, 2) 1966.

Favier, J., *Philippe le Bel*, Paris 1978.

Favreau-Lilie, M. L., *The Military Orders and the Escape of the Christian Population from the Holy Land in 1291*, in JMH, 19 (1993), n. 3, pp. 201–227.

Fedalto, G., *La Chiesa latina in Oriente*, 3 voll., San Giovanni Lupatoto (VA) (*Studi religiosi*, 5) 1981.

Fedou, M., *La vision de la Croix dans l'oeuvre de S. Justin "philosophe et martyr"*, in «RA», 19 (1984), pp. 29–110.

Filoramo, G., *La gnosi ieri e oggi*, in *Gnosi e vangeli gnostici*, pp. 21–35.

Flamant, J. and Pietri, Ch., *La dissoluzione del sistema costantiniano: Giuliano l'Apostata (361–363)*, in *La nascita di una cristianità*, pp. 325–340.

Flori, J., *Culture chevaleresque et quatrième croisade: quelques réflexions sur les motivations des croisés*, in *Quarta crociata*, vol. I, pp. 370–387.

Flury-Lemberg, M., *Sindone 2002. L'intervento conservativo. Preservation. Konservierung*, Turin 2003.

Focant, C., *Pubblicano*, in DEB, pp. 1376–1377.

—*Zeloti*, in DEB, p. 1072.

Foerster, W., *μs...*, in GLNT, coll. 909–934.

Forcellini, N., *Lexicon totius latinitatis*, Patavii 1940.

Fraisse-Coué, C., *Il dibattito teologico nell'età di Teodosio II: Nestorio*, in *La nascita di una cristianità*, pp. 468–518.

Frale, B., *L'ultima battaglia dei Templari. Dal codice ombra d'obbedienza militare alla costruzione del processo per eresia*, Rome 2001.

—*Il papato e il processo ai Templari. L'inedita assoluzione di Chinon alla luce della diplomatica pontificia*, Rome 2003.

—*The Chinon Chart. Papal Absolution to the Last Templar Master Jacques de Molay*, in JMH, 30 (2004), pp. 109–134.

—*I Templari*, Bologna 2004.

—*Du catharisme à la sorcellerie: les inquisiteurs du Midi dans le procès des Templiers*, in CdF, 41 (2006), pp. 169–186.

—*L'interrogatorio ai Templari nella diocesi di Bernardo Gui: un'ipotesi per il frammento del Registro Avignonese 305*, in *Dall'Archivio Segreto Vaticano. Miscellanea di testi, saggi e inventari*, vol. I, Vatican City (CAV, 61) 2006, pp. 199-272.

—*La quarta crociata e il ruolo dei Templari nei progetti di Innocenzo III*, in *Quarta crociata*, I, pp. 447–484.

Frei, M., *Il passato della sindone alla luce della palinologia*, in *La sindone e la scienza*, pp. 191–200.

—*Identificazione e classificazione dei nuovi pollini della sindone*, in *La sindone, scienza e fede*, pp. 277–284.

Frolow, A., *La Vraie Croix et les expéditions d'Héraclius en Perse*, in RÉB, 11 (1953), pp. 88–105.

—*La relique de la Vraie Croix. Recherches sur le*

développement d'un culte, Paris 1961.

Gadille, J., *Le grandi correnti dottrinali e spirituali nel mondo cattolico*, in *Liberalismo, industrializzazione*, pp. 111–132.

Gaier, C., *Armes et combats dans l'universe médiéval*, in *Bibliothèque du Moyen Age*, 5 (1995).

Gervase of Tilbury, *Otia Imperialia* III, in *Scriptores rerum Brunsvicensium*, Hanover 1707, pp. 966–967.

Gesù e i messia di Israele. Il messianismo giudaico e gli inizi della cristologia, Atti della II giornata di studio sulla storia del cristianesimo, Napoli, 1o dicembre 2005, ed. A. Guida and M. Vitelli, Trapani ("*oí chrístíanoí*", 4) 2006.

Ghiberti, G., *La sepoltura di Gesù*, Rome 1982.

—*Sindone, vangeli e vita cristiana*, Rome 1997.

—*Dalle cose che patì (Eb 5,8). Evangelizzare con la sindone*, Cantalupa (To) 2004.

Géraud, H., *Chronique latine de Guillaume de Nangis, de 1113 à 1300 avec les continuations de cette chronique de 1300 à 1368*, 2 voll., Paris 1843.

Gianotti, G.F. and Pennacini, A., *Società e comunicazione letteraria di Roma antica. III: Storia e testi da Tiberio al V secolo d.C.*, Turin 1986.

Gianotto, C., *Gli scritti di Nag Hammadi e le origini cristiane*, in *Gnosi e vangeli gnostici*, pp. 36–46.

Gillet, H.M., *The Story of the Relics of the Passion*, Oxford 1935.

Gilmour-Bryson, A., *The Trial of the Templars in the Papal States and the Abruzzi*, Vatican City (*Studi e Testi*, 303) 1982.

Giovanni Damascene, *Tractatus de imaginibus*, in PG 94, I, 19; oratio I, pp. 1204–1283; oratio II, pp. 1285–1318; oratio III, pp. 1318–1420.

Giudei e cristiani nel I secolo. Continuità, separazione, polemica, ed. M.B. Durante Mangoni and G. Jossa, Trapani ("oí chrístíanoí", 3; *Nuovi studi sul cristianesimo nella storia / Antichità*, series edited by Sergio Tanzarella) 2006.

Giuseppe Flavio (Flavius Josephus), *Antichità giudaiche*, vol. 2, ed. L. Moraldi, Turin 1998.

Gli apocrifi. L'altra Bibbia che non fu scritta da Dio, ed.

E. Weidinger, Italian ed. E. Jucci, Casale Monferrato 1992.

Gli uomini di Qumran, ed. F. García Martinez and J. Trebolle Barrera, Brescia 1996.

Gnosi e vangeli gnostici, in Co, 159 (may-june 2007).

Godefroy, F., *Dictionnaire de l'ancienne langue française et de tous ses dialectes du IXe au XVe siècle*, Paris 1880.

Goldstein, I., *Zara fra Bisanzio, regno Ungaro-Croato e Venezia*, in *Quarta crociata*, I, pp. 359–370.

Gordillo, M., *Giovanni Damasceno*, in EC, vol. VI, coll. 547–552.

Gordini, G. D. *Giuseppe d'Arimatea*, in BS, vol. VI, coll. 1292–1295.

Gove, H. E. et al., *A Problematic Source of Organic Contamination in Linen*, in NIMPR, 123 (1997), pp. 504–507.

Grabar, A., *Recherches sur les origines juives de l'art paléochrétien*, in "CA.A.MA", 14 (1964), pp. 49–57.

Grässe, J., *Orbis Latinus Lexicon lateinischer geographischer Namen des Mittelalters und der Neuzeit*, 3 voll., Braunschweig 1972.

Gregory the Great, *Epistolae*, lib. IX, indictio II, epist. LII (ad Secundinum), in PL 77, col. 971; Epist. LIV (ad Januarium), in PL, 33, col. 204.

Griffe, E., *Le catharisme dans le diocèse de Carcassonne et le Lauragais au XIIe siècle*, in *Cathares en Languedoc*, pp. 215–236.

Grondijs, L. H., *L'iconographie byzantine du crucifié mort sur la croix*, Bruxelles 1941.

Grossi, V., *Lo gnosticismo e i Padri della Chiesa*, in *Gnosi e vangeli gnostici*, pp. 69–80.

Gualdo, G., *Sussidi per la consultazione dell'Archivio Vaticano*, Vatican City (CAV, 17) 1989.

Guarducci, M., *Epigrafia greca*, vol. 4, Rome 1967–1978.

—*L'epigrafia greca dalle origini al tardo impero*, Rome 1987.

Guerreschi, A. and Salcito, M., *Tra le pieghe di un mistero*, in "*Archeo,*" n. 278 (april 2008), pp 62–71.

Guerriero, E., *Il sigillo di Pietro*, Turin 1996.

Gugumus, J. E. *Orsola e compagne*, in BS, coll. 1252–1267.

Guiraud, J. (ed.), Les Registres d'Urbain IV (1261–1264),

vol. 3, Paris 1901–1906: vol. IV: Tables, Paris 1958.

Hachlili, R., *Ancient Jewish Art and Archaeology in the Land of Israel*, München 1991.
—*Burial practices at Qumran*, in RQ 62 (1993), pp. 245–264.
Hammer-Purgstall, J. von, *Mémoires sur deux coffrets gnostiques du Moyen Âge du Cabinet de M. le Duc de Blacas*, in *Baphometica*, pp. 84–134.
Heers, J., *Il clan familiare nel medioevo. Studi sulle strutture politiche e sociali degli ambienti urbani*, It. Trans. A. Masturzo, Naples 1976.
Hefele, C. J. and Leclercq, H., *Histoire des Conciles*, vol. 5, Paris 1912.
Heller, J. H. and Adler, A. D. *Blood on the Shroud of Turin*, in *Applied Optics*, 19/16 (aug. 1980), pp. 2742–2744.
Hengel, M., *Gli zeloti. Ricerche sul movimento di liberazione giudaico dai tempi di Erode al 70 d.C.*, Brescia 1996.
Henriet, P., *Du nouveau sur l'Inquisition languedocienne*, in *Cathares en Languedoc*, pp. 159–173.
Hiestand, R., *Kardinalbischof Matthäus von Albano, das Konzil von Troyes und die Entstehung des Templerordens*, in ZKG, 99 (1980), pp. 17–37.
Horowitz, S., *Quand les Champenois parlaient le Grec: la Morée franque au XIIIe siècle, un bouillon de culture*, in *Cross Cultural Convergencies in the Crusader Period*, by A. Graboïs, New York 1995.

Le Icone, ed. K. Weitzmann, Milan 1981.
Icone, ed. O. Popova, E. Smirnova, and P. Cortesi, Milan 1995.
L'identification scientifique de l'Homme du Linceul, Jésus de Nazareth, Actes du Symposium Scientifique International, Rome 1993, Paris 1995.
Ignatius of Antioch, *Letter to the Smyrneans*, in PG 5, coll. 839–858.
Introvigne, M., *Il «Codice da Vinci»: fiction, provocazione o realtà storica?*, in *Gnosi e vangeli gnostici*, pp. 116–129.

Jackson, J. P. and Propp, K., *On the Evidence that the Radiocarbon Date of the Turin Shroud Was Significantly*

Affected by the 1532 Fire, in *AXEIPO.OIHTOS*, pp. 61–82.

Jackson, J. P. Jumper, E. J. Mottern, B. and Stevenson, K. E. *The Three Dimension Image on Jesus Burial Cloth, Proceedings of the U.S. Conference on the Shroud of Turin*, Albunquerque 1977.

Jackson, R., *Hasadeen Hakadosh: The Holy Shroud in Hebrew*, in *L'identification*, pp. 27–33.

—*Jewish Burial Procedures at the Time of the Christ*, in *Sudario del Señor*, pp. 309–322.

—*The Shroud of Turin: In Light of First Century Jewish Culture*, in ΑΧΕΙΡΟΠΟΙΗΤΟΣ, pp. 165–169.

Janin, R., *Constantinople byzantine. Développement urbain et répertoire topographique*, Paris 1964.

—*Les églises et les monastères des grands centres byzantins*, Paris 1975.

Janssens, Y., *Héracléon. Commentaire sur l'évangile selon saint Jean*, in LM, 72 (1959), pp. 101–151.

Jászai, G., *Crocifisso*, in EAM, vol. V, pp. 577–586.

Jéglot, C., *Le crucifix*, Paris 1934.

Johannet, J., *Un office inédit en l'honneur du culte des images, oeuvre possible de Théodore Studite*, in *Nicée II*, pp. 143–155.

Johnstone, P., *Byzantine Tradition in Church Embroidery*, London 1967.

Josephus, *The Jewish War*, ed. H. St. J. Thackeray, 2 voll., London 1976–1979.

Jossa, G., *Introduzione. L'idea del Messia al tempo di Gesù. L'orientamento della storiografia contemporanea*, in *Gesù e i messia di Israele*, pp. 15–29.

—*La separazione dei cristiani dai giudei,* in *Giudei e cristiani*, pp. 105–126.

Les Journaux du Trésor de Philippe VI de Valois suivis de l'Ordinarium Thesauri de 1338–1339, by J. Viard, Paris (*Documents inédits sur l'Histoire de France*) 1988.

Jugie, M., *Iconoclastia*, in EC, vol. VI, coll. 1541–1546.

—*Immagini, culto delle*, in EC, vol. X, coll. 1663–1667.

Jung, W., *Nicolai (Christoph) Friedrich*, in DBE, vol. VII, p. 446.

Kaplan, G., *Le Linceul de Turin ent tant que support d'informations*, in *Nouveaux regards*, pp. 19–22.

Kazhdan, A. P., *Bisanzio e la sua civiltà*, It.trans. G. Arcetri, Bari 1995.

Kenyon, K. M., *Jerusalem: Excavating 3.000 Years of History*, London 1967.

Kitzinger, E., *Byzantine Art in the Making. Main Lines of Stylistic Development in Mediterranean Art 3rd–7th Century*, London 1977.

Koch, H. A., *Hammer-Purgstall, Joseph Frh. von*, in DBE, vol. IV, p. 401.

Kohlbeck, J. A. and Nitowski, E. L., *New Evidence May Explain Image on Shroud of Turin*, in BAR, 12/4 (jul-aug. 1986), pp. 23–24.

Kollek, T. and Pearlmann, M., *Jérusalem. Ville sacrée de l'humanité. 40 siècles d'histoire*, Jérusalem 1978.

Landucci, P. C. *Giovanni, Evangelista, apostolo, santo*, in BS, vol. VI, Rome 1966, coll. 757–785.

Laperrousaz, E. M. *Esseni*, in DEB, pp. 515–516.

—*Morto, manoscritti del mar,* in DEB, pp. 890–892.

—*Tempio*, in DEB, pp. 1265–1266.

Laperrousaz, E. M. and Nahon, G., *La position des bras des squelettes dans les tombes de Qoumrân et d'Ennezat (Puy de Drôme)*, in RÉJ, 64, 1–2 (1995), pp. 227–238.

Le Boulluec, A., *Eterodossia e ortodossia*, in *Il nuovo popolo*, pp. 260–265.

Le Goff, J., *Documento/monumento*, in *Enciclopedia*, ed. R. Romano, vol. V, Turin 1978, pp. 38–48.

Lea, C., *A History of the Inquisition of the Middle Ages*, vol. 3, New York 1888–1889.

Lebreton, G., *Il mondo giudaico*, in *Storia della Chiesa*, vol. I, pp. 60–68.

Leclercq, H., *Judaisme*, in DACL, vol. VIII, t. 1, coll. 1–254, coll. 239–240 and 240–247.

Légasse, S., *Paolo e l'universalismo cristiano*, in *Il nuovo popolo*, pp. 106–158.

Legras, A. M. and Lemaitre, J. L., *La pratique liturgique des Templiers et des Hospitaliers de Saint-Jean de*

Jerusalem, in
L'ecrit dans la société médiévale, textes en hommage à Lucie Fossier, Editions du CNRS, Paris 1991, pp. 77–137.

Léonard, G., *Introduction au cartulaire manuscrits du Temple (1150–1317)*, Paris 1930.

Leoni, B., *La croce nell'archeologia*, in EC, vol. IV, Vatican City 1950, coll. 964–970.

Liberalismo, industrializzazione, espansione europea (1830–1914), ed. J. Gadille and J. M. Mayeur, It. ed. P. Stella, in Storia del cristianesimo. Religione-politica-cultura, XI, Rome 2003.

Liddel, H. G. and Scott, R., *Dizionario illustrato greco-italiano*,
It.ed. Q. Cataudella, M. Manfredi and F. Di Benedetto, Florence 1975.

Lidov, A., *The Mandylion and Keramion as an Image-archetype of Sacred Space*, in *Eastern Christian Relics*, pp. 268–280.

Lightfoot, J. B., *The Apostolic Fathers, II, S. Ignatius-S. Polycarpus*, London 1885.

Lipinski, É., *Ebreo*, in DEB, coll. 444–445.

—*Sangue*, in DEB, p. 1161.

Lizérand, G., *Le dossier de l'affaire des Templiers*, Paris 1923 (reprinted 1964).

Loiseleur, J., *La doctrine secrète des templiers*, Paris 1872.

Longnon, A., *Documents relatifs au Comté de Champagne et Brie (1172–1361)*, vol. I, Paris 1901.

Loomis, R. S., *The Grail from Celtic Myth to Christian Symbol*, Princeton 1991.

Lyons, M. C. and Jackson, D. E. P., Saladin. *The Politics of the Holy War*, Cambridge 1982.

Maier, J., *Gesù Cristo e il cristianesimo nella tradizione giudaica*, Brescia 1994.

Maleczek, W., *Innocenzo III e la quarta crociata. Da forte ispiratore a spettatore senza potere*, in *Quarta crociata*, vol.I, pp. 389–422.

Mannier, E., *Ordre de Malte. Les Commanderies du Grand-Prieuré de France d'après les documents inédits conservées aux Archives Nationales à Paris*, Paris 1872.

Marastoni, A., *Le scritte sulla S. Sindone: lettura e relativa problematica*, in *La sindone. Scienza e fede*, pp. 161–164.

Marguerat, D., *Ebrei e cristiani: la separazione*, in *Il nuovo popolo*, pp. 190–222.

—*Gesù di Nazareth*, in Il nuovo popolo, pp. 25–71.

Marinelli, E. and Petrosillo, O., *La sindone, storia di un enigma*, Milan 1998.

Marinelli E., *La Sindone. Analisi di un mistero*, Milan 2009.

Marini, M., *Memorie storiche*, in *Regestum Clementis papae V*, Rome 1885, pp. CCXXVIII–CCXLIX.

Marion, A. and Courage, A. L. *Nouvelles découvertes sur le suaire de Turin*, Paris 1997

—*Discovery of Inscriptions on the Shroud of Turin by Digital Image Processing*, in «OE», vol. 37 (August 1998), n. 8, pp. 2308–2313.

Marion, J. L., *Le prototype de l'image*, in *Nicée II*, pp. 451–470.

Markwardt, J., *Was the Shroud in Languedoc during the Missing Years?*, in *AXEIPO.OIHTOS*, pp. 177–182.

Marrou, H. I., *L'Église de l'Antiquité tardive (303–604)*, Paris 1985.

Marshall, H., Luke *Historian and Theologian*, Exeter 1970.

Martini, R., *La condanna a morte di Gesù fra "colpa degli ebrei" e "responsabilità dei Romani"*, in SDHI, 69 (2003), pp. 543–557.

Mayer, A., *Pauliciani*, in EC, vol. IX, coll. 996–997.

Mély, F., *Exuviae sacrae Constantinopolitanae. La croix des premiers croisés, la Sainte Lance, la Sainte Courounne*, Paris 1904.

Ménard, L., *Histoire civile, ecclésiastique et littéraire de la ville de Nismes*, vol. I, Paris 1750.

Mercati, A., *The New List of the Popes*, in *Mediaeval Studies*, IX (1947), pp. 71–80.

Mercati, G., *Anthimi Nicomediensis episcopi et martyris da sancta Ecclesia*, in *Note di letteratura biblica e cristiana antica*, in ST, 5 (1901), pp. 87–98.

Merlo, G. G., *Eretici ed eresie medievali*, Bologna 1989.

Meschini, M., *Note sull'assegnazione della viscontea Trencavel a Simone di Monfort nel 1209*, in MÉFR, 116 (2004), pp.635–655.

Messina, R. and Orecchia, C., *La scritta in caratteri ebraici sulla fronte dell'Uomo della Sindone: nuove ipotesi e problematiche*, in *Sindon*, n.s., giugno 1989, pp. 83–88.

Metcalf, D. M., *The Templars as Bankers and Monetary Transfers between West and East in the 12th Century*, in *Coinage in the Latin East, The Fourth Oxford Symposium on Coinage and Monetary History*, ed. by P. W. Edbury and D. M. Metcalf, Oxford 1980.

Michelet, J., *Le Procès des Templiers*, 2 voll., *Collection des Documents inédits sur l'Histoire de France*, Paris 1841–1851.

Mignard, P., *Monographie du coffret de M. le Duc de Blacas*, in *Baphometica*, pp. 136–221.

Milani, C., λ/ρ *nei papiri: un aspetto dell'interferenza linguistica*, in OM, pp. 221–229.

Miglietta, M., *Riflessioni intorno al processo a Gesù*, Milan, 1994.

—*Il processo a Gesù di Nazareth,* Rome 1995.

Morgan, R., *Did the French Take the Shroud to England? More Evidence from the Templecombe Connection*, in *ΑΧΕΙΡΟΠΟΙΗΤΟΣ*, pp. 133–140.

Motin, S., *La métrologie du tissue de Turin*, in *ΑΧΕΙΡΟΠΟΙΗΤΟΣ*, pp. 107–111.

Motyer, J.A., *Pettorale del Sommo Sacerdote*, in GEIB, p. 91.

Moule, C.F.D., "The Son of Man: Some of the Facts" in NTS, 41 (1995), pp. 277–279.

Müller, W., *Festliche Begegnungen. Die Freunde des Turiner Grabtuches in zwei–Jahrtausenden*, Band I-II, Frankfurt am Main 1989.

Narratio de imagine Edessena, in PG, 113, pp. 422–454.

La nascita di una cristianità (250–430), in *Storia del cristianesimo. Religione-politica-cultura*, vol. II, ed. C. Pietri and L. Pietri, It. ed. A. Di Berardino, Rome 2000.

Naveh, J., The *Ossuary Inscriptions from Giv'at ha-Mivtar*, in IEJ 20 (1970), pp. 33–37.

Naz, R., *Images*, in DDC, vol. V, coll. 1257–1258.

Nicée II, 787–1987, *Douze siècles d'images religieuses*, by

F. Boespflug and N. Lossky, Paris 1987.

Nicol, D. M., *Venezia e Bisanzio*, it. trans. L. Perria, Milano 1990.

Nicolaj, G., *Lezioni di diplomatica generale. I: Istituzioni*, Rome 2007.

Nikolaos Mesarites, *Die Palast-revolution des Johannes Komnenos*, ed. A. Heisenberg, Würzburg 1907.

Nouveaux regards sur le Linceul de Turin. Carte d'identité du Christ, Paris 1995.

Il nuovo popolo dalle origini al 250, in *Storia del cristianesimo. Religione-politica-cultura*, ed. L. Pietri, vol. I, Rome 2003.

Ordericus Vitalis, *Historia Ecclesiastica* by A. Le Prevost, Paris 1838–1855.

Orbe, A., *Cristologia gnostica. Introducción a la soteriologia de los siglos II y III*, vol. 2, Madrid 1976.

Les ordres religieux militaires dans le Midi (XIIe-XIVe siècle), ed. A. Demurger, in CdF, 41 (2006).

Ostrogorsky, G., *Storia dell'impero bizantino*, It. ed. P. Leone, Turin 1968.

Ozoline, N., *La Théologie de l'icône*, in *Nicée II*, Paris 1981, pp. 403–438.

Pagano, S., *I documenti del processo a Galileo Galilei*, Vatican City (CAV, 21), 1984.

—*Leone XIII e l'apertura dell'Archivio Segreto Vaticano*, in *Leone XIII e gli studi storici. Atti del Convegno Internazionale Commemorativo*, Vatican City, 30–31 October 2003, ed. C. Semeraro, Vatican City 2004, pp. 44–63.

P. Papini Stati Silvae, recensuit Aldus Marastoni, editio stereotypa correctior adiecto fragmento carminis de bello germanico, Leipzig (*Bibliotheca scriptorum graecorum et Romanorum Teubneriana, Deutsche Akademie der Wissenschaften zu Berlin. Zentralinstitut für alte Geschichte und Archäologie bereich Griechisch–Römische Kulturgeschichte*) 1970.

Partner, P., *I Templari*, It. trans. L. Angelini, Turin 1993.

Paschalis Schlömer, B., *Le "sindon" et la "Véronique"*, in

ΑΧΕΙΡΟΠΟΙΗΤΟΣ, pp. 151–164.

Pastore Trossello, F., *La struttura tessile della sindone*, in *La sindone: indagini scientifiche, atti del IV Congresso nazionale di Studi sulla Sindone*, Siracusa, 17–18 ottobre 1987, ed. S. Rodante, Cinisello Balsamo 1988, pp. 64–71.

Patlagean, E., *Contestazioni ed eresie in oriente e in occidente. I: A Bisanzio: contestazioni e dissidenze*, in *Apogeo del papato*, pp. 434 442.

Pellicori, S. and Evans, M. S., *The Shroud of Turin through the Microscope*, in *Archaeology*, 34/1 (Jan-Feb. 1981), pp. 34–43.

Penna, A., *Apocrifi, libri*, in EC, vol. I, coll. 1627–1633.

—*Pietro, apostolo*, in BS, vol. X, Rome 1968, coll. 588–612.

Penna, R., *I ritratti originali di Gesù il Cristo. Inizi e sviluppi della cristologia neotestamentaria*, 2 voll., Cinisello Balsamo 1996–1999.

Peretto, E., *L'inno cristologico di Col I, 15–20. Dagli gnostici ad Ireneo*, in *Augustinianum*, 15 (1975/3), pp. 257–274.

Pesci, B., *Bolsena*, in EC, vol. II, coll. 1817–1819.

Petersen, L. and Wachtel, K., *Prosospographia imperii Romani,*
saec. *I, II, III, pars VI*, Berolini-Novi Eboraci (Berlin-New York)1998.

Peterson, E., *Giudeocristiani,* in EC, vol. VI, coll. 705–708.

—*Mani e manicheismo*, in EC, vol. VII, coll. 1959–1963.

—*Ofiti*, in EC, vol. IX, coll. 80–81.

—*Sethiani*, in EC, vol. XI, coll. 433–434.

Petrosillo, O. and Marinelli, E., *La Sindone. Storia di un enigma,*
Milan 1998.

Pfeiffer, H., *Das Turines Grabtuch und das Christusbild. Das Grabtuch. Forschungsberichte und Untersuchungen*, Frankfurt am Main 1987.

—*La sindone di Torino e il Volto di Cristo nell'arte paleocristiana, bizantina e medievale occidentale*, in *Emmaus*, 2 (1982).

—*Le voile de sainte Véronique et le Suaire entre les treizième et quatorzième siècles*, in *AXEIPO.OIHTOS*, pp. 127–131.

Piana A., *Sindone: gli anni perduti*, Milan 2008.

Pieralli, L., *La corrispondenza diplomatica dell'imperatore bizantino con le potenze estere nel tredicesimo secolo (1204–1282). Studio storico-diplomatistico ed edizione critica*, Vatican City (CAV, 54) 2006.
Pietri, Ch., *I successi: la soppressione del paganesimo e il trionfo del cattolicesimo di Stato*, in *La nascita di una cristianità*, pp. 381–413.
—*La conversione: propaganda e realtà della legge e dell'evergetismo*, in *La nascita di una cristianità*, pp. 187–223.
—*Lo sviluppo del dibattito teologico e le controversie nell'età di Costantino: Ario e il concilio di Nicea*, in *La nascita di una cristianità*, pp. 243–280.
—*Roma christiana. Recherches sur l'Église de Rome, son organisation, sa politique, son idéologie de Miltiade à Sixte III (311–440)*, I, Rome («BÉFAR», 224) 1975.
Piquet, J., *Des banquiers au moyen âge: les templiers*, Paris 1939.
Platelle, H., *Luigi IX*, in BS, vol. VI, coll. 320–338.
Potthast, A., *Regesta Pontificum Romanorum inde ab a. post Christum natum MCXCVIII ad a. MCCCIV*, vol. 2, Graz 1957.
Pratesi, A., *Genesi e forme del documento medievale*, Rome 1987.
Il primato del vescovo di Roma nel primo millennio. Ricerche e testimonianze, Atti del symposium storico-teologico, Roma, 9–13 ottobre 1989, ed. M. Maccarrone, Vatican City (*Pontificio Comitato di Scienze Storiche. Atti e Documenti*, 4) 1991.
Puech, É., *Les nécropoles juives palestiniennes au tournant de notre ère*, in *Dieu l'a resuscité d'entre les morts*, Paris 1982, pp. 35–55.
—*Inscriptions funéraires palestiniennes: tombeau de Jason et ossuaires (Planches V–VIII)*, in RB, 90 (1983), pp. 481–533.
—*Notes sur le fragment d'apocalypse 4Q246 – "le fils de Dieu"*, in RB, 101 (1994), pp. 533–558.
—*Notes sur 11Q19 LXIV 6–13 et 4Q524 14, 2–4. À propos de la crucifixion dans le Rouleau du temple et dans le Judaïsme ancien*, in RQ, 18 (1997–1998), pp. 109–124.

Quarta crociata. Venezia-Bisanzio-Impero latino, relazioni presentate alle giornate di studio organizzate per l'ottavo centenario della Quarta crociata, 2 voll., ed. G. Ortalli, G. Ravegnani e P. Schreiner, Istituto Veneto di Scienze, Lettere ed Arti, Venice 2006.

Qumran e le origini cristiane, Atti del 6o Convegno di studi neotestamentari (L'Aquila, 14–17 settembre 1995), ed. R. Penna, Bologna 1997.

Radermakers, J., *Croce*, in DEB, pp. 378–379.

—*Giovanni*, in DEB, pp. 637–638.

Raes, G., *Rapport d'analyse*, in *La Santa Sindone*, pp. 79–83.

Raffard de Brienne, R., *Les duc d'Athènes et le Linceul*, in *AXEIPOΠOIHTOΣ*, pp. 171–176.

Rametelli, I., *Filosofia e gnosi*, in *Ennio Innocentium, in septuagesimo quinto aetatis suae amici et sodales fraternitatis aurigarum*, Rome 2007, pp. 69–94.

Rapp, F., *Il consolidamento del papato: una vittoria imperfetta e costosa*, in *Dalla Riforma della Chiesa alla Riforma protestante*, pp. 82–144.

Ratzinger, J. *Jesus von Nazareth. Von der taufe im Jordan bis zur Verklärung*; It. trans. C. Galli e R. Zuppet, *Gesù di Nazareth*, Vatican City 2007.

Ravasi, G., *Il Pentateuco (introduzione e note)*, in *La Bibbia*, pp. 1–8.

Raynouard, F., *Monuments historiques relatifs à la condemnation des Chevaliers du Temple*, Paris 1813.

Reinach, S., *La Tête magique des Templiers*, in RHR, 63 (1911), pp. 25–39.

Reisland, B., *Visible Progress of Paper Degradation Caused by Iron Gall Inks*, in *The Iron-Gall Ink Meeting, Newcastle upon Tyne, 4th-5th September 2000*, ed. A. Jean and E. Brown, Newcastle 2001, pp. 67–72.

Riant, P., *Exuviae sacrae Constantinopolitanae, fasciculus documentorum minorum ad byzantina lipsana in Occidentem saeculo XIII translata spectantium, vel historiam quarti belli sacri imperiisque gallo-graeci illustrantium*, Genevae 1877.

—*Études sur les derniers temps du royaume de Jérusalem*, in "AOL", 14 (1878).

—*Des depouilles religieuses enlevées à Constantinople au XIIIa siècle par les Latins*, Paris 1975.

Richard, M., *L'introduction du mot «hypostase» dans la théologie de l'Incarnation*, in MSR, 2 (1945), pp. 5–32.

Ries, J., *Introduzione. La controversia sugli idoli, l'antropologia patristica e le origini dell'iconografia cristiana*, in *L'arte paleocristiana*, pp. 9–16.

Riesner, R., *Esseni e prima comunità cristiana a Gerusalemme. Nuove scoperte e fonti*, It. trans. E. Coccia, Vatican City 2001.

Rigato, M. L., *Il titolo della croce di Gesù. Confronto tra i Vangeli e la Tavoletta-reliquia della Basilica Eleniana a Roma*, Rome (*Tesi Gregoriana. Serie Teologia*, 25) 2005.

Rinaldi, P., *Un documento probante sulla localizzazione in Atene della Santa Sindone dopo il saccheggio di Costantinopoli*, in *La sindone. Scienza e fede*, pp. 109–113.

Rinaudo, J. B., *Nouveau mécanisme de formation de l'image sur le Linceul de Turin, ayant pu entraîner une fausse radiodadation médiévale*, in *L'identification*, pp. 293–299.

Rius-Camps, J., *The Four Authentic Letters of Ignatius the Martyr*, Rome 1979.

Rodd, R., *The Princes of Achaia and the Chronicle of Morea. A Study of Greece in the Middle Ages*, 2 voll., London 1907.

Rodorf, W., *Martyre*, in DS, vol. X, Paris 1980, pp. 718–732.

Rohault de Fleury, Ch., *Mémoire sur les instruments de la Passion de Notre Seigneur Jésus-Christ*, Paris 1870.

Runciman, S., *History of the Crusades*, It. *Storia delle crociate*, It. trans. E. Bianchi, A. Comba, F. Comba, vol. 2, Turin 1966.

Sabbatini Tumolesi, P., *Gladiatorum paria: annunci di spettacoli gladiatorii a Pompei*, Rome 1980.

Sacchi, P., *Storia del secondo tempio. Israele tra VI secolo a.C. e I secolo d.C.*, II ed., Turin 2002.

St. Basil the Great, *Homily on Gordianus the martyr*, in PG, 31, 490.

—*A treatise on the Holy Spirit*, in PG, 32, 18, 45.

Sansterre, M., *Eusèbe de Césarée et la naissance du "césaropapisme"*, in *Byzantion*, 42 (1972), pp. 131–195;

532–594.

La Santa Sindone, ricerche e studi della Commissione d'esperti nominata dall'Arcivescovo di Torino, Card. Michele Pellegrino, nel 1969, in SRDT, January 1976.

Savio, P., *Pellegrinaggio di San Carlo Borromeo alla Sindone di Torino*, in *Aevum*, 4 (1933), pp. 423–454.

—*Ricerche storiche sulla Santa Sindone*, Turin 1957.

—*Ricerche sul tessuto della Santa Sindone*, Grottaferrata 1973.

Scannerini, S., *Mirra, aloe, pollini e altre tracce. Ricerca botanica sulla sindone*, Leumann (To) 1997.

Scavone,D. C., *British King Lucius, the Grail and Joseph of Arimathea. The Question of Byzantine Origins*, in *Publications of the Medieval Association of America*, 10 (2003), pp. 101–142.

—*The Shroud of Turin in Constantinople. The Documentary Evidence*, in «Sindon», n.s., n. 1, giugno 1989, pp. 113–128.

Schaeder, H. H., *.a.a....., .a...a...*, in GLNT, vol. VII, coll. 833–848.

Schanmberger, J., *Der 14. Nisan als Kreuzigungstag und die Synoptiker*, in *Bib* 9 (1928), pp. 57–77.

Schiller, G., *Ikonographie der christlichen Kunst*, Gütersloh 1968.

Schilson, A., *Lessing, Gotthold Ephraim*, in LTK, vol. VI, coll. 851–852.

Schlumberger, G., *Sigillographie de l'Empire Byzantin*, Paris 1884.

Schönborn, C., *L'icona di Cristo. Fondamenti teologici*, It. trans. M. C. Bartolomei, Cinisello Balsamo 1988.

Scopello, M., *Correnti gnostiche*, in *Il nuovo popolo*, pp. 317–350.

Segalla, G., *La "terza" ricerca del Gesù storico: il Rabbi ebreo di Nazareth e il Messia crocifisso*, in SP, 40 (1993), pp. 463–515.

—*La verità storica dei Vangeli e la "terza ricerca" su Gesù*, in *"Lateranum"*, 61 (1995), pp. 195–234.

—*Vangeli canonici e vangeli gnostici. Un confronto critico*, in *Gnosi e vangeli gnostici*, pp. 47–68.

Servois, G., *Emprunts de Saint Louis en Palestine et en Afrique*, in *Bibliothèque de l'Ecole de Chartes*, 1848, IV s.,

t. IV, pp. 113–131.

Sève, R. and Chagny Sève, A. M., *Le procès des Templiers d'Auvergne*, Paris 1986.

Shalina, I., *The Icon of Christ the Man of Sorrow and the Image–Relic of the Constantinopolitan Shroud*, in *Eastern Christian Relics*, pp. 324–336.

Siffrin, P., *Pallio*, in EC, vol. IX, coll. 646–647.

Simonetti, M., *Studi sull'innologia popolare cristiana dei primi secoli*, in *Atti dell'Accademia Nazionale dei Lincei, Memorie della Classe di scienze morali, storiche e filologiche*, serie \ VIII, a. CCCXLIX (1952), vol. IV, pp. 341–484.

—*Studi sull'arianesimo*, Rome 1965.

—*Eracleone e Origene*, in VC, 3 (1966), pp. 111–141 e 4 (1967), pp. 23–64.

—*Note di cristologia gnostica*, in RSLR, 5 (1969), pp. 529–553.

—*Ignazio di Antiochia*, in GLS, vol. II, pp. 1084–1088.

—*Cornelio*, in EP, vol. I, pp. 268–272.

Simonson, S., *The Apostolic See and the Jews. History, Studies and Text*, Wetteren (*Universa*, 109) 1991.

Sindone. Cento anni di ricerca, ed. B. Barberis and G. M. Zaccone, Rome 1998.

Sindone 2000. Atti del Congresso Internazionale, Orvieto, 27–29 agosto 2000, Ed. E. Marinelli, San Severo (Fg) 2002.

La sindone e la scienza, Atti del II Congresso Internazionale di sindonologia, Turin 1978.

La sindone. Scienza e fede, Atti del I Convegno Nazionale di sindonologia, Bologna, 27–29 novembre 1981, ed. L.Coppini and F. Cavazzuti, Bologna 1983.

Sindone e scienza. Atti del III Congresso Internazionale di studi sulla Sindone, Turin, 5–7 giugno 1998, ed. P.L. Baima Bollone, M. Lazzaro, and C. Marino, Turin 1998 (CD Rom edition).

Siniscalco, P., *Sull'evangelizzazionee la cristianizzazione nei primi secoli. Una rassegna bibliografica*, in *Saggi di storia della cristianizzazione antica e altomedievale*, ed. B. Luiselli, in *Biblioteca di Cultura Romanobarbarica*, 8 (2006), pp. 67–92.

Skubiszewski, P., *Cristo*, in EAM, vol. V, pp. 493–521.

Soyez, E., *La croix et le crucifix. Étude archéologique*, Amiens 1910.

Spadafora, F., *Veronica*, in BS, vol. XII, coll. 1044–1048.

Sterlingova, I., *The New Testament Relics* in *Xristianskie relikvii v Moskovskom kremle, redaktor–sostavitel'* A.M. Lidov, Moskva 2000, pp. 83–93.

Stiernon, D., *Jamnia*, in DHGÉ, vol. XXVI, coll. 863–882.

Storia della Chiesa, ed. A. Fliche and V. Martin *I: La Chiesa primitiva. Dagli inizi alla fine del II secolo, ed.* G. Lebreton and G. Zeiller, It.ed. A.P. Frutaz, Cinisello Balsamo 1995.

Storici arabi delle crociate, ed. F. Gabrieli, Turin 1973.

Stöve, E., *Magdeburger Centuriatoren*, in LTK, vol. VI, col. 1185.

Sudario del Señor, Actas del I Congreso Internacional sobre el Sudario de Oviedo, Oviedo, 29–31 Octubre 1994, Oviedo 1996.

Suetonius with an English Translation, by J. C. Rolfe, vol. 2, London 1979.

Sulzeberger, M., *Le symbole de la Croix et les Monogrammes de Jésus chez les premières chrétiens*, in *Byzantion*, 2 (1925), pp. 337–448.

Sylva, D. D., *Nicodemus and His Spices (John 19,39)*, in NTS 34 (1988), pp. 148–151.

Tamburelli, G., *Applicazione dell'elaborazione tridimensionale sindonica ad immagini ottenute per contatto*, in *La Sindone. Scienza e fede*, pp. 285–292.

—*Studio della Sindone mediante il calcolatore elettronico*, Milan 1983.

Teodorsson, S. T., *The Phonology of Attic in the Hellenistic Period*, Goteborg 1978.

Testa, E., Il Golgota e la croce. Ricerche storico-archeologiche, Jerusalem ("SBF, Collectio Minor," 21) 1978.

—*Il simbolismo dei giudeo-cristiani*, Jerusalem 1981.

Testi gnostici in lingua greca e latina, ed. M. Simonetti, Milan 1993.

Testore, C., *Il culto della croce*, in EC, vol. IV, Vatican City 1950, coll. 959–960.

The Horns of Hattin, ed. B. Z. Kedar, Gerusalemme, 1988.

The Military Orders: Fighting for the Faith and Caring for the Sick, by M. Barber, Ashgate 1994; II: *Welfare and Warfare*, by H. Nicholson, Ashgate 1998.

Thesaurum Graecae Linguae, Paris 1848–1854.

Thiede, C. P. and D'Ancona, M., *Testimone oculare di Gesù. La nuova sconvolgente prova sull'origine del Vangelo*, It. ed. F. Bianchi, Casale Monferrato 1996.

Thurre, D., *I reliquiari al tempo delle Crociate da Urbano II a san Luigi (1096–1270)*, in *Le crociate*, pp. 362–367.

Timossi, V., *Analisi del tessuto della S. Sindone, in La Santa Sindone nelle ricerche moderne*, *Atti del Convegno Nazionale di Studi sulla Santa Sindone*, Turin 1942.

Tixeront, I., *Histoire des dogmes dans l'Eglise ortodoxe*, vol. III, Parigi 1912.

Tommasi, F., *"Pauperes commilitones Christi". Aspetti e problemi delle origini gerosolimitane*, in *Militia Christi e crociata nei secoli XI–XIII*, *Atti della XI Settimana Internazionale di studio, Mendola (28 agosto–1o settembre) 1989*, Milan 1992, pp. 443–475.

—*I Templari e il culto delle reliquie*, in *I Templari: mito e storia*, *Atti del Convegno Internazionale di studi alla Magione templare di Poggibonsi-Siena (29–31 maggio 1987)*, ed. G. Minnucci and F. Sardi, Sinalunga 1989, pp. 191–210.

Tommaso da Celano, *San Francesco. Vita prima*, tr. and notes A. Caluffeti and F. Olgiati, Torriana 1993.

Tosatti, M., *Inchiesta sulla sindone. Segreti e misteri del sudario di Cristo*, Milano 2009.

Traniello, F., *Giovanni XXIII*, in EP, vol. III, pp. 646–657.

Tréffort, C., *L'Église carolingienne et la mort. Christianisme, rites funéraires et pratiques commemoratives*, in *Collection d'Histoire et d'Archéologie Médiévales*, 3, 1996.

Trocmé, E., *Le prime comunità: da Gerusalemme ad Antiochia*, in *Il nuovo popolo*, pp. 75–105.

Trudon des Ormes, A., *Étude sur les possession de l'Ordre du Temple en Picardie*, in *Mémoires de la Société des Antiquaires de Picardie*, IV s., II, 1894.

Tucci, U., *La spedizione marittima*, in *Quarta crociata*, vol. I, pp. 3–18.

Turchi, N., *Reliquie*, in EC, vol. X, Vatican City 1953, coll. 749–761.

Tyrer, J., *Looking at the Turin Shroud as a Textile*, in SSI, 6 (March 1983), pp. 35–45.

Tzaferis, V., *Jewish Tombs at and near Giv'at ha-Mivtar, Jerusalem*, in IEJ 20 (1970), pp. 18–32.

Upinsky, A. A., *La démonstration scientifique de l'authenticité: le statut scientifique, la reconnaissance, l'identification*, in *L'identification scientifique*, pp. 293–299.

Uspenskij, L., *La teologia dell'icona. Storia e iconografia*, It. trans. A. Lanfranchi, Milan 1995.

Vaccari, A., *Sindone*, in EC, vol. XI, coll. 692–697.

Valenziano, C., *Liturgia e Antropologia,* Bologna 1997.

Il Vangelo di Pietro, ed. M. G. Mara, Bologna 2003.

Vauchez, A., *Contestazioni ed eresie in oriente e in occidente. II: In occidente: dalla contestazione all'eresia*, in *Apogeo del papato*, pp. 442–455.

Vial, G., *Le Linceul de Turin. Étude technique*, in BCIELT, 67 (1989), pp. 11–24.

Vian, G. M., *La donazione di Costantino*, Bologna 2004.

Vignolo, R., *Giovanni*, in GLS, pp. 847–855.

Vignon, P., *The Shroud of Christ*, London 1902.

Villanueva, J. L., *Viaje literario á las Iglesias de España*, vol. V, Madrid 1806.

Volbach, F., La Croce. *Lo sviluppo nell'oreficeria sacra*, Vatican City 1938.

Wehr, W., *Trinità, arte*, in EC, vol. XII, coll. 544–545.

Weitzmann, K., *The Mandylion and Constantine Porphyrogennetos*, CA, XI (1960).

—*Le icone del periodo delle Crociate*, in *Le icone*, pp. 201–236.

Whanger, A. D. and Whanger, M.W., *A Comparison of the Sudarium of Oviedo and the Shroud of Turin Using the Polarized Image Overlay Technique*, in *Sudario del Señor*, pp. 379–381.

Wilkins, D., *Concilia Magnae Britanniae et Hiberniae*, 2 voll., London 1737.

Wilson, I., *Le suaire de Turin. Linceul du Christ?*, édition

française by R. Albeck, Paris 1984.
—*Holy Faces Secret Places. An Amazing Quest for the Face of Jesus*, New York 1991.
Wiseman, D. J. and Wheaton, D. H., *Weights and Measures*, in J. D. Douglas et al., *New Bible Dictionary*, London 1967, pp.1321–1322.
Wolf, G., *The Holy Face and the Holy Feet: Preliminary Reflections before the Novgorod Mandylion*, in *Eastern Christian Relics*, pp. 281–290.

Zacà, S., *Tessuto sindonico. Aspetti medico-legali*, in *Sindon*, n.s., nn. 9–10, December 1996, pp. 57–64.
Zaccone, G., *Sulle tracce della sindone. Storia antica e recente*, Turin 1997.
—*La fotografia della sindone del 1898: recenti scoperte e conferme nell'archivio Pia,* in *Sindon*, n.s., n. 3, December 1991, pp.69–94.
—*Le manuscrit 826 de la Bibliothèque municipale de Besançon*, in *ΑΧΕΙΡΟΠΟΙΗΤΟΣ*, pp. 211–217.
Zaninotto, G., *La Sindone di Torino e l'immagine di Edessa*, in *Sindon* n.s., 1986, pp. 117–130.
—*La traslazione a Costantinopoli dell'immagine edessena nell'anno 944, Atti del Convegno Internazionale di Sindonologia*, Milan 1988, pp. 344–352.
Zocca, E., *Icone*, in EC, vol. VI, coll. 1538–1541.

Index